THE MESSAGE OF THE CROSS

Norman Schafer
125 W Wiser Lake Rd.
Ferndale, WA 98248

JIMMY SWAGGART

THE MESSAGE OF THE CROSS

Jimmy Swaggart Ministries
P.O. Box 262550 • Baton Rouge, Louisiana 70826-2550
Website: www.jsm.org • Email: info@jsm.org
(225) 768-7000

ISBN 978-1-934655-96-2
09-122 • COPYRIGHT © 2013 Jimmy Swaggart Ministries®
13 14 15 16 17 18 19 20 21 22 23 24 / CW 2 / 13 12 11 10 9 8 7 6 5 4 3 2

TABLE OF CONTENTS

INTRODUCTION

Jesus Christ is the New Covenant. This means that He doesn't merely have the New Covenant or merely proclaim the New Covenant, but rather is the New Covenant. The meaning of this Covenant was given to the Apostle Paul, the meaning of which is the Cross of Christ, which Paul gave to us in his 14 Epistles.

The Cross of Christ is the Gospel. This means that it does not merely contain the Gospel but, in fact, is the Gospel. Paul said:

"Christ sent me not to baptize, but to preach the Gospel: not with wisdom of words, lest the Cross of Christ should be made of none effect" (I Cor. 1:17). In this one Scripture we are plainly and clearly told exactly what the Gospel of Jesus Christ is. It is the Cross of Christ.

THE NEW COVENANT

The New Covenant is different than any other Covenant which God has ever made with humanity. It is different in the fact that it cannot fail. While it is between God and man as all other Covenants made my God, still, it cannot fail.

The reason it cannot fail is because it is all in Christ. Christ is both God and Man, so He fills both roles. Man may accept the Covenant, or he may reject the Covenant, but that does not affect the Covenant. Because it is in Christ, Paul could call it, and rightly so, *"The Everlasting Covenant"* (Heb. 13:20). Man may fail and, in fact, will fail, but The Man Jesus Christ will not and, in fact, cannot fail.

THE MESSAGE OF THE CROSS

One might say and be Scripturally correct that THE MESSAGE OF THE CROSS is THE NEW COVENANT. It is the most complex Work ever carried out by God and, at the same time, the most simple. We have tried to bring this great Work under four headings. They are:

1. Jesus Christ is the Source of all things that we receive from God (Jn. 1:1, 14, 29; 14:6, 20; Col. 2:10-15).

2. The Cross of Christ is the Means and the only Means by which all of these wonderful things are given unto us (Rom. 6:1-14; Gal. 6:14; Col. 2:14-15).

3. With our Lord as the Source and the Cross as the Means, the Cross of Christ, without fail, must be the Object of Faith (I Cor. 1:17, 18, 23; 2:2).

4. With our Lord as the Source, the Cross as the Means, and the Cross the Object of our Faith, and exclusively the Object of our Faith, then, the Holy Spirit, Who works exclusively within the parameters, so to speak, of the Finished Work of Christ, will work grandly on our behalf. If our Faith is placed anywhere other than the Cross of Christ, the Holy Spirit will not and, in fact, cannot function and work on our behalf. He is the One Who works on our behalf, Who Alone can make us what we ought to be, and Who works exclusively within the boundaries of the Cross of Christ (Rom. 8:1-14; Eph. 2:13-18).

THE WORD OF GOD

The Story of the Bible is the Story of *"Jesus Christ and Him Crucified,"* even as *"Jesus Christ and Him Crucified"* is the Story of the Bible. This means that ninety-nine percent of the Word of God is given over exclusively to telling Believers how to live for God. The sad truth is most modern Christians, and I speak of those who truly know the Lord and love the Lord supremely, do not know how to live for God. I realize that is a statement that will raise some eyebrows; however, it happens to be true. THE MESSAGE OF THE CROSS will tell you how to live for God, how to order your behavior, how to have victory over the world, the flesh, and the Devil, and how to live this life.

Were most Christians to be asked the question, *"Do you know how to live for God,"* I think you would be met mostly with a blank stare. Then, after a few moments of hesitation, most would ask what you mean by such a question. The reason it causes most Christians to think twice is simply because deep down in their hearts, they realize that they really do not know how to live for God. Many would say that they know how, but they have trouble putting it into words, and that is true with many. However, I think if you will read carefully what we have to say in this Book, this question as to how to live for God will be thoroughly answered, which can revolutionize your life.

"Let King Jesus reign in your heart today,
"As your Lord and King, let Him hold full sway:
"Whatsoever the cost, follow at His Call:
"Let King Jesus reign, yield to Him your all."

"Let King Jesus reign, swear allegiance true,
"Choose to do His Will, let Him reign anew:
"Hail Him as your King, Christ the Crucified;
"Let King Jesus reign, twas for you He died."

"Let King Jesus reign, ere your life is o'er,
"Hold the standard high, trust Him evermore:
"Lay your trophies down at His Pierced Feet,
"Then with Christ your Lord life will be complete."

THE MESSAGE OF THE CROSS

Jesus Christ Is The Source Of All Things We Receive From God

JESUS CHRIST IS THE SOURCE OF ALL THINGS WE RECEIVE FROM GOD

As we begin the treatment of this most important subject, *"THE MESSAGE OF THE CROSS,"* we must begin with Christ, Who He is and What He has done for us.

WHO IS JESUS CHRIST?

Let's quickly state, *"Jesus Christ is the Son of the Living God,"* in reality, *"God manifest in the flesh."* He is *"the King of kings and Lord of lords, the Jehovah of the Old Testament, and the Saviour of man."*

Were Jesus Christ a mere man, albeit ever so talented, ever so educated, ever so charismatic, and ever so intelligent, that would be one thing. However, if Jesus Christ is the Son of the Living God, and He most definitely is, then that's something else altogether.

Please note the following:

• The only way to God is through Jesus Christ (Jn. 14:6).

• The only way to Jesus Christ is by the Means of the Cross (Lk. 14:27).

• The only way to the Cross is a denial of self (Lk. 9:23).

Jesus Personally stated, and unequivocally so:

"I am the Way, the Truth, and the Life *(proclaims in no uncertain terms exactly Who and What Jesus is)*: no man comes unto the Father, but by Me *(He declares positively that this idea of God as Father, this approach to God for every man is through Him – through what He is and what He has done)*" (Jn. 14:6).

It is Jesus Christ Who paid the price at Calvary's Cross for man's Redemption. No one else paid that price simply because no one else could pay that price. He Alone paid it; therefore, to be Saved, one must accept Christ. There is no other way.

It must be understood, if any doctrine is wrong about Jesus, then whatever else it is they say and do is of no consequence. As stated, He Alone is *"the Way, the Truth, and the Life."* Let us say it again:

Everything that we receive from God the Father, and I mean everything, comes to us by and through the Lord Jesus Christ. He is the One Who paid the price that that door may be opened. No one else did because no one else could.

John the Beloved probably gave the greatest definition of Who Christ is of any writer in the Word of God. He did so as the Spirit of God moved upon him and in such a way that it defies all description. Let's look at it phrase by phrase. It is taken directly from the First Chapter, even beginning with the First Verse of the Gospel that bears his name.

IN THE BEGINNING WAS THE WORD

The phrase, *"In the beginning was the Word,"* refers to the Incarnate Christ but speaks of His Existence before the Incarnation.

The word, *"Beginning,"* does not imply that He had a beginning because, as God, He had no beginning, but it refers to the time of Creation and corresponds with Genesis 1:1.

Williams says: *"As speech reveals mind, so Jesus as the Word reveals God. But to reveal God He must Himself be God, for only God could reveal God."*[1]

It is extremely interesting that the Holy Spirit through John describes Jesus as the *"Word,"* i.e., *"the Eternal Logos."* This can refer to an expression of thought but is never used by New Testament writers in that fashion. They always use it in the realm of *"speech,"* *"utterance,"* or *"word,"* or so the Greek scholars claim.

For instance, in the record of the Creation in Genesis, Chapter 1, the proclamation of Creation is described eight times by the expression, *"And God said."* The *"Word"* which was uttered was so powerful that it could only come from the Omnipotent Word.

As an example, the Jewish translators and commentators had so thoroughly grasped the idea that they were accustomed to substituting the phrase, *"Memar-Jah," "The Word of the Lord,"* for the Name of the Most High.

They seemed to feel that the Lord could be better understood in the form of this expression, which proclaimed, at least in their minds, His Eternal and Absolute Being.

THE ETERNAL WORD OR LOGOS

As well, the Eternal Word, or *"Logos,"* was not placed in suspension during the thirty-three and one-half years of the Incarnation of Christ. Even though He was Very Man, still, He was Very God. As someone has well said, *"While Jesus laid aside the expression of His Deity, He never for a moment lost possession of His Deity."* Consequently, the *"Word"* He was and, therefore, gave before the Incarnation carried through the Incarnation, thus never ceasing to exercise the functions which belonged to His Eternal Glory.

Reynolds said, *"He was 'in the beginning,' and therefore existed before all Creation. He did not 'become.' He was not 'made.' He 'was!'"*[2]

AND THE WORD WAS WITH GOD

The phrase, *"And the Word was with God,"* expresses the idea of the Trinity.

This tells us that Jesus, i.e., *"the Word,"* ever-existed (was), and that He had a personal existence, for He was with God.

The Greek scholars say that this statement as given by John is difficult to translate. It is equivalent to, *"Was in relationship with God,"* or, *"Stood over against,"* not in space or time, but eternally and constitutionally. In other words, it is more than just merely being with God, as we think of such a term, but actually having the same relation, which the next phrase declares.

AND THE WORD WAS GOD

The phrase, *"And the Word was God,"* does not mean that before the Incarnation He was God, but ceased to be during the Incarnation, but rather the opposite. He *"was"* God before the Incarnation; He *"was"* God during the Incarnation; He *"was"* God after the Incarnation; and He *"was"* and *"is"* God from eternity past to eternity future.

Williams says: *"In His Existence Eternal, in His Person Distinct, in His Nature Divine, so that His Personality was not of time, for prior to Creation He was with God (Jn. 17:5; Col. 1:17; Heb. 1:2). Thus He existed before the world began to exist; and this existence – being a conscious Personal One as distinct from the Father – necessitated His Personal Glory as God, i.e., 'Son of God'; and so being God, that relationship was in its nature eternal."*[3]

THE SAME WAS IN THE BEGINNING WITH GOD

"The same," i.e., this very Person, the Lord Jesus Christ, was in eternity with God. The Holy Spirit emphasizes this in order to declare His Eternal Relationship as the Son with the Father.

However, there is no indication that the Logos was a second God or merely Divine or God-like, neither is He described as proceeding out of or from God, nor is He to be called *"the God absolute,"* as opposed to all His Manifestations; but the *"Logos"* is said to be *"God"* — God in His Nature and Being. Reynolds said: *"He stands over and against the Eternal God in mutual communion with the Absolute and the Eternal."*[4]

To attempt to understand the Trinity, the *"Father"* is *"God"* but not first God.

The *"Son"* is *"God"* but not *"second God."*

The *"Holy Spirit"* is *"God"* but not *"third God."*

There is only One God but manifested in Three Persons, God the Father, God the Son, and God the Holy Spirit.

As God, They had no beginning and have no ending. As God, They are uncaused, unformed, and unmade. As God, They always were and always shall be. As God, They are self-sufficient and have need of nothing.

ALL THINGS WERE MADE BY HIM

The phrase, *"All things were made by Him,"* tells us that all things came into being through Him and without Him, not one single thing came into being.

This denies the theory of the eternity of matter, which was held by some in ancient times and continues to be claimed by some.

An absolute distinction, therefore, exists between Jesus and Creation.

As well, the pronoun, *"Him,"* referring to Jesus, makes it distinct that the *"Word"* is a Person.

The two words, *"All things,"* refer to every item of Creation, one by one, rather than all things regarded in totality. This tells us, at least according to the limit of our comprehension, that Jesus painstakingly saw to the individual Creation of each being, plant, planet, star, etc. As Paul said, *"For by Him were all things created, that are in Heaven, and that are in Earth, visible and invisible, whether they be thrones, or dominions, or principalities, or powers: all things were created by Him, and for Him"* (Col. 1:16).

In Verse 1, we are also told how He did this. The *"Logos,"* or *"Word,"* is the organ or instrument by which everything, one by one, was made. Paul wrote in Hebrews:

"Through Faith we understand that the worlds were framed by the Word of God *(refers to Creation, along with everything that goes with Creation)*, so that things which are seen were not made of things which

do appear. *(God began with nothing, thereby, speaking into existence the things needed to create the Universe)*" (Heb. 11:3).

AND WITHOUT HIM WAS NOT ANYTHING MADE THAT WAS MADE

The phrase of our heading says the same thing as the first phrase but in an opposite manner in order to stress the emphasis of Jesus as Creator.

The words, *"Without Him,"* mean that independently of His Cooperation and Volition, nothing, not even one single thing, was made.

When one considers the order of Creation and how it functions according to set laws and never varies from these laws, continuing to fulfill the creative order, one cannot help but be totally awed.

Other than the absolute absurdity and stupidity which characterize the vapid philosophy of evolution, the sheer affront to God as Creator by the propagation of this lie, and a lie it is, is the greatest insult of all. Actually, evolution is an insult to intelligence in any capacity. The idea that something on its own can be brought out of nothing is the beginning of this lie. In other words, evolution has no explanation for the first cause. We know what the first cause is, *"In the beginning God . . ."* (Gen. 1:1). As well, the thought that something can gradually come from disorganized matter into a well-ordered structure, which is the very heart of evolution, is the very opposite of that which really happens. If left unattended and uncultivated, there is always a regression instead of a progression. That is the reason the Lord told Adam and Eve, *". . . Be fruitful, and multiply, and replenish the Earth, and subdue it: and have dominion over the fish of the sea, and over the fowl of the air, and over every living thing that moves upon the Earth"* (Gen. 1:28).

"In Him was Life; and the Life was the Light of men" (Jn. 1:4).

The phrase, *"In Him was Life,"* presents Jesus, the Eternal Logos, as the First Cause.

While it is true that Creation exists in Him, still, to use the term only in that manner is error. Life exists in Him, which brought about the Creation. As well, this brought Him into relationship with a special part of His Creation, which is man, with whom was all His Delight.

Many men can create things, even as God, albeit on a much lower scale. However, inasmuch as man contains no life solely derived within himself, whatever he creates is dependent on the first cause, Who is God.

As an example, when man created the airplane, or anything else for that matter, he had to power that invention by some type of source which only comes from God, and which is dependent, as well, on other laws created by God.

However, the *"Life"* which is in Christ is derived solely from Him, with Him dependent on nothing outside of Himself.

Actually, this is the reason for man's terrible dilemma. At the Fall, he lost the *"Life"* imparted to him by God and has nothing left but death; consequently, man is born dying. As well, death inculcates itself in all of Creation in this world simply because of the Fall. The Life it had derived from God was lost; consequently, inasmuch as there is no other life, man must die, as well as all he touches.

AND THE LIFE WAS THE LIGHT OF MEN

The phrase, *"And the Life was the Light of men,"* proclaims two things:

1. Before the Fall, Jesus was the *"Light of men,"* which means there was no other life and no other light.
Reynolds said, *"The Life which was in the Logos 'was, has always been, is now, will ever be the Light of men.'"*[5]

When men fell from that Light Source, they had to fall into darkness because there was no other light; consequently, there could be no other *"light."* The *"Life"* and *"Light"* are exclusively in Him.

2. When the *"Light"* at the Fall was lost due to the *"Life"* being rejected, God immediately set about to restore the *"Life,"* which would automatically bring the *"Light."*

There is *"Life"* in Creation, with men attempting to worship that *"Life,"* not realizing or believing that it is derived from God. That is why Paul said, *"Professing themselves to be wise, they became fools,*

"And changed the glory of the uncorruptible God into an image made like to corruptible man, and to birds, and four-footed beasts, and creeping things."

He then said, *"Who changed the Truth of God into a lie, and worshipped and served the creature more than the Creator, Who is blessed forever. Amen"* (Rom. 1:22-23, 25).

The phrase, *"Light of men,"* is an extremely interesting statement. This *"Light"* cannot be unless it is derived from the *"Life"* which is in Jesus. And yet, men attempt to find *"Light"* in various other places. This is because of the way that man fell.

Satan told man a lie and was successful in getting him to believe it. He told Adam and Eve, *"... then your eyes shall be opened, and you shall be as gods, knowing good and evil"* (Gen. 3:5).

However, their eyes were not opened, but rather closed, i.e., the *"Light"* was gone!

BELIEVING A LIE

As well, by disobeying God and, in effect, rebelling against Him, they did not gain godhood as promised by Satan, but rather fell to the level of demonhood. This is the reason that demon spirits make their abode in the bodies and minds of much of humanity, either through direct possession or through influence and oppression.

As well, the Fall was of such magnitude and to such a degree that there is no way man can fully comprehend its extent. He cannot tell how far he has fallen because he has no idea of his original state; consequently, there is no way to make a comparison. Man knows that something is wrong, but due to having no *"light,"* he does not know exactly what it is. He continues to think it can be corrected by education, money, or various different philosophies. Hence, he opts for modern psychology even though it does not work, and he knows it does not work.

He thinks he is only slightly maladjusted and can be quickly rehabilitated. Consequently, he talks about the *"psychology of life,"* which is man's answer to man's dilemma, or *"the strength from within,"* as if he can solve his own problems. However, this he cannot do, despite the fact of thousands of years of trying.

Into this torment of failure, God became Man and came into this world as the *"Last Adam."* As such, He brought back *"Life,"* which the first Adam lost, and with it, the *"Light."* Outside of Christ, there is no *"light"* of men.

THE INCARNATION

"And the Light shines in darkness; and the darkness comprehended it not" (Jn. 1:5).

The phrase, *"And the Light shines in darkness,"* speaks of the Incarnation of Christ and His Coming into this world. Because it is derived from His *"Life,"* His *"Light"* drives out *"darkness."* As we have repeatedly stated, that *"Light"* is Jesus. There is no other, not Joseph Smith, Buddha, Carl Marx, Confucius, Muhammad, etc. All others are false, and He Alone is the Light.

This is the reason that the Gospel of Jesus Christ must be taken to all points of the world, even as Jesus said, *". . . unto the uttermost part of the Earth"* (Acts 1:8). The reason is obvious; there is no other light.

If Jesus is presented, the Light will *"shine"*; if not, the darkness will remain.

That is the reason we plead, even to the point of begging for funds to air the television programming in every city in the world that will open its door to us. We do this for two reasons:

1. This, *"the taking of the Gospel to the world,"* is the business of every Believer. He brought the *"Light"* down to this sin-cursed world, but it is our responsibility to carry forth that Light. I speak of every single Believer, irrespective as to who or where they are.

2. Above this burden and Call, which are incumbent upon every Believer, I, along with some few others, have a special Call from the Lord respecting television and radio. In other words, He has especially called me to do this thing; consequently, it is something I must do! I have no alternative or choice, and neither do I desire such. As a result, we have seen hundreds of thousands, if not millions, and I exaggerate not, brought to a Saving Knowledge of Jesus Christ, for which we give the Lord all the praise and all the glory. To be frank, that is the reason Satan has fought so hard, attempting to get our telecast removed from the air. Regrettably, Satan has used the church in this effort of darkness even more than the world.

THE CHURCH

This means that most of that which calls itself *"church,"* may, in fact, be church, but not that which belongs to God. Satan has a *"church"* as well! It looks very similar to the real thing, which is Satan's intention, but its real purpose is to stop the Gospel instead of proclaiming the Gospel.

Yes, there are some few good Churches, and thank God for those, but that number is few and, sadly and regrettably, getting less and less all the time. I personally feel that the modern church is in worse condition spiritually than it ever has been since the Reformation.

THE MESSAGE OF THE CROSS

I believe that this is the reason the Holy Spirit is promoting the Message of the Cross at this particular time. In fact, the

Church began with the Message of the Cross. This great Revelation, which is the meaning of the New Covenant, was given to the Apostle Paul, and he gave to us in his 14 Epistles.

After the original Apostles and those who knew them died off, little by little the Church began to go into spiritual declension. In about the year 600, it finally morphed into that which is now known as the Catholic church. I realize that the Catholic church claims that it started with Peter; however, the first man, the Bishop of Rome, to be referred to as *"Pope"* was in the early 600's. Then, in the early 1600's, the Reformation took place. It was basically based upon the great subject of *"Justification by Faith."* This means that Justification is not in the church but only in Christ and what He did for us at the Cross.

That was followed in the late 1700's and 1800's by the great Holiness Message, which stressed Sanctification. At the turn of the Twentieth Century, the Church experienced the beginning of the fulfillment of Joel's Prophecy concerning the outpouring of the Holy Spirit in the latter rain. The Pentecostal Message touched the world with the Gospel. I know because the Lord permitted us to have a part in this effort. In fact, in the 1980's, our telecast was aired over a great part of the world, translated into several languages. We saw literally hundreds of thousands brought to a Saving Knowledge of Jesus Christ.

However, sad to say, the Pentecostal denominations are little more preaching the Baptism with the Holy Spirit. In fact, many of them are denying that Tongues are the initial, physical evidence that one has been baptized with the Spirit. Now, into this comes the Message of the Cross, meaning that the Church has now come full circle. In fact, THE MESSAGE OF THE CROSS, I believe, is that which the Holy Spirit is presently saying to the Churches (Rev., Chpts. 2-3).

The phrase, *"And the darkness comprehended it not,"* has reference to the fact that Satan did everything within Hell's power to stop the *"Light from shining,"* but in that, he failed.

The Greek word for *"comprehended"* is *"Katalambano,"* and means, *"To seize upon; to keep down or under; to stop."*

As stated, the Evil One did everything he could to stop the shining of that Light, but in that, he failed. He did not overcome the Word, but, in truth, the Word overcame him and on the Cross spoiled all satanic powers (Col. 2:14-17).

As well, this is not something to be done in the future, but something, in fact, which is already done. *". . . For this purpose the Son of God was manifested, that He might destroy the works of the Devil"* (I Jn. 3:8).

From the time of Christ, the world has improved in many ways because of the entrance of the *"Light,"* which comes from His *"Life."* Had it not been for the Dark Ages, which were brought about by Satan's church, the advancement would have been made much sooner. I speak of the Catholic church, which, for hundreds of years, successfully hid the Bible, i.e., *"Light,"* from man. Regrettably, much of the Protestant world is likewise following in this train.

Even some Pentecostal denominations, who claim to know and have the Holy Spirit, have by and large turned their backs on the Holy Spirit and the Word of God. As such, if, in fact, that is the case, they have become Satan's church. They stop the Gospel instead of proclaiming the Gospel.

THE ANSWER

Nevertheless, wherever the *"Light"* shines, the powers of darkness are destroyed, and man is bettered in every conceivable way possible.

Through the years, I, as well as other Preachers, have seen multiple tens of thousands of people delivered from the vilest of sins and bondages by the mighty Power of God. I speak of acute alcoholism, with such bondage being broken. I've seen drug addicts delivered, even in the last stages. I speak, as well, of those delivered from the terrible bondage of religion, which, in many cases, is worse than all other bondages. Only Jesus Christ can do such a thing, not man or all his efforts, irrespective as to what they may be. Truly, Jesus Christ and what He did for us at the Cross is the Answer, the Solution, and, in fact, the Only Answer.

LET THIS MIND BE IN YOU

The phrase, *"Let this mind be in you,"* refers to the Self-emptying of Christ, which is to be in Believers as well.

After exhorting the Philippian Saints in Philippians 2:2-4 to think the same thing, to have the same love, to be in heart agreement, and in lowliness of mind to consider one another as excelling themselves, Paul says, *"Let this mind be in you which was also in Christ Jesus."*

This exhortation reaches back to Philippians 2:2-4 for its definition and ahead to Philippians 2:6-8 for its illustration. The Apostle does not give all that is in the Mind of Christ in these Verses. He selects these Qualities of our Lord which fit the needs of the Philippians at that moment. That which Paul speaks of as being in the Mind of Christ, and which the Philippians were to include in their own spiritual lives, consisted of a spirit of humility and self-abnegation and an interest in the welfare of others. These graces were illustrated in our Lord's Act of becoming Incarnate in the human race and becoming the Substitutionary Atonement for sin.

This lack of unity among the Philippian Saints became the occasion for perhaps the greatest Christological Passage in the New Testament as it regards the Incarnation. Among scholars, it is known as the Kenosis Passage, speaking of the Self-emptying of the Son of God as He became Incarnate in humanity, with the word, *"Kenosis,"* being the Greek word meaning, *"To empty."*

THE VIRTUES OF CHRIST

The expression, *"This mind,"* could be translated in a number of ways, each of which, while holding the main idea, yet brings out a slightly different shade of meaning.

For instance: *"Be constantly thinking this in yourselves;*

be having this mind in you; reflecting your own minds, the Mind of Christ Jesus; let the same purpose inspire you as was in Christ Jesus."

The sum total of the thought in the exhortation seems to be that of urging the Philippians to emulate in their own lives the distinctive Virtues of the Lord Jesus spoken of in Philippians 2:2-4. It is the habitual direction of our Lord's Mind with reference to self that is in the Apostle's thinking, and an attitude of humility and self-abnegation for the benefit of others, which should be true also of the Philippians. This gives us the key to unlock the rich treasures of the great doctrinal portion of the Letter we are now to study.

CHRIST JESUS

The phrase, *"Which was also in Christ Jesus,"* portrays Christ as the supreme example.

Of course, all of this was for one purpose, and we speak of the Incarnation of our Lord, to effect the Redemption of humanity by going to the Cross. We will find out in these Passages that this involved far more than appears on the surface. Irrespective, all that was done, all of its great magnitude, the mystery of the Incarnation, and what it all means, was but for one purpose, the Redemption of mankind, which necessitated the Cross with all its horror, pain, suffering, and humiliation. Consequently, to say that this is an example, even the supreme example, is perhaps the grossest understatement that has ever been uttered. In fact, it is beyond the pale of understanding regarding the human mind.

Whatever particular shades of meaning one may find in these Passages, Paul's essential Message (identical with the thought expressed in II Corinthians 8:9) is not difficult to discover if it be remembered that his primary purpose is practical in nature. He is dealing with a problem which threatens to dissolve the unity of the Believers at Philippi. Over against the mood of some to assert themselves selfishly, Paul sets the Spirit of Christ as the supreme example of obedience.

IN CHRIST JESUS

The words, *"In Christ Jesus,"* show that the corresponding words, *"In You,"* cannot mean, *"Among you,"* but in yourselves, in your heart. The Apostle refers us to the supreme example of unselfishness and humility, the Lord Jesus Christ.

He bids us to mind the things which the Lord Jesus minded, to love what He loved, and to hate what He hated. The thoughts, the desires, and the motives of the Christian should be the same thoughts, desires, and motives which filled the sacred Heart of Jesus Christ our Lord. We must strive to imitate Him and to reproduce His Image, not only in the outward but in the inner life. Especially here, we are bidden to follow His Unselfishness and Humility.

HOW CAN THIS BE DONE?

The only way that Christlikeness in this manner, and in every manner, can be carried out in the life of the Believer is that we have a correct interpretation of the Cross. This refers to what Jesus did in that great Sacrifice, understanding our part in that and why it was done, and placing all our trust in this Finished Work. If the Cross is that to which He came, and that's exactly why He came, then it is the Cross in which the need of humanity was met. That must be the starting place and the stopping for all Believers. Actually, the word, *"Stop,"* probably is not the better word to use, it being literally impossible to exhaust the potential of the Finished Work of Christ.

The reader must ever understand that everything in pre-Christ history strains toward the Cross, while everything now strains from the Cross. If the Believer does not base everything on the Cross and in the capacity of the Cross, and we mean everything, thus denying a proper foundation, all else believed will be skewed as well!

EQUAL WITH GOD

Paul said, *"Who, being in the Form of God, thought it not robbery to be equal with God,"* which proclaims two assertions. They are:

Jesus previously existed in the Form of God, and He did not regard His Existing in a manner of equality with God as a prize to be grasped or held on to. *"Being in the very Nature of God"* is literally, *"Existing in the Form of God."* To say that He was existing in the essential Form of God is tantamount to saying that He possessed the Nature of God. However, this does not need to be regarded as precisely the same as *"the Form of God,"* for one's essential nature can remain unchanged, though the manner in which that nature is expressed can vary greatly through changing times and circumstances.

This statement by Paul has been variously interpreted. Does it mean something that has ceased or something to be ceased? This uncertainty has led to three possibilities:

1. The preincarnate Christ already possessed equality with the Father and resolved not to cling to it.

2. Christ had no need to grasp at equality with God, for He already possessed it.

3. Christ did not reach for His Crowning prematurely as Adam did, but was willing to wait till after His Suffering.

Point number one seems to be the correct answer.

THE FORM OF GOD

The phrase, *"Who, being in the form of God,"* refers to Deity, which Christ always was.

"Form" in the Greek is *"Morpha,"* and means, *"Shape or nature."* However, the Greek word has no reference to the shape of any physical object. Actually, it was a Greek philosophical term.

Consequently, Vincent said, *"We must here dismiss from our minds the idea of shape, at least as we normally think of such. The word is used here in its philosophical sense to denote that expression of being which carries in itself the distinctive nature and character of the being to whom it pertains, and is thus permanently identified with that nature and character."[6]*

He then said, *"As applied to God, the word is intended to describe that mode in which the essential Being of God expresses itself."[7]*

In English, we actually have no word which can properly convey this meaning, and neither is it possible for us to formulate the reality. *"Form"* inevitably carries with it to us the idea of *"shape."* It is conceivable that the essential Personality of God may express itself in a mode apprehensible by the perception of pure spiritual intelligences. However, the mode itself is neither apprehensible nor conceivable by human minds.

AN EXTENDED MEANING

This mode of expression, *"The Form of God,"* might be said to be the *"setting"* of the Divine Essence. One might say that Jesus is not identical with the Essence itself, Him being God in His Own right, but is identified with this Essence as its natural and appropriate expression, answering to it in every particular. One might also say that before the Incarnation, Jesus was a Perfect Expression of a Perfect Essence. This means that it is not something imposed from without, but something which proceeds from the very depth of the Perfect Being, and into which that Being unfolds, as light from fire.

(Essence is the properties or attributes by means of which something can be placed in its proper class or identified as being what it is.)

Thus, the Greek word for *"form"* refers to that outward expression which a person gives of his inmost nature. This expression is not assumed from the outside but proceeds directly from within.

Before the Incarnation, our Lord was in the Form of God. The word, *"God,"* is without the definite article in the Greek

Text (the God), and, therefore, refers to the Divine Essence. Once again, this means that He was God in His Own Right, that is, if it's proper to use such terminology. There's only One God, which means the Godhead cannot be separated as it regards Deity, but yet, is manifested in Three Persons, *"God the Father, God the Son, and God the Holy Spirit."*

Thus, our Lord's Outward Expression of His Inmost Being was, as to its nature, the expression of the Divine Essence of Deity. Since that outward expression, which this word, *"Form,"* speaks of, comes from and is truly representative of the inward being, it follows that our Lord, as to His Nature, is the Possessor of the Divine Essence of Deity. Being that, it also necessarily follows that He was and is Absolute Deity Himself, a Co-participant with God the Father and God the Holy Spirit in that Divine Essence, which constitutes God as God.

THE TIME OF WHICH THIS SPEAKS

The time at which the Apostle says our Lord gave expression to His Essential Nature, that of Deity, was previous to His Coming to Earth to become Incarnate as the Man Christ Jesus. However, by the use of the Greek word translated, *"Being,"* Paul informs his Greek readers that our Lord's Possession of the Divine Essence did not cease to be a fact when He came to Earth to assume human form. The Greek word translated, *"Being,"* is not the simple verb of being, but a word that speaks of a previous condition protracted into the present. That is, our Lord gave expression to the Essence of Deity, which He possesses, not only before He became Man but, also, after becoming Man, for He was doing so at the time this Philippian Epistle was being written.

To give expression to the Essence of Deity implies the possession of Deity, for this expression, according to the definition of our word, *"Form,"* comes from one's inmost nature.

In fact, this word alone (form) is enough to refute the claim of modernism that our Lord emptied Himself of His Deity when He became Man.

THE ANGELS

This expression of the Essence of His Deity, which our Lord
gave in His Preincarnate State, was given through a spiritual
medium to spiritual intelligences, the Angels. Human beings
in our present state of being cannot receive such impressions
since we are not equipped with the spiritual sense of perception which the Angels have.

What Peter, James, and John saw on the Mount of
Transfiguration was an outward expression of the Essence of
Deity, but given through a medium by which the physical sens-
es of the Disciples could receive the expression given.

However, when we Believers receive our Glorified Bodies,
we will then be equipped to receive the expression of Deity,
which the Angels have already received, through a like spiritual medium. In other words, in the coming Resurrection,
the Saints with Glorified Bodies will then have the ability to
properly receive and understand the expression of Deity. To
be frank, if man, even the godliest man, presently saw God in
His Undiluted Divine Essence, man could not stand it in any
capacity.

One might say that in this statement given in Philippians
2:6, Paul was saying that God the Father and Jesus Christ are
"of one substance."

EXACTLY WHAT DOES GOD LOOK LIKE?

In the words of Albert Barnes, *"What was the 'form' Jesus
had before His Incarnation? What is meant by His having been
then in the Form of God?"* Perhaps no satisfactory answer can
be given to these questions.

Jesus Himself speaks (Jn. 17:5) of *"the Glory which He had
with the Father before the world was."* The language naturally
conveys the idea that there was then a manifestation of the

Divine Nature through Him, which, in some measure, ceased
when He became Incarnate. As well, there was some visible
splendor and majesty, which were then laid aside, although He
continued to be God. What manifestation of His Glory God
may make in the heavenly world, of course, we, as human beings, as stated, cannot know nor understand. Nothing forbids
us, however, to suppose that there is some such visible manifestations; some Splendor and Magnificence of God in the view of
the angelic beings such as becomes the great Sovereign of the
Universe — for He *". . . dwells in Light which no man can approach unto"* (I Tim. 6:16).

It is said here that before His Incarnation, the Lord Jesus
possessed that *"Glory,"* that visible manifestation, or splendor,
indicating the Nature of God.

I merely ask the question, *"Is it possible that God has a
Spirit Body, whatever that might mean?"* (Jn. 4:24).

EQUAL WITH GOD

The phrase, *"Thought it not robbery to be equal with God,"*
refers to a Judgment based upon facts.

The word, *"God,"* is used again without the article — the
God. Had the article preceded it, the meaning would be,
"Equal with God the Father." The word, *"God,"* here refers to
Deity, not seen in the Three Persons of the Godhead, but to Deity seen in its Essence. Equality with God does not refer here
to the Equality of the Lord Jesus with the other Persons of
the Trinity, nor does it refer to His Equality with Them in the
"possession" of the Divine Essence. Possession of the Divine
Essence is not spoken of here, but the *"expression"* of the Divine Essence is referred to, although *"possession"* is implied by
the *"expression."* Equality with God refers here to our Lord's
Co-participation with the other Members of the Trinity in the
expression of the Divine Essence. This is a very important
point, for when we come to consider the fact that our Lord laid
aside something, we will see that it was not the *"possession,"*

but rather the *"expression"* of the Divine Essence.

ROBBERY?

The Greek word, *"Robbery,"* has two distinct meanings, *"A thing unlawfully seized,"* or, *"A treasure to be clutched and retained at all hazards."*

When a Greek word has more than one meaning, the rule of interpretation is to take the one which agrees with the context in which it is found. The Passage which we are studying is the illustration of the virtues mentioned in Philippians 2:2-4, namely, humility and self-abnegation for the benefit of others.

If our Lord did not consider it a thing to be unlawfully seized to be equal with God in the expression of the Divine Essence, then He would be asserting His Rights to that expression. He would be declaring His Rightful Ownership of that prerogative.

However, to assert one's right to a thing does not partake of an attitude of humility and self-abnegation. Therefore, this meaning of the word will not do here. If our Lord did not consider the expression of His Divine Essence such a treasure that it should be retained at all hazards, that would mean that He was willing to wave His Rights to that expression if the necessity arose.

This is the essence of humility and of self-abnegation. Thus, our second meaning is the one to be used here (Wuest).[8]

HUMAN NATURE

Another step in Jesus' Humiliation was that He was made in the outward form of a man. His Inner Nature remained Divine. His Outward Temporary Form, however, was different, changed to that of a man.

Jesus was, in fact, God become man; the Incarnation was not a phantom; His Humanity was real.

In other words, He was not fifty percent God and fifty

percent Man. He was Very God, meaning, *"Total God,"* although freely giving up some of the expressions of Deity, and Very Man, i.e., *"Total Man."*

EQUALITY WITH GOD

To make it easier to understand the phrase, *"Thought it not robbery to be equal with God,"* I think it can be explained according to the following:

• Jesus is God: in fact, He had always been God and despite the Incarnation, was still God. Despite the fact of His becoming human, even with all its limitations, it in no way took from Him the possession of His Deity. Also, despite becoming Fully Man, He in no way felt it was an insult to the Godhead to continue to declare His Essential Essence of Deity.

• He became a Man, Fully Man, Total Man, Absolute Man, *"The Man Christ Jesus."* However, even though He willingly laid aside His Expression of Deity, He never laid aside His Possession of Deity. He was just as much God while Man as He had been God before becoming Man. His Essence never changed despite the fact that He no longer used the Power of His Deity, at least, during His Earthly Life of some thirty-three and a half years.

JESUS CHRIST THE SOURCE
OF ALL BLESSINGS

He is the Source simply because He paid the price at Calvary's Cross. In fact, while Jesus Christ is the Source of all the things we receive from God, as well, He Alone is the Way to God (Jn. 14:6). So, it doesn't matter what one gets right in other areas of life and living, and it doesn't matter what good things a religious denomination may proclaim. If they are wrong about Christ, then they are wrong about everything. Jesus Christ must be given His Rightful Due. Once again, we state that this is an absolute necessity simply because He Alone paid the price that had to be paid.

HE MADE HIMSELF NOTHING

Paul said, *"But made Himself of no reputation, and took upon Him the form of a servant, and was made in the likeness of men"* (Phil. 2:7).

The description now moves to Christ's Incarnate State. Two phrases carry the main thoughts:

1. He made Himself nothing. . . .

2. He humbled Himself. . . . This latter phrase is found in the next Verse.

The first phrase is literally, *"But Himself He emptied."* It uses a verb that has lent its name to the so-called *"kenosis"* theories that probe the nature of Christ's *"Emptying Himself."* Although the Text does not directly state that Christ emptied Himself *"of something,"* such would be the natural understanding when this verb is used. Furthermore, the context has most assuredly prepared the reader for understanding that Christ divested Himself of something. What it was, the following phrase implies:

THE FORM OF GOD

The One Who was existing in the Form of God took on the form of a servant. The word, *"Taking,"* does not imply an exchange, but rather an addition. The *"Form of God"* could not be relinquished, for God cannot cease to be God. However, our Lord could and did take on the very form of a lowly servant when He entered human life by the Incarnation.

It is sometimes suggested that the term, *"Servant,"* refers to the exalted Servant of Jehovah, but this Passage seems intended to emphasize His Condescension and Humble Station. Consequently, what an example our Lord provides considering the spirit of humility! Inasmuch as Angels also are servants, the statement makes it clear that Christ became part of humanity: *"Being made in human likeness."*

Thus, by Paul using the word, *"Likeness,"* it is implied that even though Christ became a Genuine Man, there were certain respects in which He was not absolutely like other men. Paul may have had in mind the unique union of the Divine and human Natures in Jesus or the absence of a sin nature.

In summation, Christ did not empty Himself of the Form of God (His Deity), but of the manner of existence as equal to God. He did not lay aside the Divine Attributes, but *"the insignia of majesty."*

Christ's Action has been described as the laying aside during the Incarnation of the independent use of His Divine Attributes.

NO REPUTATION

The phrase, *"But made Himself of no reputation,"* literally means, *"He emptied Himself."*

Instead of asserting His Rights to the expression of the Essence of Deity, our Lord waived His Rights to that expression, being willing to relinquish it if necessary, which He did. He did not consider the exercise of that expression such a treasure that it would keep Him from setting that expression aside and making Himself of no reputation. So, on behalf of fallen humanity, He willingly and freely *"emptied Himself."*

The Divine Majesty of which He emptied Himself was His Own Rightful Prerogative, and His Humiliation was His Own Voluntary Act.

Alford says, *"He used His equality with God as an opportunity not for self-exaltation, but for self-abasement."*[9]

In fact, Christ's Self-humiliation proved His Deity, for this renunciation would have had no value if Christ were not God. He became Man but in contrast with the first man, He did not grasp at equality with God by robbery. On the contrary, He emptied Himself of all His Outward Glory of the Form of God and revealed Himself to the world in the form of a slave.

By robbery, Adam sought to exalt Himself to the dishonoring of God; the Last Adam humbled Himself to the honoring of God. The first Adam exalted Himself and was humbled; the Last Adam humbled Himself and was exalted.

OF WHAT DID HE EMPTY HIMSELF?

Christ subsisting in the Form of God, i.e., the visible glories shining forth from His Divine Essence as God, is here set in contrast with His assuming *"the form of a servant,"* which, in its turn, declares the existence of His Human Nature. Thus, the *"form of God"* declares His Deity and the *"form of a servant"* His Humanity.

He did not hold fast and bring down to Earth the visible demonstration of His Deity — for such is the import of the word, *"Robbery"* — although it was shown out for a moment on the Mount of Transfiguration — but emptied Himself of that outward Glory in order to become Man and by His Death on the Tree secure the eternal advantage of those who would accept His Sacrifice. He fought not on His Own Glory but on the glory of others.

The question here is not between His being on an equality with God and His emptying Himself — for He never emptied Himself of His Godhead — but the contrast is between His being in the Form of God and in the form of a servant. Equality with God declares His Being; the Form of God expresses the manifestations of that Being. It was of the outward demonstrations of His Deity that He emptied Himself.

THE SEVEN STEPS

The seven downward steps of His Great Renunciation are followed here by the seven upward steps of His Glorious Ascension (Vss. 9-11). They are as follows:

1. His Renunciation (Vs. 6).
2. Emptied Himself.

3. Servant's Form.

4. Became in man's likeness.

5. Humbled Himself.

6. Bowed to death.

7. And what a death! The death of the Cross!

The seven upward steps of His Exaltation are:

1. God highly exalted Him.

2. Granted Him the Name which is above every Name.

3. Universal dominion.

4. Over beings in Heaven.

5. Over beings on Earth.

6. Over beings under the Earth.

7. Divine Glory: all tongues will confess by and by that Jesus of Nazareth is Jehovah, and such confession will honor and not dishonor God.

THE FORM OF A SERVANT

He took the form of a servant at the time when He assumed humanity, as it is said, *"Being made in the likeness of men."* It is as follows:

- His Subjection to the Law (Lk. 2:21; Gal. 5:4).
- His Subjection to His Parents (Lk. 2:5).
- His Position as a Carpenter (Mk. 6:3).
- His Sale for the price of a slave (Ex. 21:32).
- His Death, the death of a slave, and His Dependence as a Servant on God, all illustrate His Form as a servant (Isa. 49:3, 7).

This proves:

- He was in the form of a servant directly when He became man.
- He was in the Form of God before He was in the form of a servant.
- He truly subsisted in the Divine Nature as in human nature, for He was as much in the Form of God as in the form of a servant, and was so truly in the Form of God as to be on an equality with God. He therefore could have been none other

than God (Isa. 46:5; Zech. 13:7) (Williams).[10]

HIMSELF

So, we continue to come to the question, *"Of what did Christ empty Himself?"*

Was it His Deity, His Nature, His Divine Prerogative, or His Equality? Paul simply says that Christ emptied Himself.

The verb used here simply means, *"To pour out,"* with Christ Himself as the Object. Thus, Christ emptied Himself of Himself.

At no time did He allow selfish considerations to dominate His Spotless Life.

The words, *"Made Himself,"* mean, *"To make empty, to make vain or void."* The word does not occur elsewhere in the New Testament except in the Passage before us. The essential idea is that of bringing to emptiness or nothingness; hence, it is applied to a case where one lays aside his rank and dignity and becomes in respect to that, *"As nothing."* That is, he assumes a far less rank and station.

As someone has said, *"When the sun is obscured by a cloud or in an eclipse, there is no real change of its glory, nor its beams extinguished, nor is the sun itself in any measure changed. Its luster is only for a time obscured."* So it might have been in regard to the manifestation of the Glory of the Son of God.

A FAR GREATER WEIGHT

This one thing is certain, whatever the phrase means, *"But made Himself of no reputation,"* it is far more than the mind of man can even begin to grasp. The reason should be obvious.

Where it is possible for us to see what He became, it is, in fact, impossible for us to know in totality what He was before His Self-emptying. As a creature, we cannot really even begin to grasp the Glory and the Grandeur of the Creator, and He was definitely the Creator (Jn. 1:1-3). To be frank, even if shown such, we do not presently have the capabilities of grasping that which we would be shown, even if that were possible. Actually, when we're given a glimpse into the spirit world of the Glory of God, we are as much at a loss to comprehend it even as the Prophets were in trying to explain it.

If the reader doubts my words, let him look again at the First Chapter of Ezekiel, or Chapters 4 and 5 of Revelation concerning what John saw. Paul didn't even bother to attempt to explain his *"Visions and Revelations."* He just said that he saw things *". . . and heard unspeakable words, which it is not lawful for a man to utter"* (II Cor. 12:1-4).

Even as I dictate these words, I sense the Presence of God.

WHAT DO WE GET OUT OF THIS SELF-EMPTYING OF CHRIST?

If we see only greatness and glory, I think we miss the point. It is *"Love"* we must see! It was Love that did all of this, a Love that is beyond the comprehension of man.

A fallen race was doomed — doomed to die eternally lost. Having forfeited that which was given to them by God, man found himself in a position from which he could not be extricated, at least by his own machinations. So, if he was to be Saved, God would have to do the deed Himself.

In His Greatness and Glory, God could easily have regenerated man without the sin question being addressed; however, His Nature and Holiness could not allow such. The sin question had to be addressed and answered, and addressed in full, in other words, no shortcuts. There was no other way.

• God could simply have allowed man to die in his lostness, which, of necessity, would demand his spending eternity in the Lake of Fire. That would have satisfied the sin debt on an individual basis regarding each human being. The wages of sin is death, which means separation from God, and eternal separation from God would have paid the penalty.

• However, Love could not allow such to happen. It must

be understood that man was not created by God as a result of need. God does not need anything. He created man from a position totally and completely of Love.

LOVE

Some have claimed that God created man because He wanted or needed fellowship. Once again, God has never needed anything, much less fellowship. No! He created man simply and totally from a position of Love, and as such, He would *"crown him with glory and honor"* (Ps. 8:5). So, if Love created Him, then Love must rescue Him.

However, to rescue man, even though God had spoken all of Creation into existence (Heb. 11:3), He could not speak Redemption into existence, that is, and be true to His Nature. A debt had been incurred, a terrible debt of sin, and that debt must be paid. The only way it could be paid was by death, for that was the penalty (Gen. 2:15-17; Ezek. 18:4; Rom. 6:23). As stated, man could not redeem himself because he had no sacrifice which would serve the purpose. He could not give himself because, due to the Fall, he was sullied, corrupt, and totally depraved, therefore, unsuitable as a sacrifice, at least that which God could accept.

There was only one way: God would become Man and accomplish what the first man, Adam, failed to do.

As a man, He would face the onslaughts of Satan, never one time using His Deity, but definitely using the Power of the Holy Spirit (Jn. 1:32-34). However, that is not as clear-cut as it at first seems.

For the Holy Spirit to function in the manner He must function, that is, if the Ministry of Christ was to be what it should be, our Lord would have to perfectly yield in every manner and way to the Spirit and to the Father.

Christian man, even the most consecrated, yields imperfectly even at our best, whereas Jesus yielded perfectly at all times.

WAS JESUS DIFFERENT FROM US?

I think one would have to say essentially, *"No"*! While He was not born with a sin nature as are all other human beings, still, that should not have made a difference. He had to be a man like all other men, or else, His Work and Function would be to no avail. That's why the Holy Spirit through Paul referred to Him as *"the last Adam"* (I Cor. 15:45).

Some scholars argue that Jesus could not have sinned. In other words, it would not have been possible for Him to have sinned.

That is basely incorrect! Had it been impossible for Him to have sinned, the whole thing would have been a farce. While God certainly cannot sin, it definitely is possible for man to sin. Therefore, the possibility had to be there with Christ as well.

Emptying Himself of the expression of His Deity, thereby, becoming a Man, subjected Him to all that which is possible with man. Hence, He would say, *"I thirst,"* when, of course, God cannot thirst (Jn. 19:28). As well, He grew hungry, and God cannot hunger (Mat. 4:2). Also, Jesus grew tired as a human being will, but God cannot tire, at least in that fashion (Jn. 4:6).

Yes, it would have been possible for Jesus to have sinned, but He did not sin despite every effort of Satan to make Him fail.

SATAN HAS NO PART IN ME

Had Jesus failed even one time in thought, word, or deed, we could not have been Saved. He kept the Law perfectly in every respect, the only Man Who ever did such a thing. Consequently, when He came to the conclusion of His Earthly Life and Ministry, He could say, *". . . for the prince of this world comes* (Satan), *and has nothing in Me"* (Jn. 14:30).

He had no relationship with Satan or sin whatsoever and had nothing of Satan in Him. He was not subject to death because He had not sinned.

In the Fall, Satan gained a pseudo-sovereignty over man on the principle of possession and consent of a responsible agent or government by consent of the governed. This means that, in a sense, fallen man gives Satan the right to hold him in bondage. By refusing to accept Christ, man, in essence, gives his consent to Satan to make him a slave.

There are some who claim that God permitted Satan to defeat himself by causing him to kill an innocent victim (Jesus) over Whom he had no claim.

That could only be correct in the sense that Christ allowed such to happen. No man could have killed Christ, and neither could Satan kill Christ without His Consent. In fact, Jesus did not die on the Cross until the Holy Spirit told Him to die (Heb. 9:14).

Now, we know that death is of Satan caused by sin. We also know that Satan had no control over Christ whatsoever, and, as well, Jesus had never sinned, so there were no wages of sin, which was death, in His Life.

As stated, the only way that Satan could be said to have killed Christ is for the Lord to have allowed such.

So, what Jesus did regarding His Incarnation, His Life, His Ministry, and more particularly, His Death on the Cross and Resurrection, all as a Man, are beyond comprehension.

THE FORM OF A SERVANT

The phrase, *"And took upon Him the form of a servant,"* is actually the translation of the word, *"Servant,"* which Paul used in Philippians 1:1 to describe himself, a bond slave.

The manner in which the Greek phrase is structured means that our Lord took upon Himself the form of a servant or slave, which was the cause of the emptying. Consequently, the translations so far could read, *"Emptied Himself, having taken the form of a bond slave."*

As we have previously stated, the word, *"Form,"* refers to the outward expression one gives of his inward being. The words, *"Form of a bond slave,"* therefore, mean that our Lord gave outward expression to His Inmost Nature, the outward expression being that of a bond slave. When expressing Himself as a bond slave come to serve, He necessarily exchanged one form of expression for another. In Verse 6, He was in His Preincarnate State expressing Himself as Deity. In Verse 7, He expresses Himself in Incarnation as a bond slave. This is the direct opposite of what took place at the Transfiguration.

This *"form,"* not being identical with the Divine Essence but dependent upon it, and necessarily implying it, can be parted with or laid aside. Since Christ is One with God and, therefore, pure being, absolute existence, He can exist without the form. This Form of God Christ laid aside in His Incarnation.

AN ILLUSTRATION OF THE SERVANT

An illustration of this self-emptying of the Son of God is found in John 13:1-17. Our Lord, seated at the table, the Master and Lord of the Disciples, is illustrative of Him in His Preincarnate Glory, giving outward expression of the Glory of His Deity to the Angels.

Our Lord, girded with a towel and washing the feet of the Disciples, is illustrative of His taking the outward expression of a servant in His Incarnation. His Outer Garments, laid aside for the time being, point to His setting aside the outward expression of His Preincarnate Glory while He expressed Himself as a bond slave.

The fact that He was still their Master and Lord while kneeling on the floor doing the work of an oriental slave speaks of the fact that our Lord's Assumption of Humanity did not mean that He relinquished His Deity. He was just as much God while on Earth in His Humiliation as He was before He came and as He is now. His Act of taking His Outer Garments again tells of the resumption of the expression of His Glory after the Resurrection (Wuest).[11]

The word, *"Servant,"* does not mean that Jesus became an actual slave of any single man — though His Service was expressed to individual men (Lk. 22:27) — but was the Actual *"Servant"* of mankind in general.

The phrase, *"Form of a servant,"* should be allowed to explain the phrase, *"Form of God,"* in Verse 6. The form of a servant is that which indicates a condition of a servant in contradistinction from one of higher rank. It means to appear as a servant, to perform the offices of a servant, and to be regarded as such. He was made like a servant in the lowly condition which He assumed.

HUMILIATION

There are some who have interpreted this statement as given by Paul as meaning that He became the Servant or Minister of God and that in doing it, it was necessary that He should become a Man, but the objection to this is obvious.

It greatly weakens the force of the Apostle's argument. His object is to state the depth of humiliation to which Christ descended; and this was best done by saying that He descended to the lowest condition of humanity and appeared in the most humble garb. The idea of being a *"Servant or Minister of God"* would not express that, for this is a term which might be applied to the highest Angel in Heaven. Though the Lord Jesus was not literally a servant or slave, yet what is affirmed here was true of Him in the following respects:

• He occupied a most lowly condition in life.

• He condescended to perform such acts as are appropriate only to those who are servants. *". . . I am among you as He Who serves"* (Lk. 22:27).

• His Demeanor was that of a servant in every respect. Actually, this was one of the reasons that the religious leaders of Israel so totally rejected Him. He was not at all of the aristocracy and not at all of the upper class but, in fact, was looked at as a *"Peasant."*

THE LIKENESS OF MEN

The phrase, *"And was made in the likeness of men,"* presents the Lord entering into a new state of being when He became Man. However, His becoming Man did not exclude His Position of Deity. He was and is today a Person with two Natures, that of absolute Deity (Very God) and that of absolute Humanity (Very Man).

"Likeness," in the Greek Text, refers to *"that which is made like something else."* Our Lord's Humanity was a real likeness, not a phantom or an incomplete copy of humanity, but this likeness did not express the whole of Christ's Being.

His mode of manifestation resembled what men are, but His Humanity was not all that there was of Him. He was also Deity. Wuest says, *"He was not a Man merely as such, but the Son of God manifest in the flesh and nature of man."*[12]

The phrase, *"The likeness of men,"* has reference to the Humanity of Jesus, which had a beginning in time and should be taken in the sense of Galatians 4:4: *"God sent forth His Son, born of a Woman."*

THE MAN CHRIST JESUS

Baillie said, *"The Church has never taught that the human element in Jesus, His Manhood, was or is coeternal with God, but that it is exactly like ourselves and belongs to the order of created things."*[13] In other words, Jesus was not always Man even though He was always God. He became a Man at a point in time.

However, none of this can be taken to be anything less than man. Christ's Humanity was no mere mask or disguise. He was *"really like men as He was truly Man"*; but *"He was also more than a Man, without which fact there would be no resemblance but mere identity."* Jesus Christ was Truly Man, but it was in and through Him that the Revelation of God came. This makes Him unique and distinct from man — He is *"Very Man and Very God."* The only way Paul can express this Truth is to speak of His

Likeness to man. Christ took upon Himself not merely the fact of a human person but, as well, a human nature. So, one could say, even as we have said, that He is One Person in two natures.

Lightfoot says, *"Christ, as the Last Adam, represents not the individual man, but the human race."*

HUMAN LIMITATION

In attempting to explain the Deity and the Humanity of Christ, we must be very careful that we not weaken the great Testimony of His Humanity. Certainly, it fixes our thoughts on this, at least that our Lord, by becoming Man, had for His, truly for His, the experience of the human limitation, human weakness and impoverishment, human dependence, and human subjection, singularly contrasting with the Glory of the Form of God. Thus, this humanity became His.

It was so emphatically real, and at the Incarnation, it became so emphatically the form of existence on which He entered, that it is the thing eminently to be regarded and reverently to be dwelt upon. Instead of His Fullness, this emptiness, as the Holy Spirit through the Apostle proclaims it, is to draw and fix our regard. Instead of the Form of God, there arises before us this true human history, this lowly manhood — and it took place by His Emptying Himself.

Various persons in schools have thought it right to go further. The word used here, *"In the likeness of men,"* has appeared to them to suggest that if the Son of God did not renounce His Godhead, the Divine Nature in Him must have bereaved itself of the Divine Attributes or withheld itself from the use and exercise of them so that the all-fullness no longer was at His Disposal. In this line, they have gone on to describe or assign the mode of self-emptying, which the Incarnation should imply.

THE DIVINE MYSTERY

However, it does not appear to me that one can lay down

positions as to the internal privations of One Whose nature is owned to be essentially Divine without falling into confusion and darkening of counsel. Perhaps we may do well to cherish the impression that this self-emptying on the part of the Eternal Son of God for our Salvation involves realities which we cannot conceive or put in any words. There was more in this emptying of Himself than we can think or say.

He emptied Himself when He became Man. Here we have the eminent example of a Divine mystery, which being revealed remains a mystery never to be adequately explained, and which yet proves full of meaning and full of Power.

The Word was made flesh. He through Whom all worlds took being was seen in Judea in the lowliness of that practical historical manhood. We are hard put to explain this, but if we believe it, all things become new for us: the meaning it proves to have for human history is inexhaustible.

He emptied Himself, *"taking the form of a servant,"* or bond slave. For the creature is in absolute subjection alike to God's Authority and to His Providence, and so Christ came to be. He entered on a discipline of subjection and obedience. In particular, He was made after the likeness of men. He was born as other children are even though He Alone experienced a unique conception. He grew as other children grow; body and mind took shape for Him under human conditions.

HE HUMBLED HIMSELF

Paul said, *"And being found in fashion as a Man, He humbled Himself, and became obedient unto death, even the death of the Cross"* (Phil. 2:8).

After describing the fact of the Incarnation, Paul turns to the consideration of the depths of humiliation to which Christ went: *"He humbled Himself"* and went to *"Death on a Cross."*

The concluding phrase in Philippians 2:7 states what Christ actually was. The opening phrase of Philippians 2:8 looks at Him from the standpoint of how He appeared in the estimation of men.

As far as His External Appearance was concerned, He was *"found"* by them as a mere man. Outwardly considered, He was no different from other men. Even this was great condescension for One Who possessed the Form of God, but Christ's Incomparable Act did not end there. He further humbled Himself by *"becoming obedient to death."* He was so committed to the Father's Plan that He obeyed it even as far as death (Heb. 5:8). Neither was this all, for it was not ordinary death but the disgraceful death by Crucifixion, a death not allowed for Roman citizens, and to Jews, indicative of the Curse of God (Deut. 21:23; Gal. 3:13).

THE CROSS

The mention of the *"Cross"* connoted probably the cruelest form of capital punishment. Crucifixion had been practiced by the Phoenicians and Persians and was taken over by the Romans. In Rome, it was punishment reserved for slaves and foreigners, but yet, the type of death which God commanded of His Son, the Lord Jesus Christ, that is, if mankind was to be redeemed. Actually, the process was twofold:

1. It had to be a Cross, actually demanded by God, which we will deal with momentarily.

2. There had to be a certain type of Sacrifice, which only the Son of God could fill. So, the act of Crucifixion itself, although necessary, could not save anyone. The total Plan of Redemption demanded not only death by Crucifixion but, as well, a perfect Sacrifice, which no human being other than Christ could fulfill.

FOUND IN FASHION

The phrase, *"And being found in fashion as a Man,"* presents the word, *"Fashion,"* as the translation of a Greek word that refers to an outward expression that is assumed from the outside and does not come from within. The Greek word for *"Form,"* as we saw, refers to an outward expression that came from one's inward nature, thereby, describing His Deity. That means that our Lord's Expression of His Deity was not assumed from the outside but came from His Inmost Nature. Likewise, His Outward Expression as a bond slave came from His Inmost Nature.

However, His Expression of His Humanity came not from His Inmost Nature as God, but was assumed in the Incarnation.

The contrast here is between what He was in Himself, God, and what He appeared in the eyes of men. The word, *"Fashion,"* therefore, referred to that which is purely outward and appeals to the senses.

Our Lord's Humanity was real. He was really a Man, but He was not a real man in the sense that He was like others of the human race, only a Man. In His Incarnation, He was always more than man. There was always that single personality with a dual nature.

His Deity did not make Him more or less than a man, and His Humanity did not make Him less than absolute Deity. He became in the likeness of man, and He was found in fashion as a Man.

"Likeness" states the fact of His real resemblance to men in mode of existence, and *"fashion"* defines the outward mode and form as He appeared in the eyes of men. However, He was not found in fashion as a man, but rather *"Man."* The indefinite article (a) should not be in the translation. He was found in outward guise as *"Man,"* not *"a man."* He was actually *"The Man"* because He was also *"God,"* even though He had assumed human nature, but yet, without its sin.

A DIVINE MIRACLE

"Fashion" denotes the way Christ appeared in men's eyes. His contemporaries saw Jesus as they saw other men, subject to human drives and suffering (Heb. 4:15).

Isaiah said of Him, *". . . He has no form nor comeliness; and when we shall see Him, there is no beauty that we should desire Him"* (Isa. 53:2).

In fact, one could say that a Divine Miracle is required to see God in this Servant. Faith that He is the Full and True Revelation of God comes *". . . not of blood, nor of the will of the flesh, nor of the will of man, but of God"* (Jn. 1:13).

The confession that He is the Christ springs from a Revelation of the *"Father which is in Heaven"* (Mat. 16:16-17).

Paul puts it elsewhere, *"No man can say that Jesus is the Lord, but by the Holy Spirit"* (I Cor. 12:3).

PAUL'S DESCRIPTION

And so, He was *"found in fashion as Man."* Could words express more strongly how wonderful it is in the Apostle's eyes that He should so be found? He lived His Life and made His Mark in the world in human fashion — His Form, His Speech, His Acts, and His Way of Life declared Him Man.

But being so, He humbled Himself to a strange and great obedience, subjection. In that subjection, obedience is the part of every creature, but the obedience that Christ was called to learn was special. A heavy task was laid upon Him.

He was made under the Law, and bearing the burden of human sin, He wrought Redemption. In doing so, many great interests fell to Him to be cared for. This was done by Him, not in the manner of Godhead, which speaks and it is done, but with the pains and labor of a Faithful Servant.

"I have a Commandment," He said as He faced the Jews who would have had His Messianic Work otherwise ordered (Jn. 12:49).

THE HUMILITY OF CHRIST

The phrase, *"He humbled Himself,"* means, *"To be made low or to bring low, but yet to do so willingly."* What a description of the Son of God.

However, this self-humbling does not refer to the self-emptying of Verse 7. That was a self-humbling in His Character as God. Here the self-humbling is the Act of our Lord as the Son of Man. As we shall see, it was the humiliation of the Death of the Cross. This we must consider: if it was humiliating to our Lord in His Humanity, how much more was it so in His Deity. In fact, humiliation was characteristic of Him as a Man. He did not aspire to high honor; He did not affect pomp and parade; He did not demand the service of a train of menials; but He condescended to the lowest conditions of life (Lk. 22:27).

The words here are very carefully chosen by the Holy Spirit as given by the Apostle. In the former case (Vs. 7), when He became a Man, He *"emptied Himself,"* or laid aside the symbols of His Glory; now, when a Man, He further humbled Himself. That is, though He was God appearing in the form of Man — a Divine Person on Earth — yet He did not assume and assert the dignity and prerogatives appropriate to a Divine Being, or even an honored human being, but put Himself voluntarily in a condition of obedience. For such a Being to obey Law implied voluntary humiliation, and the greatness of His Humiliation was shown by His becoming entirely obedient, as stated, even till He died on the Cross.

THE PARTICULAR TIMES IN WHICH HE LIVED

The world at the time of Christ functioned on the basis of pomp, ceremony, dignity, station, and status. About a third of the population of the Roman Empire at that time were slaves. So, the very spirit of the age pointed toward catering to those of rank and station. In fact, Roman citizens were divided into three classes, Senatorial, Equestrian, and Plebeian, and the whole system of government harmonized with this triple division.

The Senatorial class was composed of descendents of senators and those upon whom the emperors conferred the privilege of wearing the tunic with broad purple border, the sign of membership in this order.

The Equestrian class was made up of those of lesser rank, but yet, who were wealthy. They had the privilege of wearing the narrow purple band on the tunic.

The Plebeians, which consisted of the general Roman public, wore no band of any nature on their garments.

The spirit of the age had also greatly infected Israel.

THE PHARISEES AND SADDUCEES

Within Israel at the time of Christ, there were found two major parties, one strict and the other lax in the observance of Mosaic Law. The leaders of the former were the highly popular Pharisees, who, according to their name, were the *"Separatists,"* separated from the common and lawless masses, at least according to their interpretation. They tried to surpass each other in their zeal for the traditional ordinances and pious observances, although it was also possible at times to find real piety among them. However, they appear at their worst in the New Testament records where they are described as taking a hostile attitude toward the higher and the highest form of Divine Revelation, and I speak of Christ Himself.

THE SADDUCEES

Their rivals, the Sadducees, were less fanatical in their observance of the demands of the Law and more willing to compromise with the spirit of the times. To this part belonged many of the more prominent Priests.

Out of this mix came the Jewish Sanhedrin to the highest tribunal of some 71 members, and also of the lower tribunals of 23 members, of which Jerusalem had two. It constituted the ruling hierarchy of Israel. It was made up of both Pharisees and Sadducees, but more so by the Pharisees. It is said that in the time of Salome, they were so powerful that *"the Queen ruled only in name, but the Pharisees in reality."*

So, in the time of Christ, the Sanhedrin was formally led by the Sadducean High Priests, but practically ruled by the Pharisees. Most, if not all, of its members were extremely wealthy. Consequently, the status or station in Israel went down from this ruling body through the ranks of these two parties, which, in effect, separated themselves from the *"common masses,"* as they were called. In fact, during the time of Christ, the religious leaders of Israel, actually consisting of these of which we have mentioned, held themselves aloof from the common people. They would not think of mixing with them, much less personally giving spiritual instruction. Worse yet, they had no real spiritual instruction to give inasmuch as they really did not know God.

JESUS

Into this status conscious hierarchy of Israel came Christ. He was a Peasant, the Son of a carpenter, at least, that was what was thought. As such, He had no contact whatsoever with this ruling hierarchy, consequently, not at all a product of its schools, etc. As a result, He was looked at by the ruling hierarchy of Israel as an unlettered, untutored, and, therefore, ignorant product of the masses. He held no station, no status, no place, and no position. Consequently, He was automatically labeled as *"One of no consequence."*

Worse yet, He was brought up in this despised village of Nazareth, prompting the reply of Nathaniel, *". . . Can there any good thing come out of Nazareth . . . ?"* (Jn. 1:45-46).

Nazareth lay close to several main trade routes for easy contact with the outside world. In fact, it is believed that a Roman garrison was stationed nearby as well. The place was scorned by strict Jews because of this outside influence, and worst of all, the Roman influence, if, in fact, a Roman garrison indeed was stationed nearby. Even though born in Bethlehem, Jesus spent nearly 30 years in Nazareth (Lk. 2:39).

The schooling that Jesus formally had was that of the

ordinary village child, which means He was taught to read and write (Lk. 4:17; Jn. 8:6-8). However, on the commencing of His Ministry, even His Own Townsfolk would not receive Him.

THE NAZARENES

After the beginning of His Ministry when He first ministered to them, and already having heard reports of great things done elsewhere, they at first listened to Him with admiration. Then, as the magnitude of the claims He was making became apparent to His Audience, a very different spirit took possession of them.

"Who was this Who spoke this? Was it not Joseph's son?" (Lk. 4:22). There seemed to be disappointment, as well, that Jesus showed no disposition to gratify them by working before them any of the Miracles of which they had heard so much (Lk. 4:23). Consequently, He told His Hearers that He had not expected any better reception. In reply to their reproach that He had wrought Miracles elsewhere but had wrought none among them, He quoted examples of Prophets who had done the same thing, Elijah and Elisha (Lk. 4:24-28).

This completed the exasperation of the Nazarenes who, springing forward, dragged Him to the brow of the hill on which their city was built, and would have thrown Him down had something in the aspect of Jesus not restrained them.

HIS TEACHING AND PREACHING

The Scripture says, *"He taught them as having authority, and not as the Scribes"* (Mk. 1:22).

The Scribes gave forth nothing of their own. They but repeated the statements of the so-called great authorities of the past. Consequently, it was a surprise to the people to find in Jesus One Whose Wisdom, like waters from a clear fountain, came fresh and sparkling from His Own Lips. The authority also with which Jesus spoke commanded attention. He sought

support in the opinion of no others but gave forth His Statements with firmness, decision, dignity, and emphasis.

This, as well, angered the Pharisees and Sadducees, who,
in fact, He ignored, seeking not at all their approval or advice. Consequently, He clashed with them more and more as
they sought to find means to oppose and accuse Him, accepting Him not at all. In fact, they *"took counsel to destroy Him"*
(Mk. 3:6).

At the beginning of His Ministry, He attracted great crowds
of people, with untold numbers being healed of every manner
of disease, and even the dead being raised. This gained Him
a wide popularity, at least at first. However, as the opposition
increased, the last year of His Ministry saw the crowds dimin-
ishing somewhat, with Him more and more privately teaching
His Disciples.

The Scriptures plainly say, *"They hated Me without a cause"*
(Ps. 35:19; 69:4; 109:3; 119:161; Jn. 15:25).

Even though we have only touched the surface, perhaps
we can still see somewhat the magnitude of the humiliation
He suffered, not only becoming Man, but rather a Man most
humiliated.

OBEDIENCE

The phrase, *"Became obedient unto death,"* does not mean
that He became obedient to death. He was always the Master
of Death. In fact, He died as no other individual ever died or
ever will die. He died of His Own Volition. He actually dismissed His Human Spirit, but not until the Holy Spirit told
Him to do so (Heb. 9:14).

The word, *"Unto,"* is the translation of a Greek word which
means, *"Up to the point of."* Our Lord was obedient to the Father
up to the point of dying. In fact, He said, *". . . Lo, I come to do
Your Will, O God . . ."* (Heb. 10:9).

Yet Christ subjected Himself to death *". . . that through
death He might destroy him who had the power of death, that*

is, the Devil; and deliver them who through fear of death were all their lifetime subject to bondage" (Heb. 2:14-15). It must be emphasized that Christ's Acts of self-humiliation and obedience to death were voluntary — of Himself, as stated, He laid down His Life (Jn. 10:17-18) — while, at the same time, such were in accord with the Will of the Father.

Should it be said that if He was God Himself, He must have been Himself the Law-Giver, we may reply that this rendered His Obedience the more wonderful and the more meritorious. If for an important purpose a monarch should place himself in a position to obey his own laws, nothing could show in a more striking manner their importance in his view.

The highest honor that has been shown to the Law of God on Earth was that it was perfectly observed by Him Who made the Law — the great Mediator. In fact, He obeyed even when obedience terminated in death.

In the case of Jesus, all of this was wholly voluntary. He placed Himself in the condition of a Servant to do the Will of God and then never shrank from what that condition involved.

THE DEATH OF THE CROSS

The phrase, *"Even the death of the Cross,"* presents the character of His Death. It was the death of a Cross, its nature one of ignominy and degradation. It was the kind of death meted out to criminals and only to those who were not citizens of the Roman Empire. *"The death of the Cross"* indicates the climax of Christ's Self-abasement, for it was the most ignominious, as stated, of all the modes of death then known. In fact, the Law of Moses had spoken a curse upon such a death (Deut. 21:23). Thus, the Cross was surrounded by the deepest shame (Heb. 12:2).

However, by His Obedience even unto *"the death of the Cross,"* Christ *". . . has abolished death, and has brought Life and immortality to light through the Gospel"* (II Tim. 1:10). Consequently, *"The Cross of Christ has come to be His Crown of Glory"* (Rom. 5:19).

WAS SUCH A DEATH NECESSARY?

Yes, it was!

If it is to be noticed, Paul did not say, *"The death on the Cross,"* but rather, *"The death of the Cross."* The idea is He came to die on the Cross. That was the purpose of His Incarnation, the very purpose of His Coming, and the very purpose of it all.

As we have previously said, His Death by Crucifixion was not an execution in the truest sense of the word. In other words, He did not run afoul of Roman or Jewish law, thereby, suffering this ignominious death. While they definitely played their part in this travesty, still, it was the Will of God for Him to die accordingly. Jesus said of this situation, *"Woe unto the world because of offences! for it must needs be that offences come; but woe to that man by whom the offence comes!"* (Mat. 18:7).

If the church misunderstands the Sacrificial Atoning Death of Christ in any manner, negative results will always follow. The purpose of the Great Plan of God as it regarded the Redemption of fallen humanity was always the *"Cross"* (Gen. 3:15; I Pet. 1:19-20; Rev. 13:8). All the predictions of the Prophets, whether directly or indirectly, pointed toward the *"Cross"* (Isa., Chpt. 53). The Incarnation of Christ (God becoming Man) was all for the purpose of the *"Cross"* (Mat. 20:28; Mk. 10:45; I Tim. 2:6). Even though He performed Miracles and healed the sick, still, His Major Purpose was always the *"Cross"* (Mat. 16:21-25).

WHY WAS THE CROSS NECESSARY?

Death is the signature of failure and disgrace. Even with sinless creatures, it seems so. Their beauty and their use are past; their worth is measured and exhausted; they die. More emphatically in a nature like ours, which aims at fellowship with God and immortality, death is significant this way and bears the character of doom.

So, we are taught to think that death entered by sin, but the valid death of crucifixion inflicted for the worst crimes is most significant this way. What it comprehended for our Lord, although necessary, we cannot measure. We know that He looked to it with the most solemn expectation, and when it came, the experience was overwhelming (Lk. 22:39-45). He submitted to the doom and blight of death, and through death, He made Atonement and finished transgression.

CRUCIFIXION, THE WORST FORM OF DEATH

The Incarnation was the way in which our Lord bound Himself to our woeful fortunes, and carried to us the benefits with which He would enrich us; and His Death was for our sins, endured that we might live.

This type of death was necessary for several reasons:

• Death was mandated for all who broke the Law (the Law of Moses, i.e., *"Law of God"*), and all had broken that Law, with the exception of the Lord Jesus Christ (Rom. 3:10; 6:23).

• The crime of the breaking of the Law of God is the worst crime that one could begin to imagine. Sin strikes at the very Holiness and Righteousness of God and is destructive of all things (Jn. 10:10). Consequently, the Death of Christ on the Cross, the worst form of death, showed the awfulness of that monster called sin (Deut. 21:22-23; Gal. 3:13). It showed the necessity of the worst type of punishment, a punishment, incidentally, that should have been ours.

• As well, when Jesus went to the Cross, He did so as a Sacrifice. In the offering up of Himself as a Sacrifice, He had to atone for the vilest sins, the worst sins, and the most heinous sins that could ever be imagined. Consequently, for that to be done, the Cross was a necessity.

In view of the tremendous significance of this, which, in fact, is the most important thing in the history of man, perhaps it would help us to look at this great Sacrifice of Christ more closely.

ATONEMENT

Considering that Jesus atoned for all sin by His Death on the Cross, past, present, and future, at least for all who will believe (Jn. 3:16), perhaps the word, *"Atonement,"* explains best all the rudiments of Redemption.

The word, *"Atonement,"* is one of the few theological terms which derived basically from Anglo-Saxon terminology. It means, *"A making at one,"* and points to a process of bringing those who are estranged into a unity. The word is used frequently in the Old Testament but is found only once in the New Testament, and would perhaps even then have been better translated, *"Reconciliation."*

Its use in theology is to denote the Work of Christ in dealing with the problem posed by the sin of man and in bringing sinners into right relation with God.

It was used frequently in the Old Testament because the Work of Redemption was, in effect, a futuristic Work, which would not be brought about until Jesus came and paid the price on Calvary's Cross.

 Redemption in the New Testament is a fact, hence, there are other words which describe it to a greater degree, such as Reconciliation, Justification, Adoption, Propitiation, etc. Nevertheless, the word, *"Atonement,"* probably helps individuals to understand the Sacrifice of Christ better than any other word.

Its use in theology is to denote the Work of Christ in dealing with the problem posed by the sin of man and in bringing sinners into right relation with God.

THE NEED FOR ATONEMENT

The need for Atonement is brought about by three things:
1. The universality of sin.
2. The seriousness of sin.
3. Man's inability to deal with sin.
The first point is attested in many places: *"There is no man*

who does not sin" (I Ki. 8:46); *"There is none who does good,
no, not one"* (Ps. 14:3); *"There is not a righteous man on Earth,
who does good, and never sins"* (Eccl. 7:20). Jesus told the rich
young ruler, *"No one is good but God Alone"* (Mk. 10:18), and
Paul writes, *"All have sinned and come short of the Glory of
God"* (Rom. 3:23). Much more could be cited.

The seriousness of sin is seen in Passages which show God's
Aversion to it. The Prophet Habakkuk prayed, *"You Who are
of purer eyes than to behold evil, and cannot look on wrong"*
(Hab. 1:13).

Sin separates from God (Prov. 15:29; Isa. 59:2). Jesus said
of one's sin, which is blasphemy against the Holy Spirit, that it
will never be forgiven (Mk. 3:29). Of Judas He said, *"It would
have been better for that man if he had not been born"* (Mk.
14:21). Before being Saved, men are *"estranged and hostile in
mind, doing evil deeds"* (Col. 1:21). There awaits the unrepentant sinner only *"a fearful prospect of Judgment, and a fury of
fire that will consume the adversaries"* (Heb. 10:27).

Man cannot deal with the situation. He is not able to keep
his sin hidden (Num. 32:23), and he cannot cleanse himself of
it (Prov. 20:9).

No deeds of law will ever enable man to stand before God
justified (Rom. 3:20; Gal. 2:16). If he must depend on himself,
then man will never be saved. Perhaps the most important
evidence of this is the very fact of the Atonement. If the Son
of God came to Earth to save men, then men were sinners and
their plight serious indeed.

ATONEMENT IN THE OLD TESTAMENT

God and man are hopelessly estranged by man's sin, and
there is no way back from man's side, but God provides the
way.

In the Old Testament, Atonement is usually said to be obtained by the sacrifices, but it must never be forgotten that God
says of Atoning Blood, *"I have given it for you upon the Altar*

to make Atonement for your souls" (Lev. 17:11). Atonement
is secured not by any value inherent in the sacrificial victim,
but because sacrifice is the Divinely-appointed way of securing
Atonement. In effect, Atonement was secured by Faith in the
coming One the sacrifices represented, namely Christ.

The sacrifices point us to certain truths concerning Atonement. Thus, the victim must always be unblemished, which indicates the necessity for perfection. The victims cost something,
for Atonement is not cheap, and sin is never to be taken lightly.

BLOOD

The death of the victim was the important thing. This is
brought out partly in the allusions to *"blood,"* partly in the
general character of the rite itself, and partly in other refer-
ences to Atonement.

There are several allusions to Atonement, either affected
or contemplated by means other than the rite itself. Where
these bear on the problem, they point to death as the way.
Thus, in Exodus 32:30-32, Moses seeks to make an Atonement
for the sin of the people, and he does so by asking God to blot
him out of the Book which He has written. Phinehas made an
Atonement by slaying certain transgressors (Num. 25:6-8, 13).
Other Passages might be cited.

It is clear that in the Old Testament, it was recognized that
death was the penalty for sin (Ezek. 18:20), but that God gra-
ciously permitted the death of a sacrificial victim to substitute
for the death of the sinner. So clear is the connection that the
writer of the Epistle to the Hebrews can sum it up by saying,
"Without the shedding of Blood there is no forgiveness of sins"
(Heb. 9:22).

ATONEMENT IN THE NEW TESTAMENT

The New Testament takes the line that the sacrifices of old
were not the root cause of the putting away of sins. Redemption

is to be obtained even *"from the transgressions under the First Covenant"* only by the Death of Christ (Heb. 9:15). This means that the sacrifices only pointed to the One Who was to come, thereby, symbolic of His Death. Salvation demanded Faith in Christ rather than the sacrifice of the animal itself, which only pointed to the One Who was to come. In fact, the blood of bulls and goats could not take away sins (Heb. 10:4), meaning that these sacrifices only pointed to the One Who was to come and Who could take away sins, which He did (Jn. 1:29).

Consequently, the Cross is absolutely central to the New Testament and, indeed, to the whole Bible. All before lead up to it. All after look back to it.

Since it occupies the critical place, it is not surprising that there is a vast volume of teaching about it. The New Testament writers, writing from different standpoints and with different emphasis, give us a number of facets of the Atonement. There is no repetition of a stereotyped line of teaching. Each writes as he sees.

Some saw more and more deeply than others, but they did not see something different. In what follows, we shall consider first of all what might be termed, *"The common basic teaching,"* about the Atonement, and then some of the information that we owe to one or other of the New Testament theologians.

THE ATONEMENT REVEALS GOD'S LOVE FOR MEN

All are agreed that the Atonement proceeds from the Love of God. It is not something wrung from a stern and unwilling Father, perfectly just, but perfectly inflexible by a loving Son. The Atonement shows us the Love of the Father just as it does the Love of the Son. Paul gives us the classic exposition of this when he says, *"God shows His Love for us, in that, while we were yet sinners, Christ died for us"* (Rom. 5:8).

In the best known Text in the Bible, we find that *"God so loved the world, that He gave His Only Begotten Son . . ."* (Jn. 3:16).

In the Gospels of Matthew, Mark, and Luke, it is emphasized that the Son of Man *"must suffer"* (Mk. 8:31). That is to say, the Death of Christ was no accident: it was rooted in a compelling Divine necessity.

This we see also in our Lord's Prayer in Gethsemane that the Will of the Father be done (Mat. 26:42). Similarly, in Hebrews we read that it was *"by the Grace of God"* that Christ tasted death for us all (Heb. 2:9).

This thought is found throughout the New Testament, and we must bear it well in mind when we reflect on the manner of the Atonement.

THE SACRIFICIAL ASPECT OF CHRIST'S DEATH

Another thought that is widespread is that the Death of Christ is a death for sin. It is not simply that certain wicked men rose up against Him. It is not that His Enemies conspired against Him and that He was not able to resist them. He *"was put to death for our trespasses"* (Rom. 4:25). In other words, no one actually took the Life of Jesus from Him; in fact, He gave it up willingly (Jn. 10:18). He came specifically to die for our sins. His Blood was shed *"for many for the forgiveness of sins"* (Mat. 26:28).

He *"made purification for sins"* (Heb. 1:3). He *"bore our sins in His Body on the Tree"* (I Pet. 2:24). He is *"the Propitiation for our sins"* (I Jn. 2:2). In fact, the Cross of Christ will never be understood unless it is seen that there on the Cross, the Saviour was dealing with the sins of all mankind.

In doing this, He fulfilled all that the old sacrifices had foreshadowed, and the New Testament writers loved to think of His Death as a Sacrifice, which it definitely was. Jesus Himself referred to His Blood as *"Blood of the Covenant"* (Mk. 14:24), which points us to the sacrificial rites for its understanding.

Indeed, much of the language used in the institution of the Holy Communion is Sacrificial, pointing to the Sacrifice which was accomplished on the Cross.

THE LAMB OF GOD

Paul tells us that Christ *"loved us and gave Himself up for us, a fragrant Offering and Sacrifice to God"* (Eph. 5:2). On occasion, Paul refers not to sacrifice in general but a specific Sacrifice, as in I Corinthians 5:7, *"For Christ our Pascal Lamb* (Passover Lamb) *has been sacrificed."* Peter speaks of *"the Precious Blood of Christ, like that of a lamb without blemish or spot"* (I Pet. 1:19), which indicates that in one aspect Christ's Death was a Sacrifice. In John's Gospel we read the words of John the Baptist, *". . . Behold the Lamb of God, Who takes away the sin of the world"* (Jn. 1:29).

Sacrifice was practically the universal religious rite of the First Century. Wherever men were and whatever their background, they would discern a sacrificial allusion. The New Testament writers made use of this and employed sacrificial terminology to bring out what Christ has done for men. All that to which the sacrifices pointed and more, He fully accomplished by His Death.

THE REPRESENTATIVE NATURE OF CHRIST'S DEATH

It is agreed by most students that Christ's Death was vicarious (substitutionary). In one sense, He died *"for sin,"* and another, He died *"for us,"* but *"vicarious"* is a term which may mean much or little. It is better to be more precise.

Most scholars today accept the view that the Death of Christ is representative. That is to say, it is not that Christ died and somehow the benefits of that Death became available to men. It is rather that He died specifically for us. He was our Representative as He hung on the Cross. This is expressed succinctly in II Corinthians 5:14, *"One died for all; therefore, all have died."*

The Death of the Representative counts as the death of those He represents. When Christ is spoken of as our *"Advocate with the Father"* (I Jn. 2:1), there is the plain thought of representation. As the Passage immediately goes on to deal with His Death for sin, it is relevant to our purpose.

The Epistle to the Hebrews has as one of its major themes that of Christ as our Great High Priest. The thought is repeated over and over. Now, whatever else may be said about a High Priest, He represented men. Thus, the thought of representation may be said to be very strong in the Book of Hebrews.

SUBSTITUTION TAUGHT IN THE NEW TESTAMENT

However, we can say more:

Whereas representation is definitely taught in the New Testament, substitution is, as well, and graphically so, which, in effect, goes a step further than representation.

In the three Gospels, Matthew, Mark, and Luke, there is the great ransom saying, *"The Son of Man also came not to be served but to serve, and to give His Life as a ransom for many"* (Mk. 10:45).

The same Truth is indicated by Passages which speak of Christ as the Suffering Servant of Isaiah, Chapter 53, for of Him it is said, *"He was wounded for our transgressions, He was bruised for our iniquities: and the chastisement of our peace is upon Him; and with His Stripes we are healed . . . the LORD has laid on Him the iniquity of us all"* (Isa. 53:5-6).

The shrinking of Christ in Gethsemane points in the same direction. He was Courageous, but many far less worthy than He have faced death calmly. The agony seems to be inexplicable, other than on the grounds disclosed by Paul, that for our sake God *"made Him to be sin* (a Sin-Offering), *Who knew no sin"* (II Cor. 5:21).

In His Death, He took our place, and His Holy Soul shrank from this identification with sinners. It seems that no less than this gives meaning to the cry of dereliction, *"My God, My God, why have You forsaken Me?"* (Mk. 15:34).

The general thought of all this is that men should die, but Christ died instead, which, of course, is substitution.

WHAT THE CROSS TELLS US

Paul tells us that Christ *"redeemed us from the curse of the Law, having become a curse for us"* (Gal. 3:13). He bore our curse, which is but another way of *"substitution."*

The same thought lies behind Romans 3:21-26, where the Apostle develops the thought that God's Justice is manifested in the process whereby sin is forgive, i.e., *"the Cross."* He is not saying, as some have thought, that God's Righteousness is shown in the fact that sin is forgiven, but that it is shown in the way in which sin is forgiven. Atonement is not a matter of passing over sin as had been done previously (Rom. 3:25). The Cross shows that God is Just at the same time as it shows Him justifying Believers.

This must mean that God's Justice is vindicated in the way sin is dealt with. This seems another way of saying that Christ bore the penalty of men's sin. This is also the thought in Passages dealing with sin-bearing, as Hebrews 9:28 and I Peter 2:24. The meaning of bearing sin is made clear by a number of Old Testament Passages where the context shows that the bearing of penalty is meant.

For example, in Ezekiel 18:20, we read, *"The soul that sins shall die. The son shall not suffer for ('bear' in the Hebrew) the iniquity of the Father..., "* and in Numbers 14:34, the wilderness wanderings are described as a bearing of iniquities. Christ's bearing of our sin then means that He bore our penalty.

This is extremely important in that some are teaching that Christ actually became a sinner on the Cross by taking on the nature of Satan, which, of course, is ludicrous.

THE PRICE OF REDEMPTION

Substitutionalized behind the statement in I Timothy 2:6 is that Christ gave Himself *"a ransom for all."* The word, *"Ransom,"* given here in the Greek is, *"Antilytron,"* and is a strong compound meaning, *"Substitute-ransom."*

It is that which is given in exchange for another as the price of his Redemption. Actually, it is impossible to empty the word of substitutionary associations.

A similar thought lies behind John's recording of the cynical prophecy of Caiaphas, *"It is expedient for you that one man should die for the people, and that the whole nation should not perish"* (Jn. 11:50). For Caiaphas, the words were sheer political expediency, but John saw in them a Prophecy that Christ should die instead of the people.

This is a formidable body of evidence proving the fact of substitution on the part of Christ, but is in no way exhausted. In other words, the Word of God teaches emphatically that Jesus Christ was our Substitute. In the face of all this, it seems impossible to deny that substitution is one strand in the New Testament understanding of the Work of Christ.

DELIVERANCE

There are many truths set forth concerning the Atonement, with the Holy Spirit, in effect, addressing this all-important subject in so many ways that it should not be possible for the Bible student to misunderstand what is being said. In fact, and as should be overly obvious, the Atonement, which, of course, signifies what Jesus did at the Cross and the Resurrection as it regards the great Salvation experience, is the Foundation, the very bedrock of the Christian Faith. If men are mixed-up concerning the Atonement, in other words, if they have something wrong concerning this firm Foundation as it regards their interpretation or thinking, everything else will be somewhat wrong as well.

In fact, I personally believe that much error begins with this — an improper interpretation of the Atonement. Consequently, this must be corrected first of all before anything else can be properly addressed.

Paul sees in the Cross the way of Deliverance, in fact, the only way. This means not only Deliverance for the unsaved soul coming to Christ, to which it most certainly does refer, but, as well, for the Christian. This is where many Christians miss it. They understand the Atonement as it regards their initial Salvation experience, but have little idea as to how it affects their everyday walk before God. Therefore, they attempt to sanctify themselves by methods of their own devising, the devising of other people, etc. Irrespective, any way other than God's Prescribed Order, which is the Finished Work of Christ, which, of course, is the Atonement, is doomed to failure.

Men naturally are enslaved to sin (Rom. 6:17; 7:14), but *"In Christ,"* and only *"In Christ,"* are men free. That applies to the Christian just as well as it applies to the unsaved soul coming to Christ (Rom. 6:14-22).

Along with being free in Christ, which takes place at Conversion, similarly through Christ, Believers are delivered from the flesh. They have *"crucified the flesh"* (Gal. 5:24).

WHAT DOES CRUCIFYING THE FLESH MEAN?

Let's see first what it doesn't mean.

Believers have been attempting to do this from day one. They (and I should say, *"We"*) have tried to do this by using every method imaginable.

What is the flesh?

Paul uses the word, *"Flesh,"* in many ways. It can refer to the physical man. As well, it can refer to the sin nature. It also can refer to the efforts of individuals to sanctify themselves by their own ability, etc. So, it is used in a variety of ways.

However, the word, *"Flesh,"* as Paul uses it in Galatians 5:24, refers to the physical man, in other words, our personal ability as a human being, our talents, education, motivation, willpower, etc.

All these things are not sin within themselves. We turn them into sin if we try to live for God by the means of those things listed, plus others we haven't mentioned. Due to the Fall, the physical body and the mind of man have been made insufficient for the task. So, the Lord has provided a way of victory as well as Salvation. It is the Cross of Christ. It only requires us to place our Faith entirely within Christ and what He did for us at the Cross, and then the Holy Spirit, Who Alone can bring about that which we need, can do His Office Work in our lives.

However, if we place our faith in anything other than Christ and the Cross, this greatly limits the Holy Spirit and actually puts the Believer into a place of living in spiritual adultery (Rom. 7:1-4).

So, what does Paul mean when he, in effect, tells us that we must *"crucify the flesh with the affections and lusts"*? (Gal. 5:24).

This is done and can only be done by the Believer placing his or her Faith exclusively in Christ and the Cross, and maintaining it exclusively in Christ and the Cross (Rom. 6:1-14; 8:1-11; I Cor. 1:17, 18, 23; 2:2).

The great Apostle tells us in Galatians that we cannot live for God by the means of the flesh but only by the means of the Spirit. He said, *"If we live in the Spirit, let us also walk in the Spirit"* (Gal. 5:25).

What does he mean by that?

HOW DO WE WALK IN THE SPIRIT?

The word, *"Walk,"* as Paul used the word, refers to how we live this life, how we order our behavior, how we conduct ourselves, etc. So, this tells us that the great Apostle is addressing us as to how we live this life. We can only do so by *"walking in the Spirit."*

Now, as already asked, how do we do that?

The Holy Spirit works entirely within the parameters, so to speak, of the Finished Work of Christ. In other words, it's the Cross that gave and gives the Holy Spirit the legal means for Him to do what He wants to do within our hearts and lives.

For instance, before the Cross, due to the fact that the sin debt was unpaid, the Holy Spirit could not come into the heart and life of Believers to dwell permanently. Paul said, *"The blood of bulls and goats could not take away sins"* (Heb. 10:4). In fact, when Believers in Old Testament times died, their soul and spirit did not go to Heaven but rather down into Paradise, which was in the heart of the Earth (Lk., Chpt. 16). Once again, the reason for that was because the animal sacrifices were insufficient to take away sins. So, the Holy Spirit was very limited during those times as to what He could actually do because of the reasons given.

However, when Jesus died on the Cross, thereby, paying the sin debt in totality, this made it possible for the Holy Spirit to live within our hearts and lives, and to do so permanently (Jn. 14:16-17).

The manner in which the Believer can walk in the Spirit, and the only way, is that we place our Faith exclusively in Christ and the Cross, and maintain it exclusively in Christ and the Cross. As we have already stated, the Cross of Christ is the Means, and the only Means, by which all of these wonderful things are given to us. When the Believer places his or her Faith exclusively in Christ and the Cross, this is *"walking in the Spirit,"* in other words, the way the Spirit works. This is the only way that one can have victory over the flesh.

GOING BEYOND THE CROSS

Considering that the Cross of Christ answered every question and pointed out every way, where else is there to go? Furthermore, where do we find in the Bible that we ought to go beyond the Cross?

Some might say, *"Well, we go to the Holy Spirit."* The Holy Spirit works exclusively within the parameters of the Finished Work of Christ and will not work outside those parameters, so much so that it is referred to as a Law. Paul said:

"The Law of the Spirit of Life in Christ Jesus has made me free from the Law of Sin and Death" (Rom. 8:2). So, if you're going to go with the Holy Spirit, you have to go with the Cross.

Others would claim that we go on to the Resurrection. While, of course, the Resurrection and anything and everything that Christ did was of immense significance, still, our Redemption was not purchased at the Resurrection, but rather the Cross. Paul said:

"Christ sent me not to baptize, but to preach the Gospel: not with wisdom of words, lest the Cross of Christ should be made of none effect" (I Cor. 1:17).

If it is to be noticed, Paul did not say, *"Lest the Resurrection be made of none effect."*

The great Apostle also said, *"For the preaching of the Cross is to them who perish foolishness; but to we who are Saved it is the Power of God"* (I Cor. 1:18).

He did not say, *"For the preaching of the Resurrection. . . ."*

The great Apostle also said, *"I determined to know nothing among you save Christ and Him Crucified"* (I Cor. 2:2).

He did not say, *"I determined to know nothing among you save the Resurrection. . . ."*

THE RESURRECTION LIFE

Every Believer is importuned by the Lord to live the Resurrection Life, but how do we do that? Paul again told us how that is done. He said:

"For if we have been planted together in the likeness of His Death (the Cross), we shall be also in the likeness of His Resurrection" (Rom. 6:5).

The idea is, it is impossible to live the Resurrection Life if we do not first of all understand the Cross of Christ.

In fact, every single Doctrine in the Bible is built squarely on the Foundation of the Cross of Christ (I Pet. 1:18-20). Actually, all false doctrine begins with an improper interpretation of the Cross, a misunderstanding of the Cross, or a denial of the Cross. In fact, the Cross of Christ is so prominent in the Bible that it is impossible to ignore this which the Lord has done that man might be Saved.

Every single sacrifice given in the Old Testament from day one, which numbers into the multiplicities of millions, all and without fail typified the coming Redeemer and the price that He would pay on the Cross. In fact, there is only one Type of the Resurrection in the Old Testament that I can recall at present, and that pertains to the cleansing of the leper.

One bird was killed in running water, which typified the Cross, and the second bird was let go into the sky, typifying the Resurrection of Christ. As far as I can recall, that is the extent of the type of the Resurrection found in the Old Testament.

When one goes beyond the Cross, one loses one's way. In fact, the Cross of Christ is so prominent that in the last two Chapters in the Book of Revelation, which portrays the coming Perfect Age which will last forever and forever, Christ is referred to seven times as the *"Lamb,"* which is a portrayal of the Cross.

Why would the Holy Spirit refer to Christ at that particular time as *"the Lamb,"* considering that Satan and all the demon spirits and fallen Angels are locked away in the Lake of Fire, meaning that there is no more sin and no more temptation? Seven times Christ is referred to as *"the Lamb"* simply because the Holy Spirit wants all to know that every Saint of God will enjoy the New Jerusalem forever and forever because of what Jesus Christ did at the Cross. Let me say it again:

If one tries to go beyond the Cross, one goes into spiritual oblivion.

"O my brother, do you know the Saviour,
"Who is Wondrous, Kind, and True?
"He's the Rock of your Salvation!
"There's Honey in the Rock for you."

"Have you tasted that the Lord is Gracious?
"Do you walk in the way that's new?
"Have you drunk from the Living Fountain?
"There's Honey in the Rock for you."

"Do you pray unto God the Father,
"What will You have me to do?
"Never fear, He will surely answer,
"There's Honey in the Rock for you."

"Then go out through the streets and byways,
"Preach the Word to the many or few;
"Say to every fallen brother,
"There's Honey in the Rock for you."

THE MESSAGE OF THE CROSS

CHAPTER

2

The Cross Of Christ
Is The Only Means By Which
All Of These Wonderful Things
Are Given To Us

THE CROSS OF CHRIST IS THE ONLY MEANS BY WHICH ALL OF THESE WONDERFUL THINGS ARE GIVEN TO US

Sometime back, a young man asked me the question, *"Is it Who He was, or What He did?"*

It was asked rather sarcastically, and I knew that he was denigrating the Cross. He was trying to say that Redemption and all that it affords was because of Who Jesus Christ was and is, God manifest in the flesh.

To be sure, Jesus Christ, the Son of God, God manifest in the flesh, is the Only One Who could have carried out this great Plan of Redemption. No one else could have done this thing. Abraham could not have done it, Moses could not have done it, David could not have done it, etc. All of these were born in original sin, therefore, instantly making them ineligible to serve as the perfect sacrifice. Make no mistake about it, the Cross of Christ was to satisfy the demands of God. It had nothing to do with Satan, at least, that something was owed this evil monarch. It was that which God demanded. Think about the following for a few moments:

Jesus Christ has always been God. As God, He was unformed, unmade, uncreated, always was, always is, and always shall be, but please consider the following:

He has always been God, never ceasing to be God when He became Man. However, if Jesus Christ, the Son of the Living God, had remained in Heaven, despite the fact of His being God, not a single soul would have ever been saved. In other words, merely being God, as important and necessary as that was, saved no one.

Before man could be redeemed, God had to become Man, and He had to do so for the purpose of going to the Cross. That's the reason that we say that *"the Cross of Christ is the only Means by which all of these wonderful things from God, paid for by Jesus Christ, can be given to us."*

So, the answer to the question is that both, Who He was and What He did, were absolutely necessary. But we must remember, man is not saved because Jesus Christ is God. Man is Saved because Jesus Christ was the Perfect Sacrifice offered up at Calvary's Cross, which satisfied the demands of a thrice-Holy God. We always go back to the Cross! The Cross! The Cross!

Paul said:

"For Christ sent me not to baptize, but to preach the Gospel: not with wisdom of words, lest the Cross of Christ should be made of none effect" (I Cor. 1:17).

Anything and everything that we as Believers receive from the Lord, all, and without exception, is made possible by the Cross of Christ. This we must ever understand.

We are Saved simply because of what Jesus Christ did at the Cross. We are baptized with the Holy Spirit simply because of what Christ did at the Cross. All Blessings come through the Cross, even as all answers to prayer come through the Cross. All communion with the Lord is made possible by the Cross. Before the Cross, man could not approach God due to the fact that the blood of bulls and goats could not take away sins (Heb. 10:4). Under the old Economy of God, it was only the High Priests who could approach God, and then, only once a year, the Great Day of Atonement, and not without blood. But now, due to the Cross and what it effected, meaning that there Jesus Christ atoned for all sin, past, present, and future, at least for all who will believe (Jn. 3:16), any Believer can *"come boldly unto the Throne of Grace, that we may obtain Mercy, and find Grace to help in time of need"* (Heb. 4:16). What a privilege!

The Cross of Christ changed everything because it atoned for all sin.

THE CROSS OF CHRIST

When we speak of the Cross of Christ and what was there accomplished, we aren't speaking of the wooden beam on which Jesus died. In fact, if someone found in Jerusalem the

Cross on which Jesus died, and it could be proven as such, still, that wooden beam would not have any more power than a dead stick out in the road. It's not the wooden beam on which He died, although that was necessary, but it was what He there accomplished.

WHAT DID JESUS DO AT THE CROSS?

As stated, He atoned for all sin, past, present, and future, at least for all who will believe (Jn. 3:16). Sin provides the legal means that Satan has to hold man captive. However, with all sin atoned, which Jesus did at the Cross, this removed the legal right that Satan had to hold anyone in bondage. So, that being the case, how do we account for the entirety of the world basically being in bondage and, sadly and regrettably, even most of the church?

As it regards the unredeemed, they are in bondage to Satan, ruled by the sin nature, simply because they will not take advantage of what Jesus did at Calvary's Cross. In fact, that is the same identical reason that most Christians presently are in spiritual bondage to Satan.

Virtually the entirety of the church world will agree with the statement that, *"Jesus Christ is the Source of all things we receive from God."* However, when we say that *"the Cross of Christ is the Means, and the only Means by which we receive all of these wonderful things from the Lord,"* that's where we have a problem. In fact, the church bounces from one fad to the other.

When Frances and I were starting out in evangelistic work back in the mid-1950's, at a given point in time, Christians being demon possessed and needing demons cast out of them began to make the rounds. In other words, Christians were taught that if they had a problem with lust, then that meant they had a *"lust demon"*; if they had a problem of unforgiveness, that meant they had a *"demon of unforgiveness,"* etc. They would then have to find a preacher who understood these things, and who could lay hands on them and rebuke this demon spirit, and then they would be free.

While it sounded right to a lot of Christians, it wasn't right. There is nothing in the Word of God that substantiates such a thing. Others have claimed that one can go on a protracted fast and get victory over sin, take the Lord's Supper once each day and effect victory over sin, etc. While fasting and the Lord's Supper are viable, Scriptural prerogatives, still, there will be no victory over sin by such a method.

Sin was dealt with at the Cross of Christ and only at the Cross. So, for the Believer to have victory over sin, his Faith must be placed exclusively in Christ and the Cross. Then and only then can the Holy Spirit help him as it regards this problem that all of us face.

FULFILLING THE LAW

As it regards the Law of God, every human being in history has broken that Law, with the exception of the Lord Jesus Christ, Who kept it perfectly. The Law demanded death, which we will deal with more extensively momentarily.

Jesus kept the Law perfectly in His Life and Living, never sinning even one time in word, thought, or deed. In fact, had He sinned even one time, He could not have served as the Perfect Sacrifice. So, as our Substitute Man, He kept the Law perfectly, all on our behalf. In other words, our Faith in Him transfers us from the position of lawbreaker to the position of Law-keeper. The position of lawbreaker demands death. This means separation from God forever, which means Hellfire. The position of Law-keeper is all in Christ and what He did at the Cross.

As it regards the broken Law, of which every human being was and is guilty, Jesus satisfied that by giving Himself as a Perfect Sacrifice on Calvary's Cross. That's the reason we say that the Cross of Christ is the only Means by which we can receive from God.

Concerning the Cross, Paul said, *"Blotting out the hand-writing of Ordinances that was against us, which was contrary to us, and took it out of the way, nailing it to His Cross"* (Col. 2:14).

This Verse vividly describes the attendant circumstances of forgiveness in Christ. One is the cancellation of *"the written code . . . that was against us."*

What is cancelled is called, *"The written code,"* an expression used of any document written by hand. The reference is to the Mosaic Law, and the thought is that God has blotted it out so that it no longer stands against us. We will deal with this momentarily as to how this was done.

The idea of its cancellation or removal is that it has been removed permanently, that is, removed so that its claims against us can never again alienate us from God.

Paul's vivid metaphor of nailing the Law to the Cross has been variously explained. However, it probably has to do with an Old Testament practice called, *"The double,"* which we will also attempt to explain to a greater degree momentarily.

THE LAW OF GOD

The phrase, *"Blotting out the handwriting of Ordinances that was against us,"* pertains, as stated, to the Law of Moses. This was God's Standard of Righteousness, which man could not reach. God's Nature demands Righteousness, which refers to a strict adherence to the Law on all accounts and at all times. Man being fallen and, thereby, containing a satanic nature made it impossible for him to come up to God's Standard, or anywhere close for that matter. Consequently, this Law is conceived here as a bond, a bill of debt, if you will, standing against those who have not received Christ, whether then or now.

Of course, man little recognizes God's Standard of Righteousness; however, not recognizing this Standard in no way closes the door to the coming Judgment. Man may go on in his merry way as if this Law does not exist, trying to make himself believe that it is of no consequence, that is, if he thinks about it at all. However, the truth is, he will answer to this Law in

Jesus Christ, or he will answer to it at the Great White Throne Judgment, with the latter having no reprieve (Rev. 20:11-15).

The battleground of the Atonement is seen in Calvary's Cross. The charges against man were nailed with Christ to that rough tree. The *"handwriting of Ordinances"* is a signed bond, if you will, an IOU made to God and signed (or admitted) by mankind. By that I mean the following:

All responsible men admit the fact of sin and consent to the justice of the death penalty for it, at least if they think about it sensibly.

WHY IS MAN UNABLE TO KEEP THE LAW?

Paul gives us the answer to that in the great Book of Romans. The Holy Spirit through him said:

"**And if Christ be in you** *(He is in you through the Power and Person of the Spirit [Gal. 2:20])*, **the body** *is* **dead because of sin** *(means that the physical body has been rendered helpless because of the Fall; consequently, the Believer trying to overcome by willpower presents a fruitless task)*; **but the Spirit** *is* **Life because of Righteousness** *(only the Holy Spirit can make us what we ought to be, which means we cannot do it ourselves; once again, He performs all that He does within the confines of the Finished Work of Christ)*" **(Rom. 8:10).**

The cause of all the problems is the fall of Adam and Eve in the Garden of Eden. It so weakened the human body, plus the human mind, making it impossible to do what needed to be done. So, if it was to be done, meaning that man would be Saved, God would have to perform the task Himself, which He did.

THE APPLICATION OF GOD'S LAW PRESENTLY

Some preachers claim that these Passages as given by Paul

blot out the Law in totality for both the Saved and the unsaved.

In a measure, that is true, but only in a potential sense. In fact, even as we've already stated, Jesus did atone for all sin and for all time. However, the effectiveness of the Atonement, so to speak, only functions in the realm of those who will accept God's Pardon, which must be made on the basis of the Finished Work of Christ. In other words, the Law of God, i.e., God's Standard of Righteousness, i.e., man's debt owed to God, cannot be assuaged unless the individual accepts Christ. Otherwise, it is not blotted out, and the charges are still leveled at the Christ rejecter.

SIN

Many think that because we're living in the day of Grace, sin is excused; however, sin is never excused!

The Grace of God is tied totally to the Cross of Christ in an absolute sense and cannot be received by anyone unless the great Sacrifice of Christ is accepted. Actually, that should go without saying. God cannot wink at sin, cannot overlook sin, and cannot ignore sin, even the slightest sin, even in His Own Children. The Scripture plainly tells us, *"For if the word spoken by Angels was steadfast, and every transgression and disobedience received a just recompense of reward; how shall we escape, if we neglect so great Salvation. . . ?"* (Heb. 2:2-3).

The whole thing was settled in Christ, and is only settled in Christ, even as Paul proclaims here. Man accepts that and is Saved, or he rejects that and is lost.

So, let not anyone think that because this is the age and day of Grace that all Judgment has been suspended, the Law of God has been suspended, and man is free to sin. Nothing could be further from the truth. God hates sin now as much as He always hated sin. The God of the Old Testament is the same God of the New Testament. God does not change because God cannot change, and because God doesn't need to change. How can perfection change! If man does not accept Christ, man will answer ultimately to the Law of God at the Great White Throne Judgment. In other words, man will answer to Jesus Christ and what He did for us at the Cross, thereby, accepting Him as Saviour and Lord, or man will face Jesus Christ as the Judge at the Great White Throne Judgment, but face Christ, man will!

HANDWRITING

This speaks of the Ten Commandments, which constitute the Law of God, His Moral Standard of Righteousness, and was actually given on *". . . two Tables of Testimony, tables of stone, written with the Finger of God"* (Ex. 31:18).

In other words, what God gave to men, proverbially speaking, was written in black and white so as to be undeniable. Exodus, Chapter 20, proclaims these Commandments, written very simply and easy to understand, so that no one has any excuse for not understanding what God has said. Once again, *"It's the Law."*

Before the Law of Moses was given (the Law of God and the Law of Moses are one and the same), there was no clear definition of sin. To be sure, sin existed from the time of the Fall, and exceedingly so, but as to exactly what different types of sin were, man had no definition. Of course, the Law of God changed all of that, leaving man without excuse.

JEWS ONLY?

Some may argue that the Law of God was for Jews only, considering that it was given solely to them. However, even though it was given solely to the Jews, nevertheless, it pertained to all of humanity.

While provision was definitely made for Gentiles, still, the insistence then was not nearly as strong as it presently is regarding the Great Commission. The reasons are obvious:

While the Law was God's Standard of Righteousness,

not even the Jews could keep it, even though they were God's Chosen People. This automatically meant that the Gentiles surely couldn't.

So, why would God give a Law that was impossible to keep?

The idea is not in man's ability to keep the Law, but it was God's Standard of Righteousness. God cannot lower His Standard, irrespective of man's ability or inability. However, the Lord did provide a way out, exactly as Paul is saying in the Verse of our study.

THE LAW WAS GIVEN FOR SEVERAL REASONS

• As a Standard of Righteousness for the entirety of the world: in fact, these were the first Laws that were truly fair and equitable for all of mankind. To be sure, there were all types of laws before the Law of Moses, but they were greatly weighted in favor of certain classes of people.

• The Law was given that man would have no excuse as to what God required.

• The Law was given to define sin, even the categories.

• The Law was meant to show man his inability to live up to what God demanded. To be sure, it served its purpose well!

• The Law contained Righteousness because it was formulated by God, but it demanded perfect obedience in order for such Righteousness to be obtained. Due to man's fallen nature, which we have briefly addressed, such was impossible.

• The Law was designed that man may see his inability and, thereby, throw himself on the Mercy and Grace of God provided through the Lord Jesus Christ, of which all the sacrifices were Types.

• Consequently, the Law was designed not to push man away from God, even though man was woefully inadequate, but rather to draw him to God, admitting his inadequacy and seeking Mercy and Grace.

• The penalty of the Law was death, but Christ took the

penalty upon Himself. Therefore, man will not have to suffer
its penalty, but only if man accepts God's Offer of Salvation
through Christ.

CONTRARY TO US

Continuing to speak of the Law, the phrase, *"Which was
contrary to us,"* proclaims that which is obvious.

Paul has just said, *"Which was against us,"* which referred
to our debt binding us legally. The latter phrase, *"Contrary to
us,"* enlarges on that idea, emphasizing the hostile character of
the bond as a hindrance.

Law is against us simply because we are unable to keep its
precepts no matter how hard we try.

Someone has said, *"Law is against us because it comes like
a taskmaster, bidding us do, but neither putting the inclination
into our hearts nor the power in our hands. And Law is against
us because the Revelation of unfulfilled duty is the accusation
of the defaulter and a Revelation to him of his guilt. And Law
is against us because it comes with threatenings and foretaste of
penalty and pain. Thus, as standard, accuser, and avenger, it is
against us."*

The Law is contrary to us simply because we cannot meet
its demands. Still, it is not our enemy because it tells us the truth.

In fact, the Law of God was the rapturous delight of the
Psalmists and Prophets. It was God's Greatest Gift to man
before Christ because it was the knowledge of His Will and,
as stated, His Standard of Righteousness. In fact, the Law
of Moses was the first gleam of light into a darkened world;
nevertheless, light is not too very much appreciated by darkness. Light exposes what the darkness is covering, hence, the
antagonism.

So, even though the Law of God definitely was not and is
not the enemy of man, it became his enemy because man re-
belled against its precepts, which man continues to do even
unto this very hour.

THE REMOVAL OF THE LAW

The phrase, *"And took it out of the way,"* refers to the penalty of the Law being removed. That penalty was death, consequently, so severe that it beggars description.

This legal bond being contrary to us, Paul now states the way in which God removed the death penalty, by *"blotting out."* This means that the charge is *"smeared out"* as on wax. Another way of putting it is that since Christ died and since we are dead with Him by Baptism *"into His Death,"* the *"IOU"* is no longer valid. Our death (with Christ on the Cross) releases us from the obligation. Christ is the Propitiation (appeasing Sacrifice) for our debt (Rom. 3:24-25).

God could not take it away by fiat or decree. In other words, He could not remove it with His Word. Every iota of the debt of the Law owed to God by man had to be paid. So, God paid it Himself through the Death of His Only Son, which presents the greatest act of Love by far that the world has ever known or ever will know.

It is impossible for us to really know exactly what went into the words, *"And took it out of the way."* Our intellect cannot even begin to grasp the comprehension of all of this. That the Lord would do such for righteous men is one thing, but that He would do such for those who hated Him is something else altogether. His Death was definitely for a few righteous because the Old Testament proclaims some who truly loved God and sincerely endeavored to live for Him. Still, as is obvious, virtually all were in the column of animosity toward God, and still He died for them. In fact, His Death was just as much for the ones who hated Him as the few who loved Him.

THE CROSS

The phrase, *"Nailing it to His Cross,"* tells us the manner in which this was done. The Law with its decrees was abolished in Christ's Death as if crucified with Him. It was no longer in the midst or in the foreground, as a debtor's obligation is perpetually before him, embarrassing his whole life. At least, this is true for those who will believe (Jn. 3:16).

Paul tells us here that the burden and penalty of sin had been laid on Jesus Christ and borne by Him on His Cross.

In deep, mysterious, but most real identification of Himself with the whole race of man (the Representative Man), He not only Himself took our infirmities and did bear our sicknesses by the might of His Sympathy and the reality of His Manhood, but the Lord also made to meet upon Him the iniquity of us all. He, the Lamb of God, willingly accepted the load and did bear away our sins by bearing their penalty.

To philosophize on this great teaching of Scripture is not our business here. It is our business to assert it. We could never penetrate to a full understanding of the rationale of Christ bearing our sin, but that has nothing to do with the earnestness of our belief in the fact.

THE PRICE HE PAID

Enough for us that in His Person He willingly made experience of all the bitterness of sin when He agonized in the dark on the Cross, and when from out of the darkness came that awful cry, so strangely compact of wistful confidence and utter isolation, *"My God, My God, why have You forsaken Me?"* It was something deeper than physical pain or shrinking from physical death that found utterance — even the sin-laden consciousness of Him Who, in that awful hour, gathered into His Own Breast the spearpoints of a world's punishment. The Cross of Christ is the endurance of the penalty of sin and, therefore, is the unloosing of the grip of the Law upon us, insofar as threatening and punishment are concerned.

It is not enough that we should only intellectually recognize that as a principle — it is the very heart of the Gospel, the very life of our souls, and we continue to speak of the Cross of Christ.

By trusting ourselves to that great Sacrifice, the dread of punishment will fade from our hearts, the thunderclouds will melt out of the sky, the sense of guilt will not be a sting but an occasion for lowly thankfulness, and the Law will have to draw the bolts of her prison house and let our captive souls go free.

THE END OF THE LAW

Christ's Cross is the end of the Law as ceremonial. The whole elaborate ritual of the Jews had sacrifice for its vital center and the prediction of the Great Sacrifice for its highest purpose. Without the admission of these principles, Paul's position is unintelligible, for he holds, as in this context, that Christ's Coming puts the whole system out-of-date because it fulfills it all. Inasmuch as we now have the reality, we do not need the shadow. Christ is the Great High Priest. In His Presence, all human priesthood loses its consecration, for it could offer only external sacrifices and, therefore, secure a local approach to a *"worldly sanctuary."*

However, that which was only a shadow pointed to the reality which was to come in that Christ is the True Sacrifice. His Death is the real propitiation for sin, and we, in Him, become the Thank-Offerings, moved by His Mercies to present ourselves as living sacrifices.

DOES THIS MEAN THAT CHRISTIANS HAVE NO MORE OBLIGATION TOWARD THE MORAL LAW?

In fact, Christ's Cross is not only the end of the Law as ceremonial, it is also the end of the Law as a moral rule. Nothing in Paul's writings limits the restriction of the ceremonial law only. In fact, it includes the entirety of the Law.

However, such words definitely do not mean that Christians are freed from the obligations of morality, far, far from it! It does mean that we are not bound by the *"things contained in the Law,"* but yet, those things will be done because, in fact, they have already been done in Christ.

Duty is duty now because we see the pattern of conduct and character in Christ. Conscience is no longer our standard and neither is the Old Testament conception of the perfect ideal of manhood. The idea now is, since Christ has nailed the Law to His Cross, our law is the Perfect Life and Death of Christ, Who is at once the Ideal of humanity and the Reality of Deity.

THE LAW MERELY COMMANDS BUT HAS NO POWER TO HAVE ITS COMMANDMENTS OBEYED

Let us say it again: the weakness of all law is that it merely commands but has no power or claims to have those commandments obeyed. Like a discrowned king, it posts its proclamations but has no army at its back to execute them.

However, Christ puts His Own Power within us through the Person of the Holy Spirit and His Love in our hearts. So, we pass from under the dominion of an external commandment into the liberty of an inward spirit. As someone has said, *"Christ is to His Followers both 'Law and Passion,' one might say."* He gives not the *"Law of a carnal commandment but the Power of an endless life."*

The long schism between the inclination and duty is at an end insofar as we are under the influence of Christ's Cross. The great Promise is fulfilled, *"I will put My Love into their minds and write it in their hearts."* And so, glad obedience comes with the Power of the New Life for the sake of the Love of the Dear Lord Who has bought us by His Death, which supersedes the constrained submission to outward precept. In fact, a higher morality characterizes the partakers of the Life of Christ, who have His Example for our code and His Love for our motive.

"If you love Me, keep My Commandments," wins us to purer and more self-sacrificing goodness than the stern accents can ever enforce, which can only say, *"You shall — or else!"* He came *"not to destroy, but to fulfill."*

Law died with Christ on the Cross in order that it might rise and reign with Him in our inmost hearts (MacLaren).[1]

THE DOUBLE

The phrase, *"Nailing it to His Cross,"* undoubtedly has reference, as well, to the Old Testament concept, which was referred to as *"the double"* or *"possessing the double."*

After giving the great predictions concerning the coming Messiah, the Prophet Isaiah said, *"For your shame you shall have double; and for confusion they shall rejoice in their portion: therefore in their land they shall possess the double: everlasting joy shall be unto them"* (Isa. 61:7).

The idea was this:

Whenever an Israelite went bankrupt, all of his debts would be posted on a piece of animal skin and tacked up in a prominent place beside the city gate for all to see. Consequently, the shame would be obvious. As many as desired to do so, and, to be sure, all would, could look at the list of debts and ruminate concerning the amount owed, the inability of the individual to pay, etc. As stated, such always brought great humiliation and shame!

Every once in awhile, a very rich individual, to whom the amount owed was little more than pocket change, would, for whatever reason, settle the account himself.

The wealthy benefactor would go to the place where the account was inscribed upon the record and posted for all to see. He would take it down and double it over, thereby, hiding the debts, hence, it being referred to as *"the double."*

He would sign his name on the doubled over skin or parchment. Then he would take a nail of some sort and, with a hammer, would drive the nail through the doubled over parchment into the wood. Consequently, all anyone could now see was the parchment doubled over with the benefactor's name written on the front.

In other words, all to whom money was owed could come to him, and he would settle the account.

When Jesus died on the Cross, He, in effect, took all of our sins, which were so ugly, so humiliating, and so shameful, and written down for all to see. He doubled over the record and nailed it to His Cross. He then wrote His Name, so to speak, across the doubled over parchment and wrote in Blood, His Blood, *"Paid in full,"* and then, *"Jesus Christ."*

This means that every single Believer, in effect, *"possesses the double."*

THE TRIUMPH

Paul then said, *"And having spoiled principalities and powers, He made a show of them openly, triumphing over them in it"* (Col. 2:15).

Paul affirms here that Christ has *"disarmed"* these forces of evil, so to speak.

However, our Lord not only disarmed them, He also made a public spectacle of them. That is to say, He totally exposed them to public disgrace in the spirit world by exhibiting them to the Universe as His Captives. The added word, *"Triumphing over them by the Cross,"* expands this idea. The picture, which was quite familiar in the Roman world, is that of a triumphant general leading a parade of victory. The conqueror, riding at the front in his chariot, leads his troops through the streets of the city, and more particularly, the main street of the city of Rome.

Behind them trails a wretched company of vanquished kings, officers, and soldiers — the spoils of battle.

In this picture, Christ is the Conquering General. The powers and authorities are the vanquished enemy displayed as the spoils of battle before the entire Universe.

To the casual observer, the Cross appears to be only an instrument of death, the symbol of Christ's defeat. However, Paul represents it as Christ's Chariot of Victory.

THE SPOILING OF PRINCIPALITIES AND POWERS

The phrase, *"And having spoiled principalities and powers,"*

presents the same as Ephesians 6:12. These are ruling poten-
tates under Satan, actually, fallen Angels, some very powerful,
in the atmosphere of this Earth. They are, no doubt, of much
higher rank than mere demons, as should be obvious.

"Spoiled" in the Greek is, *"Apekduomai,"* and means, *"To
strip the clothes off of another or to put off."*

The word goes back to Jesus' statement, which Paul, no
doubt, had in mind, *"Or else how can one enter into a strong
man's house* (referring here to Satan and his kingdom of darkness), *and spoil his goods* (which Jesus did at the Cross), *except
he first bind the strong man? and then he will spoil his house."*
(The spoiling of Satan's house was done at the Cross. We must
not forget that. It continues unto this hour, with Believers
having the use of the Name of Jesus and the Power of the Holy
Spirit) (Mat. 12:29).

HOW DID THE CROSS ACCOMPLISH THIS TASK?

Due to the Fall in the Garden of Eden, Satan legally had a
claim on the entirety of the human race. Inasmuch as the seed
of all humanity was in Adam's loins, consequently, his sin, his
fallen nature, passed on to all. This means that every baby
born thereafter would be born *"in sin."* It is referred to as
"original sin." Sin being the legal claim that Satan had upon
humanity, he, in effect, now rules over the entirety of humanity. This incorporates all who would be born, and for all time,
at least unless something was done.

This means that man, God's Greatest Creation, originally
created even higher than the Angels (Ps. 8), is now infested
with a Satanic nature. This is the very opposite of the God-
consciousness which man enjoyed before the Fall and was intended to enjoy forever. Consequently, Satan, along with all
of his demon spirits and fallen Angels, now rules. He holds
man in captivity in totality, hence, making this world, which
God intended to be a paradise, into a veritable Hell filled with
murder, hate, covetousness, greed, selfishness, immorality of

every stripe, envy, jealousy, war, etc.

ALMIGHTY GOD?

To be sure, God is Almighty, with Satan far, far less. So, the question might be asked as to why the Lord did not stop this situation at the beginning.

As we have stated, Satan's hold on humanity was legal in that man had sinned. Consequently, God, Who made these Laws in the beginning, could not violate His Own Statutes. As long as sin remained, Satan had a right to do what he was doing.

As well, sin being an infraction of God's Laws, which, if left unchecked, will destroy the entirety of God's Creation, cannot be ignored. Sin constitutes a debt, and that debt had to be paid. To portray even in glaring detail what this debt meant, God gave the Law of Moses to Israel, which in stark clarity defined what this debt actually was, which we addressed in the previous Verse.

Considering that this debt of sin was of such magnitude, Satan felt he had won the day in his revolution against God because man was helpless to address this situation.

Angels could not redeem man because they were of another Creation. As well, man could not redeem man simply because all are born in sin, which means they are disapproved upon their birth. So, if man was to be redeemed, God Himself would have to perform the task. Thank God, that He did.

THE PRICE THAT WAS DEMANDED

In all the definitions that could be given of sin, disobedience to God, which refers to disobedience of His Clear, Concise Commands, perhaps provides the best explanation of all. Sin is a rebellious, disobedience of the clear, concise Word of God.

When this first disobedience was carried out, which concerned the *"tree of the knowledge of good and evil"* and the prohibition of the eating of its fruit, this was the first sin, at least on this Planet, from the time of Adam. It was not that this particular tree of the knowledge of good and evil carried poisonous properties, but was rather disobedience on man's part, irrespective as to what the command may have been.

When this first sin of disobedience was committed, man, of his own freewill, took himself from the Life of God, consequently, making himself void of that Life, which means that he immediately died spiritually. He is now on the side of the tempter, i.e., *"Satan and the kingdom of darkness."*

So, the question must be asked now as to what commodity would be valuable enough to purchase back the Life of God that man had forfeited.

It could not be purchased back by silver or gold, for such was now corrupted inasmuch as the entirety of the Planet was now corrupted. Consequently, anything offered of it would be polluted, which God would not accept.

This is so because God had given Adam dominion over all of His Creation; therefore, when Adam fell, the entirety of Creation fell (Gen. 1:28; Ps. 8:3-6). Consequently, Paul said, *"For we know that the whole Creation groans and travails in pain together until now"* (Rom. 8:22).

So, what could God do to salvage the situation?

THE PLAN OF GOD

To be sure, God, being Omniscient, which means that He knows all things past, present, and future, was not caught off guard at the fall of Adam and Eve in the Garden of Eden. In fact, through foreknowledge, which we will address more fully elsewhere in this Volume, He had always known this would happen and, as well, knew the Remedy (I Pet. 1:18-20).

God would have to do something that was not of this world, but yet, was. He would have to stay within the limits of the dominion originally given to Adam before the Fall. This meant, as stated, that no Angel could redeem humanity, or any other of the great Spirit Beings created by God, because they were of another Creation. Consequently, this blew to pieces the contention of the Gnostics as it regarded many layers of Angels between God and man, with all of these serving as mediators.

To solve this terrible problem, God would become Man, and the Second Man (the Last Adam) would purchase back the dominion, which had been forfeited by the first Adam.

To carry this out, He would be born of a virgin, which would bypass original sin, but, at the same time, would not spoil the type. Adam was originally created by God, which means he was not born in sin. In the Incarnation, God becoming Man, He would, likewise, be conceived by special decree (Lk. 1:26-27).

PERFECTION

As a Man, the Man Christ Jesus, while never ceasing to be God but not able to use His Powers of Deity, He must live a Perfect Life, not failing in even one point or at any one time, with only the Holy Spirit to help Him, which Born-Again Believers also have presently.

In rendering a life of perfect obedience, which was demanded, He would do the opposite of the original Adam regarding his disobedience. As well, He would seek only the Will of the Father whereas the first Adam ignored God's Will, opting for his own will instead! Jesus would not use His Power to turn the stones to bread in order to satisfy His Hunger whereas the first Adam did eat of the bread, i.e., *"of the forbidden fruit of the tree of the knowledge of good and evil."*

However, even though these things were acutely necessary, they in no way addressed the problem of sin and how this debt would be paid! This means that none of the things that Jesus did as it regarded His Perfect Life, even considering His Miracles, etc., would at all redeem fallen humanity. As stated, while they were necessary, they did not address the real issue. Consequently, to present Christ as the Great Teacher, or even as the Great Miracle Worker, if the Cross is disbelieved, denied, or even ignored, no Redemption for mankind can be effected. The intellectual Jesus will not suffice, and neither will the Miracle-working Jesus suffice. That's why Paul said:

"I determined not to know anything among you, save Jesus Christ, and Him Crucified" (I Cor. 2:2).

THE PAYMENT OF THE DEBT

The debt that was owed was not owed to Satan, but rather to God. Consequently, while the Cross definitely defeated Satan and all the powers of darkness, it was not actually instituted to address the problem according to Satan, but rather according to God. As stated, this debt was owed to God, and it was to God that this debt must be paid.

As the Life of God imparted to man had been forfeited, a life must be given in turn as payment. However, it must be a perfect life containing no sin, housed in a perfect body which had never sinned. There was no way that God could accept anything sinful as a sacrifice. That's why man could not redeem himself. As well, it had to be of this Earth because Earth was a part of the dominion given to Adam. That's why the Scripture says, *"Wherefore when He comes into the world, He said, Sacrifice and Offering you would not (meaning that the blood of bulls and goats could not suffice for sin), but a Body have You prepared Me"* (Heb. 10:5).

A PERFECT SACRIFICE

As a Perfect Sacrifice, a Sacrifice which God could accept as payment, a Perfect Body was to be offered up. It had to be a Body which was of this world because He was born of woman, which would house a Perfect Life that would be poured out on the Cross in the shedding of its Blood because the life of the flesh is in the blood. This Perfect Life given, freely offered up, would suffice as payment for the life that had been forfeited and, thereby, lost.

In the doing of this, the offering up of Himself on the Cross, Christ satisfied the entirety of the sin debt for all of humanity, and for all time, at least for those who will believe (Jn. 3:16). This satisfied the demands of the Law as well as its penalty, which satisfied the Righteousness of God.

THE GREAT ARGUMENT

Many philosophers have claimed that if man was born in original sin, which he was, because of something that Adam did over which his offspring would have no control, then man should not be held responsible. Consequently, he should not be punished!

That argument might be valid if the matter had been allowed to stand as it originally was. It is true that Adam's offspring had no choice in this matter and actually was not responsible for the original sin, which should be obvious, even though all of humanity has had to reap the bitter consequences.

However, God did not let the matter stand as it was. He did something about the situation in the giving of His Only Son in order to redeem humanity (Jn. 3:16). So, the punishment of unredeemed man is not so much that he is, in fact, unredeemed, but that he rejects God's Solution to the problem, which is the Cross of Christ.

It is true that God would definitely have been grossly unfair if He had not provided Redemption, especially considering that Adam's offspring were not responsible for the situation. However, the point is moot! God did not do that because Love cannot do that. So, as it regards those who claim that God is unfair, nothing could be further from the truth.

In fact, this argument is not new, having been used by unredeemed man all along.

Some in Israel said to the Lord, *"The Way of the LORD is not equal."*

God's Answer was instantaneous, *". . . Hear now, O House*

of Israel; is not My Way equal? are not your ways unequal?"
(Ezek. 18:25).

In fact, the Cross answers all of these questions, portraying the Love of God in a fashion that man cannot deny, at least if he is to be honest!

SATAN DEFEATED

When Jesus poured out His Life on the Cross by the shedding of His Own Precious Blood, He atoned for all sin. Because His Sacrifice of Himself was a Perfect Sacrifice, God could accept it in payment in full, which He did.

This had to be if man was to be redeemed.

As well, this is what defeated Satan and all of his powers of darkness. The payment of the sin debt *"removed all the penalty of sin."* It not only did this, but Jesus satisfied the penalty of the broken Law (God's Law) also. This caused not only the penalty of the Law to be satisfied but, as well, even removed the Law itself since He had kept all its precepts, hence, the statements of the previous Verse regarding the *"blotting out the handwriting of Ordinances that was against us."*

Satan's legal claim is now gone. This means he has no more hold over humanity, at least for those who will accept God's Solution of the Cross, which means Satan is totally defeated. Hence, after His Death on the Cross and His Resurrection, Jesus could go down into Paradise in the heart of the Earth, where all the righteous souls were held captive by Satan, and, thereby, set them free, which He did (Eph. 4:8-10).

THE CROSS

Before the Cross, all the Righteous who died did not go to Heaven, but rather down into Paradise in the Earth. Even though it was not in the burning side of Hell, still, there was only a gulf that separated these two compartments, which Satan, no doubt, hoped to ultimately make into one compartment.

Satan had a right to take these righteous souls down there, with them actually becoming his captives, because before the Cross, the sin debt was not satisfied, thereby, still owing. The animal sacrifices were only a stopgap measure, so to speak, until the Cross. To be sure, all of these people, whomever they might have been, were definitely Saved. However, their Salvation was in no way ratified until the Cross, which then destroyed all of Satan's claims. Since the Cross, the soul and spirit of every righteous person who dies instantly goes to Heaven to be with the Lord.

The Cross was the manner in which our Lord spoiled all of the kingdom of darkness, and spoiled it completely, exactly what He said He would do!

JESUS DEFEATED AND HUMILIATED SATAN
AND HIS COHORTS OPENLY

The phrase, *"He made a show of them openly,"* means that what Jesus did at the Cross was in the face of the whole Universe.

All of this declares that from Christ's Cross, a magnetic influence, so to speak, streams out upwards as well as earthwards, binding all things together in the great Reconciliation. Now He tells us that from that same Cross, darts, or conquering power, shoot downward, which subdue and despoil reluctant foes of other realms and regions than ours, insofar as they work among men.

That there are such seems plainly enough asserted in Christ's Own Words; however, it may be ridiculed or set aside, but it can never be disproved.

However, the position which Christianity takes in reference to the whole matter is to maintain that Christ has conquered the banded kingdom of evil by His Death on the Cross. As well, no man owes it fear or obedience if he will only hold fast by his Lord, maintaining his Faith in that great Finished Work.

JUDGMENT

In the Cross is the Judgment of this world, and by it is the prince of this world cast out. Jesus has taken away the power of these powers that were so mighty among men. They held men captive by temptations too strong to be overcome. However, He has conquered all these temptations, and did so upon the Cross, and therein made us more than conquerors.

Satan held men captive by ignorance of God, but the Cross reveals him by the lie that sin was a trifle and teaches us its gravity and power. By the opposite lie, man was made to believe that sin was unforgivable, but the Cross brings pardon for every transgression and cleansing for every stain.

By the Cross, the world is a redeemed world. As our Lord said in Words which may have suggested the figure of our Text, to which we have already alluded, the strong man is bound and his house spoiled of all his armor wherein he trusted. The prey is taken from the mighty, and men are delivered from the dominion of evil.

So, that dark kingdom is robbed of its subjects and its rulers impoverished and restrained, all by and through the Cross.

ISAIAH AND THE RESULTS OF THE CROSS

Some 750 years before Christ, the great Prophet Isaiah beautifully and wondrously prophesied what would take place when Jesus suffered the dire penalty on the Cross. The Holy Spirit through him painted it in pictures undeniable and in symbolism portrayed it grandly.

He said, *"To open the blind eyes, to bring out the prisoners from the prison, and them who sit in darkness out of the prison house"* (Isa. 42:7).

Jesus did this by His Death on the Cross and His Resurrection from that Death. As the Cross was Satan's defeat, it was Christ's Victory and, therefore, our victory because Christ was our Substitute Man, so to speak.

Every demon spirit was defeated at the Cross. Every fall-en Angel, every power, every principality, every ruler of the darkness of this world, and every spiritual wickedness in high places, all and in totality were defeated! This means, even as Isaiah prophesied, that no man need be bound by the pow-ers of darkness. It means that every alcoholic can go free; every drug addict can go free; and every bondage of darkness can fall off. That's the Deliverance that Jesus preached — the preaching of the Cross — which sets the captive free, even as Paul said!

THE CENTRAL PLACE OF THE CROSS

How could anyone read these Verses and not understand the central place of the Cross in the great Plan of Redemp-tion? How can anyone not see that this is the Foundation of the Church, the constitution and bylaws, so to speak, on which the whole of Christianity rests! This is where Christ did the deed and where Satan bit the dust.

If the sinner places his trust in that which the Lord did, he will instantly know Salvation and Deliverance from all the powers of darkness. If the Christian will maintain his Faith in this which Jesus has done, understanding that it is the Source of all that we have in the Lord, he can walk in victory with no sin whatsoever dominating him (Rom. 6:14). No, we are not teaching sinless perfection, even as the Bible does not teach sinless perfection, but we are teaching, because the Bible does teach, that sin is not to have dominion over us (Rom. 6:14).

Again I shout, *"It's in the Cross! It's in the Cross! It's in the Cross!"* That's where Jesus defeated and humiliated Satan, and that is where my victory and your victory were obtained.

TRIUMPH

The phrase, *"Triumphing over them in it,"* means that not

only were they whipped, but, as well, our Lord leads these foes of Righteousness as a victorious general leads his prisoners in a procession of victory.

The Cross is the cosmic battleground where Christ single-handedly defeated all the forces of Hell (Eph. 2:15-16), showing them up for what they really are — enemies of God and all good. These forces, religious and heathen, thought they were putting Christ out of the way once and for all when they screamed that He be crucified. However, what really happened was that Christ put them out of the way instead. By His Resurrection, He broke away and showed Himself superior.

Therefore, says Paul, why should anyone be bound by these worldly powers, judged by lesser authorities, or deceived by proven enemies of Christ? He exhorts all to have the enmity circumcised from their hearts, to surrender to God Alone (Rom. 12:1-2).

IN IT

A question has been raised regarding this last phrase of Verse 15. Is it *"in it"* or *"in Him"* that the victory is won?

Actually, it is both! *"In it"* refers to the Cross, but it was Christ Who died on that Cross. Actually, the Cross within itself as a wooden beam would have been of no effect. In fact, there were others on crosses who died with Jesus that day, and probably hundreds that day on crosses throughout the Roman Empire.

Actually, *"in it"* refers to what the Cross represents, what it accomplished, and what it brought about, which refers to what He did. So, the two, *"in it"* and *"in Him,"* are inseparable — the Cross and Christ!

As stated, Paul may well have had in mind the parade of Roman generals leading their totally defeated captives in chains before the cheering throng. However, be that as it may, that is of little consequence as it regards what Jesus actually did. I think we would be hard put to even grasp the beginning of the spectacle He made of Satan and all his cohorts. This one thing is sure, Satan and every demon spirit and every fallen Angel full well know what He did and, thereby, acquiesce to the mention of that Glorious Name.

IT FLOWS FROM THE CROSS

So, we learn to think of evil as conquered, and for ourselves in our own conflicts with the world, the flesh, and the Devil, as well as for the whole race of man, to be of good cheer. True, the victory is but slowly being realized in all its consequences, and it often seems as if no territory has been won. However, the main position, to be sure, has been carried and though the struggle is still obstinate, it can end only in one way. The brute dies hard, but the naked Heel of Christ has bruised his head, and though still the dragon, his death will come sooner or later, i.e., *"incarceration in the Lake of Fire forever and forever"* (Rev. 20:10).

The regenerating power is lodged in the heart of humanity, and the center from which it flows is the Cross. The history of the world thenceforward is but the history of its more or less rapid assimilation of that power and of its consequent Deliverance from the bondage in which it has been held. The end can only be the entire and universal manifestation of the Victory which was won when He bowed His Head and died. Christ's Cross is God's Throne of Triumph.

OUR PEACE OFFERING

Let us see that we have our own personal part in that Victory. Holding to Christ and drawing from Him by Faith a share in His New Life, we shall no longer be under the yoke of Law but enfranchised into the obedience of Love, which is liberty. We shall no longer be slaves of evil but sons and servants of our conquering God, Who woos and wins us by showing us all His Love in Christ and by giving us His Own Son on the Cross, our Peace-Offering. If we let Him overcome, His Victory will be life, not death.

He will strip us of nothing but rags and clothe us in garments of purity. He will so breathe beauty into us that He will show us openly to the Universe as examples of His Transforming Power. He will bind us glad captives to His Chariot Wheels, partakers of His Victory, as well as trophies of His All-conquering Love. *"Now thanks be unto God, which always causes us to triumph in Christ . . ."* (II Cor. 2:14) (MacLaren).[2]

SINLESS PERFECTION?

As we have previously stated, the Bible does not teach sinless perfection. If anyone knows anything about sin, he should understand the reason. However, the Bible does teach that sin is not to have dominion over us, which means to dominate us (Rom. 6:14).

In this Volume, I think it would be proper for us to deal with the subject of spiritual maturity.

Paul said: *"Let us therefore, as many as be perfect* (mature)*, be thus minded: and if in anything you be otherwise minded, God shall reveal even this unto you"* (Phil. 3:15).

Here, Paul exhorts those who are mature to think in harmony with what he has just said, and promises that those who think differently about minor points will be enlightened by God if their attitudes are right.

The word, *"Perfect,"* as used here, means, *"Mature."* It does not mean, *"Sinless perfection,"* but is referring to a certain level of spiritual growth and stability in contrast to the opposite.

By Paul using the Greek word, *"Teleioi,"* translated, *"Perfect,"* the Apostle, I think, just might be using a tiny bit of sarcasm toward those who had claimed sinless perfection. He is calling on them to recognize the truth as he gives it.

MATURITY

The phrase, *"Let us therefore, as many as be perfect,"* speaks of spiritual maturity.

The Apostle asserts that some of the Philippian Saints, and also he himself, were *"spiritually mature."* However, in Philippians 3:12, he denies the fact that he is yet perfect. How are we to correlate this Verse with his use of the word, *"Perfect,"* in Verse 15?

Is there a contradiction?

The answer is found in the fact that in Verse 12, Paul is speaking of a finished process and absolute spiritual maturity beyond which there is no room for improvement. This is a place that no human being has ever reached, and no one will ever reach, whereas in Verse 15, he is speaking of relative spiritual maturity where there is room for development and growth. This is clear from the fact that in the former Verse, he uses a verb in the perfect tense, whereas in the latter, he uses a noun.

Therefore, Paul exhorts the Philippian Saints, and all of us, as well, who are spiritually mature, to consider themselves so only in a relative sense and to remember that there is much room for spiritual growth in the lives of all of us.

Wuest says, *"The spiritual maturity spoken of here is as we have seen, not a state of sinlessness or flawlessness, but one of completeness, of a well-rounded Christian character, a state opposite of spiritual infancy."*[3]

A TOUCH OF SARCASM?

As we have alluded, Paul may have been speaking here with a touch of sarcasm as in I Corinthians 2:6. There were those in many congregations at that time who were influenced by contemporary Gnosticism, which we will study to a greater degree in our Commentary on Colossians. These persons thought of themselves as more sophisticated than their brethren.

In effect, therefore, Paul is saying to those who are inclined to be self-satisfied and complacent by claiming some type of spiritual perfection, *"If you are as perfect as you profess to be, you will be as eager for growth in Grace as I am."* Of course, if this indeed were the case, we can note the sarcasm. How can one grow in Grace if one is already perfect regarding growth?

The lesson we learn from all of this is that Christian maturity properly understood does not cut the nerve for aspiration for a greater degree of Christlikeness. Instead, it will whet one's appetite to be more like Jesus. In other words, proper spiritual growth into proper spiritual maturity only makes one desire more of Christ, in effect, instilling even a greater hunger and thirst for more of the Lord.

TOTAL DEPENDENCE ON CHRIST

As well, there is a sense, therefore, in which the one experiencing the Grace of Perfect Love has the Witness of the Spirit that in Christ, he is victorious over indwelling sin. At the same time, he feels no less dependent upon the only Source of Grace and Goodness that he has. He knows from where he has come, and I speak of trial and error and even much failure, and the Grace of God in bringing him through this. Therefore, there is no pride, only thanksgiving, no criticism of others who have not reached that maturity, but only encouragement, and no self-dependence, but total dependency on Christ.

Since there will no longer be any lingering desire for sin, the whole ardor of his soul will be focused upon Christ Alone.

MATURITY, IN CHRIST, IN THE CROSS

I want to again emphasize the patience, love, and compassion which one has when coming to true spiritual maturity, even as Paul evidences here. Paul used himself here as an example, so I suppose it would not be displeasing to the Holy Spirit for me to do the same in a limited way.

I empathize with all this the Apostle is saying to such a degree that I hardly know where to begin. I know what it is to be immature, and I know what it is to be mature. My heart grieves as it regards the immaturity, and I speak of the failure that such brings about, all because of a lack of understanding of the Cross, which was, no doubt, caused by much self-will.

Even as Paul will bring out in Verse 18, it is impossible for spiritual maturity to be realized outside of the Cross. The Cross of Christ is the great humbling factor, which plays such a part in one's spiritual growth, even as the Apostle outlines in the Second Chapter of the Epistle to the Philippians. If the Believer does not understand the Cross, the vicarious, atoning Work carried out there by the Christ of Glory, and all that it means to the Believer, then I think spiritual maturity is impossible of realization. The Cross of Christ is the one great key.

THE KEY IS THE CROSS

If this key is realized, this knowledge of the Cross, everything begins to fall into place, without which, nothing falls into place. This is a life that I have lived, a life of hurt, disappointment, failure, and then of victory, Power, and the True Work and Operation of the Holy Spirit. However, I did not find the latter until the veracity of the Cross was revealed unto me by the Spirit of God.

How can one walk in spiritual victory, and I mean being victorious over the world, the flesh, and the Devil? How can one overcome all manner of sin and iniquity? How can one have this *"more Abundant Life,"* which Jesus promised? (Jn. 10:10). How can one enjoy the *"rest,"* which Jesus said He would give to those who came unto Him? (Mat. 11:28-30). How can one live a life that's not dominated in any way by sin? (Rom. 6:14). With those questions burning in my heart, I sought the Lord earnestly, even to the point of acute desperation.

THE ANSWER

I wish I could say that the answer came quickly, but it didn't! In fact, regarding these questions I have just asked,

I sought His Face earnestly for some five years, and to an extent, all my life. And yet, looking back over the entirety of a life spent in attempting to serve God, I suspect, as stated, that the entirety of this experience plays into this of which I say. In other words, quite possibly, it was not merely the six years I have just mentioned, but rather the entirety of the experience which covers the entirety of my life.

Perhaps it was only in that particular six years that I really understood enough about this great Christian experience to even properly ask the right questions. As I have said repeatedly, we do not come to this place quickly or easily. That means that there are no shortcuts. It means that no Preacher can lay his hands on you and impart this of which I speak.

DEATH AND RESURRECTION

Many years ago, I heard the great Preacher, A.N. Trotter, preach a message on *"Death and Resurrection."* It moved me greatly, but yet, in looking back, I think that I only partially understood that of which he said.

He was speaking of the Cross and what Jesus did and our part in that process, even as is recorded in Romans, Chapter 6; however, he was more so speaking of our experience in Christ after Conversion. Even though every person is *"in Christ"* from the time of Conversion, why is it so difficult and hard to properly realize our place and position in Christ which was given to us by the Grace of God? Why do we almost immediately resort to the flesh? Why is there such a great dependency on self instead of the Lord? Why do we have to learn these things the hard way? I am persuaded that all must come this way in one manner or the other. Why do we learn so slowly?

I still don't have the answer to all of these questions, but I believe I do have some answers and the fact of understanding the questions more so than ever. That may not seem like much, but, to be sure, properly understanding the question is of far greater worth than most realize.

DEATH TO SELF

Death, of course, even as Brother Trotter brought it out so long ago, speaks of death to self, to personal ambition, and to the attempts of bringing about Righteousness and Holiness by our own machinations, which cannot be done. Let me again touch on the question:

Many, if not most, Christians do not even understand they are doing this, much less why they are doing it! In other words, they don't even understand that their failure is caused by their own efforts and, much less, why those efforts are wrong. This is what Paul was speaking about when he used the phrase, *"For to be carnally minded is death . . ."* (Rom. 8:6). The point is, it's bad enough to be *"carnally minded,"* but to not even know you are carnally minded is that of which I speak.

To be *"carnally minded,"* to which we have previously alluded, refers to the attempt to be holy and righteous by means other than the Holy Spirit, Who works exclusively by and through the Cross of Christ.

WHY ARE YOU FAILING?

Once the Believer is brought to the place that he knows why he is failing, then the problem can begin to be corrected. When I speak of failing, I mean that which speaks of dependence on the flesh, which means that one's Faith is not exclusively in Christ and the Cross. Once he understands this, he then understands that the Spirit of God must do these things within our lives and that He functions and works in our lives, as stated, according to our Faith in the Cross and a proper understanding of the Cross. Actually, it is virtually impossible for one to have Faith in something of which he has no understanding. Even the sinner coming to Christ must have some elementary understanding that Jesus died for him, etc. God does not require much, but He does require some understanding, which comes about through the Word of God.

As *"death"* speaks of the dying of all the carnal efforts, all the ability of self, and all the machinations of personal efforts, *"Resurrection"* speaks of one coming forth into the New Life in Christ, generated by the Holy Spirit. That's why Paul also said the following:

"If we have been planted together in the likeness of His Death, we shall be also in the likeness of His Resurrection" (Rom. 6:5).

No! Paul is not speaking here of the coming Resurrection of Life when the Trump sounds, but rather our living this Resurrection Life, which is a life of victory and not failure and defeat. It can only be done as the Believer understands that the Cross of Christ Alone is the Means, and the only Means, by which all of these wonderful things come to us.

GOD'S PLAN FOR YOU

A man found a cocoon of a butterfly. One day, he saw a small opening in the cocoon. He sat and watched the butterfly for several hours as it struggled to force its body through that little hole. Then it seemed to stop making any progress. It appeared as if it had gotten as far as it could and could go no further.

So, the man decided to help the butterfly. He took a pair of scissors and snipped off the remaining bit of the cocoon. The butterfly then emerged easily.

However, it had a swollen body and small shriveled wings. He continued to watch the butterfly because he expected that at any moment the wings would enlarge and expand to support the body, which would contract in time.

Neither happened! In fact, the butterfly spent the rest of its life crawling around with a swollen body and shriveled wings. It was never able to fly.

What he had done in his well-intentioned kindness and haste that he did not understand was that the restricting cocoon and the struggle required to get through the tiny opening

were God's Way of forcing fluid from the body of the butterfly into its wings so that it would be ready for flight once it
achieved its freedom from the cocoon.

Sometimes, struggles are exactly what we need in our lives.
If God allowed us to go through life without any obstacles, it
would cripple us. We would not be as strong as we could have
been . . . and we could never fly, spiritually speaking.

Remember, God wants you to fly, but such a state is not
achieved without struggle.

The Resurrection speaks of New Life, a new beginning,
and a maturity, actually, the type of maturity of which Paul
speaks here. The Resurrection will come, but there must be
death first — death to self, death to personal efforts, death to
the flesh, and death to the carnal mind!

DEATH IS NOT PRETTY

No one likes death, and no one likes to see one die. Consequently, the dying process of the Child of God is never pretty
but, as the butterfly, is absolutely necessary. Unfortunately,
there are many Christians who have not yet even arrived at the
dying process — dying to self — and, therefore, ridicule such
in those who are in that process. What a shame! Regrettably
and sadly, I think that most of those who do such a thing will
never reach the stage of maturity. They will do as the butterfly
who tried to short circuit the process. They will never fly, but
rather slide around at a much lower level, never knowing the
freedom, the Power, and the joy which full maturity brings —
the leaving of the boundaries of the confines of restrictions and
soaring to the rarified heights of God's Intentions.

THE DYING PROCESS

Nevertheless, the dying process is absolutely necessary, for
there can be no resurrection without a death. It's not pleas-
ant, and we like it not at all! We wish there were other ways,

and to be sure, many have come up with other ways, but all to no avail. They have thought that one could confess his way through, positive think his way through, self-esteem his way through, or come to this place through some type of spiritual manifestation such as *"holy laughter,"* being *"slain in the Spirit,"* etc. However, such cannot be done!

Jesus spelled this out very succinctly in Luke 9:23-24. He spoke of taking up the Cross daily and following Him, and losing one's life in order to find one's life. As stated, many Christians have attempted to short-circuit that process, evidently thinking they had a better way than that announced by the Lord. They have been sadly disappointed, as they always will be sadly disappointed.

It is the Way of the Cross; there is no other way as there can be no other way.

THUS MINDED

The phrase, *"Be thus minded,"* refers to the things Paul has just said. In other words, this which he has said was given to him by the Holy Spirit, is, therefore, without error, and should be heeded accordingly by every Believer. Those who would think otherwise, who would put forth another thought, such as sinless perfection or its opposite, are in error, which will always lead to extremely negative results. The reason for the negative results is twofold:

1. Any way other than that of the Lord, which is the Way of the Cross, means that it is devised of man and, as such, can lead to no positive results. All of Salvation, which includes all of its rudiments, comes in totality from God and not at all from man. Man's efforts, especially his religious efforts, which we have been studying, only lead to ruin. It is the story of Abraham, Sarah, and Ishmael all over again.

2. Error is likened as *"leaven,"* which always spreads. In other words, a little error will steadily enlarge until it totally engulfs the whole. So, when Paul said, *"Be thus minded,"* even

though the phrase is short, it carries with it a wealth of meaning, which I would hope by now is obvious.

REVELATION

The phrase, *"And if in anything you be otherwise minded, God shall reveal even this unto you,"* means that some were actually otherwise minded.

The word, *"If,"* presents not a hypothetical case but a fulfilled condition. Some of the Philippians were otherwise minded. Epaphroditus evidently had told Paul of those in the Church who were teaching sinless perfection. Paul turns these over to God.

The idea is that God will reveal the truth about the matter to them if they are willing to be taught.

The word, *"Otherwise,"* speaks of diversity in a bad sense and refers to the *"otherwise thinking"* of some of these Philippian Saints, who thought that they had reached the place beyond which there could be no spiritual development or progress. In other words, they believed in *"Sinless perfection."*

This statement as given by Paul is extremely important and deserves close attention.

We find that Christians can be wrong about some things, even as Paul describes here. It doesn't mean they aren't Saved, but it does mean that there is error contained in their thinking and if continued, as leaven, will cause great difficulties.

THE HONEST HEART

His statement also proclaims to us that if the heart is honest, earnest, and sincere, the Lord will reveal the truth to the individual in question. This is extremely important and actually applies to every single Believer because all have contained some error at one time or the other. Even Paul falls into this category, as he describes the situation to us in his account given in Romans, Chapter 7. However, again I emphasize, if the heart is honest before God, sincerely seeking Truth and sincerely wanting Truth, the Holy Spirit will ultimately reveal that Truth to the individual. It is only when our minds are closed, when we think we know all things, that the Holy Spirit is shut off from giving us that which we desperately need. In other words, if one foolishly thinks he is sinlessly perfect, this means he has no more to learn, so it's impossible to reach such a person.

Also, prejudice and bias play a great part in all of this. There are many Christians who will not hear the Truth if it comes from someone they do not like. This is a serious matter indeed simply because the Lord may not send someone else with that particular Truth. So, our hearts must remain open at all times, which means to be pliable to the Movings and Operations of the Holy Spirit.

HINDERING THE HOLY SPIRIT IN
THIS VITAL OPERATION

Due to the vast significance of which we speak, actually, that which Paul has said, let us state again that no Christian is immune from wrong thinking in some manner. No one has all the Light on all Biblical subjects, and, in fact, I don't think that anyone has all the Light on any Biblical subject. That means that there is room for growth in all of us, even the strongest, whomever that may be. So, in understanding this, we must realize at all times that we still have things to learn, and that these things we need to learn are very important. Our hearts must remain open to the Administration of the Holy Spirit.

To which I have alluded often, in 1997, the Lord began to open up to me a Revelation, or perhaps it would be better explained, Illumination on the Cross. As stated, it has been the answer to many questions through the years, and it has been the most revolutionary thing that has ever happened to me.

However, I want to emphasize that I'm not meaning that the Revelation that I was given was something new, actually,

already having been given to the Apostle Paul and quite possibly, many others as well. But yet, in the Lord being gracious
and kind to give this to me, it has only made me realize how
much yet I do not know. Actually, in my heart, it seems the
Holy Spirit has placed great emphasis on this fact, which, of
course, is obvious; at least, it is to me. I speak of so much more
I need to learn. The awareness and the knowledge of this are
more pronounced than ever. What I have learned makes me
so eager to learn more, and I speak of learning Christ. It's like
a consuming desire, a thirst that anticipates being slaked, and
a hunger which anticipates being satisfied. I know the Holy
Spirit has placed this consuming desire for more of Christ
within my heart; however, I have said all of that to say this:

THIS REVELATION

I know what this great Revelation of the Cross has done
for me. As stated, I know it's only the beginning, so to speak.
But yet, I fear that many Christians will not receive this great
Truth simply because it comes from me.
Why?
I once again go back to *"prejudice"* and *"bias."* We Christians
carry these twin evils within our hearts far, far more than
any of us realize. Consequently, when carried in this capacity, these twin evils, and evils they are, act as a barrier to the
Holy Spirit.
In fact, this problem is acute in almost all religious circles.
For instance, there are millions of Christians I think, who
would receive the Truth on the Baptism with the Holy Spirit
with the evidence of speaking with other Tongues if it came
through their particular denomination, i.e., *"church!"*
They are biased and prejudiced toward others, so this hinders them from receiving. The same could be said for Divine
Healing and many other Truths as it pertains to the Word of God.
Prejudice and bias against other particular denominations
or churches keep us from receiving Truths which other Believers

have, which we just might not have.

PREJUDICE AGAINST PAUL

With the great stand that Paul took against the Judaizers, there was tremendous prejudice against him from the Jewish sector of the Church. This is not to say that all Jews in the Church felt in a negative way toward Paul, for such was not the case. However, I think it should be obvious that some definitely were prejudiced against the Apostle. I think the Book of Hebrews is an excellent example.

Of course, there has been much argument over who actually wrote the Epistle to the Hebrews. Even though there is no concrete evidence, I personally feel that there is enough evidence to warrant the suggestion, at least, that Paul was the author. As far as I am personally concerned, I think that evidence is irrefutable.

If one is to notice, this particular Book does not begin at all as any other Epistle in the New Testament. It actually carries no salutation, such being omitted entirely.

I think it is this way because Paul didn't want the Jews to whom it was addressed, and I speak of Christian Jews, to know that he was the author. He felt that upon knowing this, many of them would be prejudiced and would, therefore, fail to heed the great Truths given therein.

PAUL AND THE WORD OF GOD

I think from this that we can see how lethal all of this actually is. Imagine some Christians not wanting to receive instruction from Paul, especially considering that what he wrote, at least in these capacities, was the Word of God! The great Truths given to this man by the Holy Spirit, and intended for the entirety of the Church for all time, would be lost on some for the reasons mentioned. What a travesty! And yet, I wonder how many of us have fallen into the same trap.

I want to receive from the Lord, and I want to receive from Him irrespective as to the direction from whence it comes or the one whom He chooses to use. Therefore, my heart must be open at all times, and even at times to the most unlikely of sources. Now, that certainly doesn't mean that we are to accept all preachers and teachers as being from the Lord. The truth is, all aren't! In fact, most aren't! So, we must be very, very careful about what we hear and from whom it is heard. So, don't misunderstand my words.

Preachers who are preaching and teaching error have no truth to impart. So, there will be no truth from that source. However, there definitely can be Revelation and Truth given by Preachers who are walking in all the Light they know and have, even though they are remiss in other areas. In other words, what they actually do know, they know it to a great extent, and they can be a great blessing to all who will listen to them in these particular categories. Let me give another example.

THE BAPTISM WITH THE HOLY SPIRIT

There are many preachers who do not believe in the Baptism with the Holy Spirit with the evidence of speaking with other Tongues, which I feel is error on their part. However, they are not opposed to this Grace of which I speak; they just don't have much understanding on the subject and, consequently, have not yet received. But yet, in the area regarding Salvation in which they are well versed, they certainly are capable of bringing forth excellent Truths in this regard, Truths, I might quickly add, which will be a tremendous benefit to those who hear them.

REJECTING THE HOLY SPIRIT

However, at the same time, for those who reject the Baptism with the Holy Spirit, and I mean reject it with anger, even as many do, I personally feel that their attitude in this respect has shut them off from even what Truths they presently may hold. I don't think these particular individuals can help anyone with anything. I trust I'm making myself clear.

For instance, a short time ago, I was looking at a pamphlet which outlined the purposes and intentions of a particular Christian college. In the section on the Baptism with the Holy Spirit, the founder wrote that anyone who believed in the Baptism with the Holy Spirit with the evidence of speaking with other Tongues was of the Devil. His statement basically was that they were of the Devil, or else, mentally unbalanced. He then went on to say that no one would be allowed in that particular school who believed such, and if found to entertain such after they had enrolled in the school, they would be summarily dismissed.

I don't think that man has anything to say to me about anything as it pertains to God. That's what I'm trying to say!

AN OPEN HEART TO GOD

Receiving from the Lord is totally different from receiving from anyone else. There are several requirements, the first, of course, being *"Born-Again."*

The entire fact of living for God, being a Christian, and of having a relationship with the Lord is all tied up and played out by being led by the Spirit. To be sure, the Spirit of God does this in many and varied ways, but whatever the way might be, everything must coincide with the Word of God. In fact, the Word is always the primary manner in which the Holy Spirit reveals Himself to the Saint. Of course, the more that we know the Word, the easier it is for us to be led by the Holy Spirit.

However, in all of this, even taking into account everything I've just said, we must have, as previously stated, an open heart. In other words, we must have a responsive heart toward God if we are to receive from the Lord and be led by the Spirit. Of course, sin stops any type of relationship with the Lord and especially being led by the Spirit. Unconfessed, unrepentant sin is the greatest barrier there is. The Scripture plainly tells us that sin *"hardens the heart"* (Heb. 3:13), and sin comes in many shapes, forms, and sizes.

SIN

Unforgiveness is sin! A bad attitude is sin! As we've already stated, bias and prejudice, at least in the manner we are discussing it here, is sin!

That's the reason the Lord plainly says, *". . . but to this man will I look, even to him who is poor and of a contrite spirit, and trembles at My Word"* (Isa. 66:2).

The word, *"Poor,"* here refers to *"poor in spirit"* exactly as it does in the Beatitudes (Mat. 5:3).

It means that the Believer is to know and understand that within himself, he is spiritually and morally bankrupt, i.e., *"poor in spirit."*

"Contrite" speaks of that which is broken and, in a sense, *"crushed."*

The whole thing speaks of humility, which can only be gained at the Cross. This is at least one of the reasons we are demanded to take up the Cross daily and follow Christ (Lk. 9:23).

Only with such a spirit can a person be led by the Spirit of God.

TO KEEP IN LINE WITH

Paul said, *"Nevertheless, whereto we have already attained, let us walk by the same rule, let us mind the same thing"* (Phil. 3:16).

Paul is saying here that we must not wait for God to reveal all the Truth on all points before we begin to give ourselves to spiritual growth. Each Believer should exercise fully the degree of maturity he already possesses, whatever that might be.

The words, *"Live up to,"* which actually mean, *"To keep in line with,"* calls for Christians to maintain a constant life in

harmony with the understanding of God's Truth we already
have, at whatever level that might be. The Holy Spirit through
the Apostle tells us that Christians, proceeding along the same
path, may be at different stages of progress and should be
faithful to as much of God's Truth as they understand. This is
the only way to continued spiritual growth, for this Christian
life is a process of growth, and as all should know, growth in
any capacity is never instantaneous but is always a process.

PRESENT ATTAINMENT

The phrase, *"Nevertheless, whereto we have already attained,"* presents a different word regarding *"attained"* than
the word translated, *"Attained,"* in Philippians 3:12. The word
there meant, *"To take or appropriate."* This word in Verse 16
means, *"To arrive at, to reach."* It speaks of progress along a
road to a certain point.

Paul is thinking of the Philippians along the Christian path.
His idea is, *"So far as we have come,"* meaning, of course, that
there is still another distance to go. He is not meaning a certain
distance to go to be Saved, but rather to become more and more
mature in the Lord. In other words, I think one is safe to say that
no Christian has all the Light on any Biblical subject; nevertheless, we are to walk according to the Light we presently have.

IF WE ERR . . .

I think the idea of all of this is that we who have entered
on the race may trust God to set us right if we err in anything,
provided only that we are persevering in the course. The as-
surance of Light from Him does not supersede the duty of perpetual and watchful effort.

There is another meaning to this as well. Though there
might be different degrees of attainment among Christians
and different views on many subjects, yet there are points on
which all can agree. There are attainments which all have

made, and in reference to the agreement, we should walk in harmony and love.

In fact, it might be and, no doubt, is that some have made much greater advances than others. They have a greater degree of the Light on a particular subject, which means they have a higher knowledge with all of its attendant Blessings. However, they did not get to this place automatically or easily. If they are truly at an advanced level, always remembering how this place and position was attained, which means through and by the Grace of God, they will be overly patient and kind with others who are walking the same road but yet have not attained the same level.

THE TRUE LIGHT OF THE GOSPEL

True Light, if followed truthfully, will always bring about humility. The reason follows along this line:

This of which we speak is not attained by study, education, intellectualism, or human ability. It is always given by the Spirit. However, the manner in which He gives this of which we speak, on whatever subject, usually comes about (and possibly always comes about) as a result of trial and error on our part — trial and error, incidentally, which, at times, have brought great difficulty and problems. In other words, most of us, I think, have attempted to develop ourselves or to go into maturity by means of the flesh, which Paul addresses greatly so in Romans, Chapter 8. True attainments in the Lord can never be reached in this manner, irrespective of our efforts. All of these things can only be brought about through and by the Holy Spirit, Who, even as we've already stated, always works by and through the Finished Work of Christ, i.e., *"the Cross."*

HOW DOES THE HOLY SPIRIT BRING
ABOUT SUCH ATTAINMENTS?

Spiritual growth could probably be summed up in the realm

of Righteousness and Holiness, with the word *"Christlikeness"* describing everything more than all. This is the direction of the Holy Spirit. The Scripture says, *"For whom He did fore-know* (knew that they would be Saved)*, He also did predesti-nate to be conformed to the Image of His Son, that He* (Jesus) *might be the Firstborn among many brethren"* (Rom. 8:29).

"Conformed to the Image of His Son" sums it all up! Even though the growth and attainment of which we speak covers many areas, possibly it can be summed up in the words just given.

However, the great question is: *"How does the Holy Spirit bring this about in our lives?"*

It's not an automatic process. In other words, the Holy Spirit doesn't just automatically do these things because we are Christians. If that were the case, every Christian would be spiritually mature, but we know that all aren't, and, in fact, only a few actually are. So, what is the problem?

Assuming that every true Christian wants to be more and more Christlike, wants to grow in Grace and the Knowledge of the Lord, let us look at the main hindrance to this effort.

The main hindrance is the *"flesh,"* which Paul very suc-cinctly dealt with in Romans, Chapter 8. This hinders our progress more than all, but the truth is most Christians simply don't know what the flesh actually is, etc.

WHAT IS THE FLESH?

The flesh is that which is indicative to a human being, in other words, what a human being can do. I speak of personal talent, education, motivation, ability, personal strength, etc. These things within themselves are not wrong; however, if we try to live for God by these particular means, we will fail every single time. We will fail because, due to the Fall, the physical body of the human being has been rendered ineffective. In other words, *"The Spirit is willing, but the flesh is weak."* And yet, most Christians are trying to live for God by the means of the flesh. In fact, most modern Christians don't even know what the flesh actually is; however, trying to live for God by the means of the flesh means that we aren't trying to live for God by the Means of the Cross. Consequently, we are going to fail, as fail we must. God's Way is the Cross of Christ. As we have repeatedly stated, every single thing we receive from God comes by the Means of the Cross. Let me give an example!

ABRAHAM AND SARAH

For almost anything we can think of as it regards spiritual things, we can find a counterpart in the Old Testament who lived out the situation in graphic detail. In other words, their life experiences provided an excellent example of this of which we speak. In this case, Abraham and Sarah provide the perfect example.

It was sometime in early 1998 (if I remember correctly). I was listening to a particular Christian radio broadcast. The Preacher in question is now with the Lord. However, he made a statement, which I knew was from the Lord, and it greatly ministered to me even though, at the time, I did not really understand exactly what he meant. For some reason, I didn't hear the balance of the program, or else, he never fully explained his statement, but I knew what he said was of tremendous significance.

He said, *"Abraham and Sarah had to deal with their sin before Isaac could be born."*

When he said these words, the Spirit of God came all over me. Actually, it was to such a degree that I had no doubt that it was the Lord, even as I began to weep because of the Presence of God.

Some may ask the question as to why this statement would affect me to such a degree.

THE EFFECT

It affected me because of my quest for an answer to the

very things we are discussing here. I knew what the man said was right even though I did not exactly know why it was right, at least at that particular time.

After that, I thought about this many times, knowing that the Holy Spirit was telling me something, but I had not then grasped what He was trying to tell me. I sought the Lord about the matter, asking Him to reveal this to me, knowing that it would contain a valuable Truth.

When I attempted to analyze the statement, *"Abraham and Sarah had to deal with their sin before Isaac could be born,"* I kept trying to figure out what sin.

In my mind and spirit, I dealt with Abraham's life, trying to come to an answer. Was it the Hagar situation?

I felt in my heart that this played a part in the scenario, but I did not feel this was what the Holy Spirit was saying. Then the Lord revealed this thing to me.

DEPENDENCE ON THE FLESH

It was not so much these acts of wrongdoing that the Spirit of God was talking about, such as Hagar, which, in reality, were only symptoms. While these were truly wrong, they were more the results of the real wrong than anything else.

"The sin of Abraham and Sarah was their dependence on the flesh, their self-efforts, and their own machinations in attempting to bring about the great Promise of God, as it regarded a baby boy being born, instead of allowing it to be done by the Holy Spirit."

That was their sin, and that is our sin as well. Only when Abraham and Sarah quit trying to bring this about by their own machinations was Isaac finally born because only then could the Spirit of God work as He desired. In other words, all the hope of the flesh had to die before the Holy Spirit could bring about the miracle birth of this child. This is exactly what happens to us as well.

Whenever we attempt to become Christlike or overcome

sin in our own way and manner, irrespective that we think it's very spiritual, we succeed in doing nothing but frustrate the Grace of God (Gal. 2:20-21).

Abraham and Sarah were frustrating the Grace of God by their own personal efforts in trying to bring about the Promise of God, just like we frustrate the Grace of God by our own efforts to bring about Holiness and Righteousness, etc.

HOW DO WE FRUSTRATE THE GRACE OF GOD?

In regards to this, Paul said:

"**I do not frustrate the Grace of God** *(if we make anything other than the Cross of Christ the Object of our Faith, we frustrate the Grace of God, which means we stop its action, and the Holy Spirit will no longer help us)*: **for if Righteousness** *come* **by the Law** *(any type of law)*, **then Christ is dead in vain.** *(If I can successfully live for the Lord by any means other than Faith in Christ and the Cross, then the Death of Christ was a waste)*" (Gal. 2:21).

The Grace of God is the Goodness of God freely giving the Saints all that we need in respect to bringing about what we ought to be in Christ. However, the Grace of God, just as the Work of the Holy Spirit, is not automatic. The Grace of God always functions through, by, of, and within the Cross of Christ, i.e., *"the Finished Work of Christ on the Cross."* That is the only manner in which God can extend to anyone His Grace.

When the sinner comes to Christ, he does so because he puts his Faith in Christ and the Cross even though he understands very little about what was done there. Even so, God honors his Faith simply because the Object of his Faith is correct and gives the sinner Grace, which is his Salvation.

After Salvation, the Grace of God continues to work in the same capacity. God gives good things to us without merit, without payment on our part, and without earning such in any way, which is impossible to do in any case. However, this Grace comes to us as Christians not because we are Christians, but because of Christ and what He did on the Cross. It is all tied to the Cross!

That means that the Believer must place his Faith in the Cross and leave his Faith in the Cross, understanding that all of the things we receive from God comes through what Jesus did on the Cross. The Grace of God can then flow unhindered, with the Holy Spirit helping us to be what we must be in the realm of Righteousness and Holiness — but only by this method. Our problem is we often frustrate this method.

The manner in which the Grace of God is frustrated is varied and many. Please allow me to use personal examples.

THE MEANS OF FRUSTRATION

Anytime a Believer does anything in the realm of spirituality, such as attending church, giving money to the Work of God, etc., as a means of making one holy or righteous, in other words, one does these things in order to be Holy, the only thing one will succeed in actually doing is to frustrate the Grace of God.

As it regards my own personal prayer life, I personally have three prayer meetings a day. However, I know that these prayer meetings within themselves do not make me holy, do not make me righteous, do not help me to earn anything, and do not make me worthy of anything.

As well, I believe I can say without fear of contradiction that I have paid tithe on every dollar I have ever made from the time I was a child. However, this did not purchase me anything with the Lord, nor did it or does it merit me anything. While the Lord most definitely will bless my prayer life and will bless my giving, still, that is totally different than Righteousness, Holiness, and Christlikeness. My Righteousness and Holiness come exclusively from Christ and my Faith in Him and what

He did for me at the Cross — and that alone. In other words, it is impossible for one to earn Righteousness, Holiness, or to even earn Christlikeness. It simply cannot be done.

PERSONAL EXAMPLE

Sometime back, Donnie showed me a book that he had purchased, which was written by a prominent minister of the Gospel. The things I'm about to say are in no way meant to demean the consecration or dedication of our dear brother. I'm certain that he loves the Lord very much, but he was dead wrong in what he was saying.

He had written a book on fasting and stated that if a person will fast 21 days, or some such time limit, this will rid that individual of the bondage of sin, etc.

Now, while fasting is most definitely scriptural, and if done in the right way, will definitely be a Blessing to the individual, still, one cannot fast one's way to victory over sin. It is the Cross Alone which deals with sin. Paul said:

"So Christ was once offered to bear the sins of many; and unto them who look for Him shall He appear the second time without sin unto Salvation" (Heb. 9:28).

This Passage refers to the Second Coming. *"Without sin,"* refers to the fact that the Second Coming will not be to atone for sin, for that was already carried out at the Cross at His First Advent. The Second Coming will bring all the results of Salvation to this world, which refers to all that He did at the Cross. We now only have the *"Firstfruits"* (Rom. 8:23).

Whenever we place our Faith in anything except the Cross of Christ, pure and simple, we *"frustrate the Grace of God."* Such greatly hinders the Holy Spirit, without Whom, we are in terrible trouble. What needs to be done in our hearts and lives can only be done by the Holy Spirit, and He works entirely within the framework of the Cross of Christ. In fact, that's what gives Him the legal means to do all that He does for us. That's the reason the Scripture also says, concerning the Holy

Spirit and the Cross:

"For the Law of the Spirit of Life in Christ Jesus has made me free from the Law of Sin and Death" (Rom. 8:2).

THE DOING OF RELIGION

Someone has said that the *"doing of religion"* is the most powerful narcotic there is. Because it pertains to good things and religious things, the very *"doing"* of these things, whatever they might be, tends to make one feel that one has earned something from the Lord, etc. Believers must know that the Lord has nothing for sale! Everything He has is in the form of a Gift, but it all comes through what Jesus did at the Cross.

That means that one cannot earn anything from God in any capacity, so we should quit trying.

We must understand that everything we receive from the Lord is a free gift but always based upon our Faith. Yet, it must be Faith in the Finished Work of Christ.

When we place our Faith in the Cross, and the Cross exclusively, knowing that everything we receive from the Lord comes from this Source, the Holy Spirit can then help us and bring us to the place that He wants us to be, i.e., *"Christlikeness!"* He cannot and, in fact, will not do it any other way.

This means that whatever He does, it is entirely a Work of the Spirit and not a mixture of the flesh and the Spirit, which God cannot accept. Salvation, and everything that goes with this glorious Grace, is all of God and not whatsoever of man.

The whole thing confuses us at times simply because the things we do are spiritual. Because they are spiritual, we tend to think of them as of the Spirit. To be sure, they are, if they're kept in their right perspective. I've mentioned the following before but please allow me to say it again:

AN EXAMPLE

A young minister was on our radio program some time

ago. I think that there was no doubt that he loved the Lord very much, which was evident in his spirit. Even though I did not really know him, one could tell by speaking with him just a few moments that he was consecrated to the Lord. However, his knowledge of the Cross and the provision there made was not as strong as it should have been.

During the course of our conversation, which was going out over our daily radio program to quite a few stations, he made this statement, or words to this effect:

"When I have a problem with sin or evil passions, I go on a three-day fast and that takes care of the situation."

No, it won't!

I was not that blunt with him, but I pray that I did say enough to let him know that what he was saying was not exactly right.

While fasting is definitely Scriptural and definitely helpful, if we attempt to use it in that manner, and I speak of trying to overcome sin, in effect, we are saying that what Jesus did at the Cross was not necessary, or else, He did not do enough. In other words, He did not complete the task; therefore, we have to add fasting to His Work in order to have victory.

While fasting will definitely help any Believer, that is, if it's done in the right way, it is not a means of overcoming sin. Once again I emphasize, were this the case, then Jesus died in vain exactly as Paul said (Gal. 2:21).

CHRISTLIKENESS

As a Believer, I want to grow in Grace and the Knowledge of the Lord. I want to be what He wants me to be. I want to be Christlike, and furthermore, I want to be more and more Christlike all the time. However, I have learned that I cannot bring this about, and please believe me, I have tried. It can only be brought about by the Spirit of God. The only part I am to play is to exhibit Faith in the Cross of Christ, understanding that my victory is in the Cross, and then the Spirit of

God can bring about the work all of us so desperately need.

THE APOSTLE PAUL

When Paul was Saved on the road to Damascus and baptized with the Holy Spirit some three days later, he set out to live for God in the only way he knew, which was the keeping of Commandments. He thought that now that he was Saved and baptized with the Spirit, surely this could be done. This is what he said, and I quote the Text plus the notes from THE EXPOSITOR'S STUDY BIBLE:

> "For I was alive without the Law once *(Paul is referring to himself personally and his Conversion to Christ; the Law, he states, had nothing to do with that Conversion; neither did it have anything to do with his life in Christ)*: but when the Commandment came *(having just been Saved and not understanding the Cross of Christ, he tried to live for God by keeping the Commandments through his own strength and power; in his defense, no one else at that time understood the Cross; in fact, the meaning of the Cross, which is actually the meaning of the New Covenant, would be given to Paul)*, sin revived *(the sin nature will always, and without exception, revive under such circumstances, which results in spiritual failure)*, and I died *(he was not meaning that he physically died, as would be obvious, but that he died to the Commandment; in other words, he failed to obey no matter how hard he tried; let all Believers understand that if the Apostle Paul couldn't live for God in this manner, neither can you!)*."

Then he said:

> "And the Commandment, which *was ordained* to life *(refers to the Ten Commandments)*, I found *to be* unto death *(means that the Law revealed the sin, as it always*

does, and its wages which are death; in other words, there is no victory in trying to live by Law; we are to live by Faith, referring to Faith in Christ and the Cross.)"

DECEPTION

"For sin *(the sin nature)*, **taking occasion by the Commandment** *(in no way blames the Commandment, but that the Commandment actually did agitate the sin nature and brought it to the fore, which it was designed to do)*, **deceived me** *(Paul thought, now that he had accepted Christ, by that mere fact alone he could certainly obey the Lord in every respect; but he found he couldn't, neither can you, at least in that fashion)*, **and by it slew** *me (despite all of his efforts to live for the Lord by the means of Law-keeping, he failed; and again, I say, so will you!)"* **(Rom. 7:9-11).**

I DON'T UNDERSTAND . . .

Then the great Apostle said:

"For that which I do *(the failure)* **I allow not** *(should have been translated, 'I understand not'; these are not the words of an unsaved man, as some claim, but rather a Believer who is trying and failing)*: **for what I would, that do I not** *(refers to the obedience he wants to render to Christ, but rather fails; why? as Paul explained, the Believer is married to Christ but is being unfaithful to Christ by spiritually cohabiting with the Law, which frustrates the Grace of God; that means the Holy Spirit will not help such a person, which guarantees failure [Gal. 2:21])*; **but what I hate, that do I** *(refers to sin in his life, which he doesn't want to do and, in fact, hates, but finds himself unable to stop; unfortunately, due to the fact of not understanding the Cross as it refers to Sanctification, this* *is the plight of most modern Christians)*" (**Rom. 7:15**).

OUR WALK BEFORE GOD

The phrase, *"Let us walk by the same rule, let us mind the same thing,"* refers in the Greek to *"direct one's life, to live."*

Actually, the word, *"Rule,"* is not in the original Greek but has been supplied by the translators. The literal Greek is, *"Walk by the same."* The context speaks of a path and could be translated, *"Let us walk the same path. . . ."*

Most of the time when the word *"walk"* is used in Scripture, it concerns itself with our conduct, our manner of life, the way we live, and the things we do. In its truest sense, it refers to following the Lord.

TWO WAYS TO WALK

One way to walk is the following of Jesus, which is the only True Way, and speaks of what Jesus did at the Cross and the Resurrection.

All other ways, irrespective as to how many they might be, are enemies of the Cross of Christ, which Paul will deal with in the next Verse.

The Early Church was constantly beset by two temptations, which, in effect, are the same presently: the tendency to swerve to the right and end in legalism, and the tendency to swerve to the left and end in lawlessness. As stated, such is the current trend today.

The thing that such people glory in is actually their shame and disgrace. Paul will say in Verse 19 that their end is destruction. Even in his present continued state of imprisonment, Paul was very much aware that tensions existed in the Churches under his care.

In the above phrase, the Apostle used two words, *"Walk"* and *"Mind."* Consequently, in this Passage, there seems to be the same double reference which has pervaded all of Paul's practical teaching. He is anxious for two things — that they should keep on in one course (walk), and that all should keep on together (mind).

In both senses, he addresses the *"perfect,"* or *"maturity."* He will have them understand that they have attained only one thing — to be on the right path, and that is for them to continue in it. He also bids them refrain from setting themselves up above *"the imperfect,"* for the very fact of division would mark them as still *"carnal,"* mere *"babes in Christ"* (I Cor. 3:1-4).

THE EXAMPLE

Paul said: *"Brethren, be followers together of me, and mark them which walk so as you have us for an example"* (Phil. 3:17).

In the early years of the Church, which actually continues unto this moment, Believers needed examples. So, Paul urged the Philippians to join together in imitating his conduct, just as he had done in his exhortation to the Church at Corinth — *"follow my example, as I follow the example of Christ"* (I Cor. 11:1).

Such advice was not egotism, for Paul's emphasis was always strongly that of Christ. Furthermore, Paul includes others in this model as he urges his readers to take note of those who were living in conformity with *"the pattern we gave you,"* i.e., *"the high standard"* (outlined in Phil. 3:7-16).

Literally, Paul wrote, *"You have us as a pattern,"* and the *"us"* includes not only himself but Timothy and perhaps Epaphroditus also. Hence, he was not claiming a unique superiority.

FOLLOWERS OF ME

The phrase, *"Brethren, be followers together of me,"* means to be *"fellow-imitators."* Paul is compelled to make his own example a norm or standard on the new life, even as every Christian ought to seek to do the same.

Paul has far more here in mind than merely trying to get

Christians to follow him. The direction he's going has nothing to do with his ego or even the localized situation. The Holy Spirit is impressing this through him for the following reasons:

Under Christ, Paul was the masterbuilder of the Church (I Cor. 3:10). As it should be understood, the Church was and is altogether different from the Israel of old, through whom and which the Lord previously worked. In fact, there were many in the Jewish segment of the Church who were attempting to pull the Church into Judaism, which Paul vigorously opposed. So, the Apostle had much more in mind than merely his conduct. He was speaking of Doctrine, as well, and I think more particularly of Doctrine. As we shall see in the next Verse, the Cross is the central point of Christianity. It is actually the Foundation of Christianity, i.e., *"what Christ did on the Cross."* Consequently, to have what Jesus did there, one must follow a Prescribed Order. This is what Paul is speaking of more so than anything else.

MARK THEM

The phrase, *"And mark them which walk so as you have us for an example,"* means, *"To fix the attention upon with the desire for or interest in."* It means, *"To observe intently."*

The idea is that the Philippians, and all others for that matter, observe his life attentively and become imitators of him. They are to do the same also with reference to those other Christians in whose lives they find an example of Paul's own manner of life. Two things are said here:

First was the new way of living, which, in effect, was after Christ and produced a walk, i.e., *"lifestyle,"* totally unlike anything else in the world. In effect, the Standard of Righteousness demanded by God in the Ten Commandments was now kept; however, they were kept by a different means than anyone had ever known. Jesus Christ had kept the Law perfectly, which, of course, included the Ten Commandments, and had never failed even one single time. As our Representative Man, God gave us the Perfection of Christ upon Faith on our part registered in Him and what He did at the Cross. Then, in our daily walk before God, and the world for that matter, Christ, Who continues to live in us through the Power, Person, and Ministry of the Holy Spirit, literally lives this life in and through us. He does for us what we cannot do for ourselves. This great victorious walk comes to us and remains with us as we exhibit Faith in the Finished Work of Christ, i.e., *"the Cross,"* by which principle the Holy Spirit works, and by which principle only He works. This is the only manner and way of victory (Rom. 8:1-2).

THE GREAT MISTAKE MADE BY MANY CHRISTIANS

When we think of Jesus saving us and then baptizing us with the Holy Spirit, we come to realize how privileged and fortunate we actually are. But then, too often, we make the mistake of thinking that because we are now Saved and Spirit-filled, we can now live this life as it ought to be lived. Consequently, we set out to do just that, and we always fail. It confuses us because we really don't understand why we fail. We have the Holy Spirit, and I'm speaking of those who have been baptized with the Holy Spirit with the evidence of speaking with other Tongues (Acts 2:4), and we know that there is Almighty Power registered in the Holy Spirit (Acts 1:8). So, with this Power to help us, we think that surely we can do all the things we need to do and live the kind of life we need to live.

When the first failure comes our way, we sort of think of it as a fluke, somewhat brushing it aside as we ask the Lord to forgive us — whatever that failure might be. Then it happens again with a repetition of Repentance and forgiveness. We then discover that the same thing has happened quite a number of times, and we resolve within our hearts that it must stop, and for all the obvious reasons. We are now Children of God, and sin is repugnant to us. Actually, to fail the Lord is a terrible thing, which registers greatly in the hearts and lives of the Believers, with them actually not able to rest until the thing is washed and cleansed by the Blood (I Jn. 1:9).

In this scenario, we resolve to *"try harder,"* whatever that means! We must read the Bible more! We must pray more! We must check our lives to see if there is some fault or difficulty that is allowing Satan access with which to overcome us.

In regard to all of this, we do try harder, and harder, and harder, but regrettably, the situation is not getting better, but rather worse.

WHAT IS ACTUALLY HAPPENING?

At this stage, we do not realize it, but we have resorted to law. While it's not the Law of Moses, it definitely is a law of our own making. Because these things we are doing are very right in their own way, actually, very Scriptural, it fools us. Again, we at times mistake forgiveness for victory. It isn't! Forgiveness is that which God has promised to all who would seek such (I Jn. 1:9), which restores the relationship between Himself and the sinning Believer. But again, it is not victory, and even though we sense and feel the joy of restored fellowship, that doesn't mean we are free from this dominion of sin of some nature with which Satan has ensnared us.

As we've already stated, we have to be very careful here because many Christians think if they're not snared by the big five (gambling, drugs, alcohol, nicotine, immorality), they are home free. We must never forget that there are other sins, as well, such as greed, covetousness, uncontrollable temper, malice, pride, etc. Satan doesn't care with which he ensnares us, just so we are snared.

This may come as a shock but if the Christian has to be snared by something, it would probably be better were it one of the big five, so to speak, because it's much easier to bring such to Repentance than it is sins of pride. Jesus said as much (Mat. 21:31).

At any rate, the reason we are failing is because we are

not looking to the Cross, but rather to law, whether we understand it or not. Law has only one effect: it just makes matters
worse. That doesn't mean that the Law itself is wrong. In
fact, the law is right, whether the ancient Law of Moses or laws
of our own devising. What is wrong is our attempting to bring
about victory through these laws, i.e., *"efforts."* Again I state,
we may not think we are attempting to do this within our own
strength, but that's exactly what's happening. We think that
because we are baptized with the Holy Spirit, He automatically exerts His Great Power on our behalf. The truth is, He
does no such thing.

WHAT IS THE PATH TO VICTORY?

There's only One Path or Way of Victory and that is Jesus.
Now, let's see what that means.
It means what Jesus did at the Cross. Our Faith is to be in
that exclusively. We must understand that this is where Satan
was totally defeated. There, all sin was addressed and atoned,
which destroyed the power of Satan, at least for those who
will believe. Whenever the Saint expresses Faith in the Cross,
which he should do on a daily basis (Lk. 9:23; Gal. 6:14), the
Holy Spirit will then exert His Great Power of which we speak,
and do so on our behalf (Rom. 8:2). To be sure, there is no
power of darkness that can overcome the Holy Spirit. However, if we try to have the victory for which we seek by our own
machinations of any kind, no matter how holy they may be in
their own right, we are going to fail every single time.

THE TRAGEDY!

What is so bad about all of this is that in the last 50 years,
there has been so little preaching and teaching on the Cross of
Christ that the church little knows its way of victory. Consequently, it casts about in every conceivable way possible, attempting to find the answer to its problems. Mostly, it does so

through humanistic psychology, which is tantamount to saying that what Jesus did on the Cross was not sufficient. Or else, it resorts to means and ways of its own devising. The great fad at the moment is the *"Purpose Driven Life"* scheme. And then, there's always, as stated, humanistic psychology. Others seek manifestations of the Holy Spirit. Of course, if it is truly a Manifestation of the Spirit, it will definitely be a Blessing to the individual. Still, one being *"slain in the Spirit,"* which the Lord at times definitely does, will not give one victory over sin. He will be blessed, but that's as far as it will go.

Part of the church tells Believers that if their *"confession"* is proper, that is the means of victory. While confession is very important, once again, there is no victory in this capacity.

Others claim that Christians, who are having problems of some nature, are having these problems because of demon spirits. They admonish them to have these demons cast out, and then their problems will be solved. While demon spirits definitely are involved in every manner of sin and failure, that's not what the Christian needs.

Even though Believers can definitely be oppressed by demon spirits, they cannot be demonically possessed.

Back in the 1970's, this was all the rage. Christians were lining up in churches all over the world, with some preacher laying hands on them and supposedly casting out the demon of fear, immorality, lust, alcohol, etc.

While the laying on of hands is definitely Scriptural and will bless the individual, still, it will not give one victory over sin.

We should stop and think a moment. If any of these things, plus a lot of things we haven't mentioned, could bring about victory in our hearts and lives, then Jesus did not need to come down here and die on the Cross (Gal. 2:21). The Lord could have just instituted whatever particular fad being presently promoted. Unfortunately, the problem is much worse than that. It took Jesus coming down and dying on a Cross in order to set captives free. Nothing else will suffice but that. The only answer, and I mean the only answer, for sin is the Cross of Christ (Rom. 6:1-14; 8:1-11; I Cor. 1:17, 18, 23; 2:2; Gal., Chpt., 5; 6:14; Col. 2:10-15).

THE REAL PROBLEM OF THE CHURCH IS SIN

The heading I have just given is not easily admitted. Most of the modern church world denies this. In fact, sin is not even mentioned anymore in most churches. The question might be asked, *"Whatever happened to sin?"* Now it's just a mistake someone makes, a bad habit, an improper confession, etc. For the Preacher to preach about sin, it may embarrass people, or it may even offend some. So, if one is going to fill up one's church with warm bodies, one does not want to mention sin because that's not what the people come to hear. They come to hear how good they are or how good they can be with a slight adjustment. So, if you don't recognize the problem, then you don't need the solution, which eliminates the Cross as well. Then again, many Christians claim that due to the fact that they are now Born-Again and Spirit-filled, they are little bothered by sin.

One leader of a major Pentecostal denomination made the statement that those in his particular denomination were seldom bothered by these types of things, etc. He admitted that once in awhile it might happen, but seldom.

I happen to have been very much acquainted with his denomination, and I knew that what he was saying was totally off the wall, so to speak. The truth was, and regrettably is, that preachers in that particular denomination were and are failing right and left. I don't say that with any joy, but regrettably, it is the truth.

In fact, the majority of the modern church is in a state of denial. It hides its head in the sand, refusing to look at the real problem, which is sin, all the time claiming it is something else.

"Our Faith is not strong enough," many claim! Others say, as we've already mentioned, *"The confession is wrong!"*

Others claim that if you'll just go to a certain meeting and have Brother so and so pray for you, your problems will then be solved. Others claim that the problem is a *"family curse,"* and this particular curse must be rebuked by preachers who understand the problem.

NO, IT IS SIN!

The real problem, as it always has been, is sin. Satan is trying to drag the Christian down, and he does so by sin in some way or the other. We can deny that fact if we want to, but it doesn't make it any less true.

Now, there is only one answer for sin, and that is what Christ did at the Cross. Nothing else will address itself to this terrible malady of darkness! Nothing else will suffice! It is only what Jesus did at the Cross and the Resurrection that addressed this terrible problem, and addressed it totally and completely. In other words, Christ left nothing undone, which means that His Work was and is a Finished Work.

This means that this thing is so bad, and I continue to speak of the problem of sin, that even though God could speak worlds into existence, He, in fact, could not speak Redemption into existence, that is, if He was to stay true to His Nature. That's a startling statement, but it happens to be true! God had to become Man, literally becoming the Second Man and the Last Adam, and serving as our Substitute and Representative Man. He paid a terrible price on the Cross of Calvary in order that this horrible problem of sin might be conquered. He did it in a most expensive manner, with the giving of His Own Life.

THE CROSS

This means that the Cross was not an accident or an incident. The Cross of Christ was planned even before the foundation of the world (I Pet. 1:18-20). In other words, Jesus came down here to die on the Cross. That was His Objective. Many other things were necessary, such as His Virgin Birth;

His Spotless, Sinless, Perfect Life; and His Perfect Keeping of the Law, but it was the Cross which broke the back of Satan, so to speak.

Therefore, the Victory is in the Cross and the Cross Alone. I speak of the Atonement, where Jesus addressed every single thing that was lost in the Fall. While we do not have all the benefits of the Atonement presently, and will not have such until the Resurrection of all Saints, still, the benefits we do have presently are so astounding that there is no reason that any Believer should be overcome by sin. The Victory is ours, all purchased by Christ.

Our problem is, the modern church little understands the veracity of the Cross and what it means for the Child of God.

SALVATION AND VICTORY

The Cross of Christ is the only way of Salvation for the sinner and the only way of victory for the Saint.

Most Christians, as we have repeatedly stated, know and understand the part the Cross plays as it regards their initial Salvation experience. However, most have no idea whatsoever as to the part it plays in our continued life as lived for the Lord. The truth is the Cross of Christ plays just as much a part in our victorious, daily walk before God as it did when we initially gave our hearts to Christ. Just as we as sinners had to believe the Lord and what He did at the Cross in order to be Saved, such Faith must continue even on a daily basis for the entirety of our lives, that is, if we are to walk in victory (Lk. 9:23-24).

FAITH

We've heard more teaching on faith in the last several decades than possibly all the remainder of the centuries of the Church put together. Some of the teaching has been very good; however, most of it, I think, has not been good at all. It has led the church away from the Cross.

When we speak of Faith, exactly what do we mean?

We talk about having *"Faith in God,"* having *"Faith in Christ,"* having *Faith in the Word,"* etc. All of these statements are correct, but if left there, they leave some things to be desired.

The reader should read the next phrases very carefully, even several times, for the significance of what is being said.

It is the Object of Faith that is so important. By that, I mean that when we talk about having Faith in Christ, we must understand that it's Faith in what He did at the Cross, which guarantees my Salvation and victory. In other words, *"Christ and Him Crucified"* must ever be the Object of our Faith (I Cor. 2:2). It is not just Jesus, as grand and glorious as that would be, but rather Jesus and what He did at the Cross. That's where our victory resides, and only where our victory resides.

THE PRICE PAID AT THE CROSS

So, when we say that we're having Faith in the Lord, it must always register within our hearts that we're speaking of the great price which He paid on the Cross of Calvary. That is where Satan was defeated, where every sin was atoned, where death was defeated, where the claims of Heavenly Justice were satisfied, and where the curse of the Law was also satisfied.

However, most Christians are running around trying to increase their Faith because they've been taught that the more Faith they have, the more great things they will receive. However, it is not the amount of Faith which causes one to receive from God, but rather the Object of one's Faith (Rom. 6:3-5; 8:1-2).

Actually, Faith in God is not difficult to have. All we have to do is simply believe Him, i.e., *"His Word,"* and that is Faith. There's nothing hard or complicated about the subject. We either believe, or we don't.

If we do believe, we must make sure that the Object of our Faith is correct, which means that we are to have Faith at all times in the Cross of Christ. Salvation comes through the Cross; the Baptism with the Holy Spirit comes through the Cross; our economic prosperity comes through the Cross; our victory in every capacity comes through the Cross; our mental well-being comes through the Cross; our answers to prayer come through the Cross; and the Grace of God comes through the Cross. In other words, every single thing we receive from the Lord comes to us because of what Jesus did at the Cross and the Resurrection. Consequently, our Faith must be in that great Finished Work, must stay in that great Finished Work, and must do so, even as we have repeatedly stated, on a daily basis (Lk. 9:23).

Basically, this is what Paul was speaking about, even as the next Verse will proclaim.

WHO WILL YOU FOLLOW?

Second, the Saints of God were admonished by Paul to follow those who believed and taught exactly as he is here proclaiming — the Message of the Cross. If the preachers or the laymen were not living the Cross life, they were not to be followed.

Where does that leave the modern church?

People are following denominations, so-called great faith teachers, fads, particular churches, and about everything one could think, with most all leading nowhere.

Paul is saying that we must follow the Preacher who is preaching the Cross, who is living the Cross, and who understands the Cross and holds it up as the Foundation of Christianity and the throughway of all Blessing.

The Apostle uses the word, *"Mark,"* which in the Greek is, *"Skopos,"* and means, *"Look at, look on, take heed and consider."* These are the ones to follow, and no one else!

That means that if the church is not a Cross church, one should not attend there. If the preacher is not a Cross preacher, he should not be heeded.

That is blunt but the best way I know to say the words. Please remember, we are speaking of the single most important thing in the world, your soul and your victory. The Cross of Christ is the answer and the only answer for that!

ENEMIES OF THE CROSS OF CHRIST

Paul said: *"For many walk, of whom I have told you often, and I tell you even weeping, that they are the enemies of the Cross of Christ"* (Phil. 3:18).

Who are these *"enemies of the Cross of Christ"*?

Now, please notice, he did not say that they were enemies of Christ, but rather, *"Enemies of the Cross of Christ."*

They are anyone, and for all time, who attempts to substitute something else in place of the Cross, who does not recognize the rightful place of the Cross as the Foundation of Christianity.

To attempt to pinpoint of whom exactly Paul was speaking begs the issue and misses the point. It doesn't really matter who he had in mind at that particular time. It refers to all who build structures other than the Cross of Christ; consequently, it covers a great many people, churches, denominations, preachers, etc.

In Paul's day it would have covered the Judaizers who were attempting to add Law to Grace, who little understood the Cross, and who little believed in what the Cross represented. It would have also referred to those who had taken liberty into license, claiming that sin little mattered. They little realized, if at all, that Jesus died on the Cross in order to deliver us from sin. In fact, even though the Cross was for many purposes, the great reason and purpose that it had to be carried out was that all sin be atoned, past, present, and future, at least for all who will believe (Jn. 3:16).

MANY WALK THE WRONG ROAD

The phrase, *"For many walk,"* speaks of those, even as we have stated, who were attempting to live for God outside of the Victory and rudiments of the Cross of Christ. In other words, their ways and means were a Crossless Christianity, i.e., *"a Crossless Christ!"* Even though they admitted that the Cross happened, in their thinking, it was only incidental and played little or no part in one's Salvation and relationship with God. Even then, there were *"many"* who walked these erroneous paths.

If it was many then, and it definitely was, what is the percentage presently, especially considering that the modern church is entering into the last day apostasy? Of course, only the Lord knows the answer to that question. However, I think it should be obvious that the *"many,"* as used by Paul then, would now be changed to *"most!"*

For instance, the entirety of the Catholic church teaches other than the Cross of Christ. While the Cross is pictured in Catholic dogma, what Jesus did there is not held up at all as the way of Salvation. It is rather the church itself and obedience to its principles and precepts, whatever they might be, that is held up as the Salvation process, and they feel free to change them as they will. In other words, if they will be faithful to the church and pray to Mary, they will be saved. Nothing could be further from the truth. One can only say, albeit regrettably, that the entirety of the Catholic church is an enemy of the Cross of Christ.

OTHER ENEMIES . . .

The modern greed gospel falls into the same category. The Cross of Christ is not the object at all in this teaching, but rather material things, i.e., *"money!"* In fact, in these circles, the Cross of Christ is actually repudiated. Many of these particular churches will not sing songs about the Cross or the Blood because that refers, they say, to weakness and not strength. They actually refer to the Cross as *"past miseries,"* which has no place in the life of the modern Christian, they say!

These blasphemers, for that's what they are, claim that we are Resurrection people, etc. They seem to forget that one cannot have Resurrection Life unless one properly accepts the Cross Life. Paul plainly stated, *"For if* (since) *we have been planted together in the likeness of His Death* (this is the Cross Life), *we shall be also in the likeness of His Resurrection* (Resurrection Life)*"* (Rom. 6:5).

As is clearly stated here, it is impossible to have Resurrection Life without first understanding and accepting the *"Cross Life."* In fact, Paul used the word, *"Planted."* This means that we must literally be planted in the Cross, which refers to all that was there accomplished, before we can have this glorious *"Resurrection Life."* Unfortunately, those who teach and preach the so-called greed gospel have tried to ignore the *"Cross Life,"* jumping instead to the *"Resurrection Life."* Of course, such cannot be done.

This is the same thing as Adam and Eve not being allowed to remain in the Garden to partake of the Tree of Life. To have done so in their sinful state would have resulted in monsters instead of the opposite. It is the same presently!

Embracing the Cross Life, which refers to placing one's Faith in what Jesus did at the Cross and understanding its veracity, qualifies one then for *"Resurrection Life."* There is no other way to God except through Christ, and there is no other way to Christ than through His Cross (Lk. 9:23).

WHAT EXACTLY IS THE CROSS LIFE?

Most Christians have an erroneous understanding of the Cross. They think of it in the realm of suffering. Of course, Christ suffered greatly on the Cross, but that's where the suffering began and ended. If we think that the Cross entails some type of suffering, this means that what Jesus did at the Cross was not enough, and we have to add ours to what He has done. Nothing could be more wrong than that.

Actually, the Cross of Christ is the fount of all Blessings, all good things, and all wonderful things. It is the Means, and the only Means, by which all of these wonderful things are given to us. Unfortunately, most Christians don't understand that.

If a Christian has a wreck in the car and is laid up in the hospital for six months, Christians will say, *"Well, that's the Cross that he has to bear,"* etc. No, that has nothing to do with the Cross of Christ. It has something to do with the wreck, etc.

Every good thing that we receive from God, and I mean every good thing, all and without exception are made possible by what Jesus did at the Cross. As we have stated over and over again, the Cross of Christ is the Means, and the only Means, by which all of these wonderful things come to us. Unfortunately, the church thinks of the Cross in an entirely different way, which Satan has been very successful in propagating. Let me say it again:

While the Cross of Christ was the most horrific place of suffering that man could ever begin to imagine, when it was done, however, it was finished. There is absolutely nothing that you and I can do to add to what Christ has already done. In fact, it's a sin to attempt to do so. So, even though Jesus suffered terribly on the Cross, as should be obvious, He did so to atone for our sins. That was the reason for the Cross. For Believers to come along, thinking that we have to add to what He has already done, is pretty close to blasphemy.

The other day, a preacher said something to me about a denomination punishing another preacher for something the man had done, some sin he had committed, etc.

I made the statement to him, *"When they did this, they were, in effect, saying that what Jesus suffered was not enough, and we have to add something to His Finished Work."*

The man stopped dead in his tracks, wheeled around and looked at me, and then said, *"You know, I've never thought of that."* I told him that such is a sin because Jesus has already suffered for us, and for us to think that something else is needed is pretty close to blasphemy.

THE BLOODY DOOR

Jesus said, *"Verily* (truthfully)*, verily* (truthfully)*, I say unto you, He who enters not by the door into the sheepfold, but climbs up some other way, the same is a thief and a robber"* (Jn. 10:1).

Jesus then said, *"Verily, verily, I say unto you, I am the Door of the Sheep"* (Jn. 10:7).

I must remind the reader that this Door is a Bloody Door.

In using this as an example, Jesus was going all the way back to the Deliverance of the Children of Israel from Egyptian bondage, which was a type of our present Salvation.

Each family was to slay a lamb in sacrifice to God, which, of course, represented the coming Christ, and then apply its blood to the doorpost of each house. The Lord then said, *"And the blood shall be to you for a token* (a symbol of the Blood which would be shed by Christ when He ultimately came) *upon the houses where you are: and when I see the blood, I will pass over you, and the plague shall not be upon you to destroy you, when I smite the land of Egypt"* (Ex. 12:13).

Again I say, if we try to go in through another door, we are a thief and a robber, at least in the Eyes of God, which, of course, God can never accept. The True Door is Jesus Christ, but more particularly, it is a Bloody Door, which speaks of His Death and Resurrection on our behalf.

THE MODERN CHURCH

The church has never been in greater trouble than presently. I realize that's quite a statement, but I believe it to be true. I believe it is true simply because the Cross is little preached or taught anymore. Of course, there are exceptions here and there, but they are few and far between. As I've stated over and over again, the church has been moved so far away from the Cross that most modern Believers have little understanding of its veracity, its Power, and what it all means as it regards Christianity. In other words, most Christians little know and understand that the Cross of Christ is the very Foundation of Christianity. All must be built on that premise, the premise of the Cross, or else, it is a house built on sand (Mat. 7:24-27).

THE REVELATION OF THE CROSS

In 1997, the Lord began to open up to me the Revelation of the Cross of Christ and how it pertains to our everyday walk before the Lord. I had always known of the veracity of the Cross as it refers to our initial Salvation. I preached strongly this great Truth, which resulted in hundreds of thousands all around the world being brought to a Saving Knowledge of Jesus Christ. However, as stated, I little knew or understood the part the Cross plays in our daily living.

This lack of knowledge caused me tremendous problems, to say the least. But, thank the Lord, after some six years of soul-searching, seeking the Face of the Lord, and imploring Him to open up the answers to me as it regarded the living of a victorious, Christian life, the Lord answered my prayer.

This Revelation didn't come all at once. In fact, it is still coming, and I believe this Revelation will ever continue to expand. Please understand when I say, *"Revelation,"* I am not speaking of something new. What the Lord gave me, He had already given to the Apostle Paul and, no doubt, many others down through the centuries. However, the truth is, the Cross of Christ has been so little preached in the last several decades that anymore, it seems like a new Message when, in reality, it is the very Foundation of the Faith.

This which happened to me is the most revolutionary thing I've ever experienced, other than my Salvation and Baptism with the Holy Spirit. It's almost like I've been *"Born-Again again!"* The Bible has become brand-new to me. In fact, I see everything in an entirely different light — the Light of the Cross — and, oh yes, I have found there the victory for which I had so long sought. A victory so total, so complete, so absolute, and so all-encompassing that I hardly know how to define or explain this of which I feel and have experienced, even with this experience continuing to expand.

THE CROSS, OUR FAITH, AND THE HOLY SPIRIT

Even though I've said it repeatedly, please allow me to say it again:
The Lord showed me that all Salvation and all Victory are

found totally and completely in the Cross (Rom. 6:3-5).

He then showed me that my Faith in totality and continuously must rest in the Cross of Christ. I must not allow my Faith to be pulled aside to other things but must anchor it in the Cross and keep it there for all time (Gal. 6:14).

He then showed me that once I understood that all Victory is in the Cross, and I then placed my Faith in the Cross, understanding its veracity, the Holy Spirit would then help me to be what I ought to be and do what I ought to do. This is for the simple reason that He works only within the confines of the Finished Work of Christ (Rom. 8:1-2).

Now, I've given this in a few words, but what it all means would take Volumes to tell. As well, these great Truths are understood totally only in the spiritual sense, in other words, they are spiritually discerned (I Cor. 2:14). That's the reason I keep saying these Truths in many and varied ways. I know that if you, the reader, will keep reading what I have to say, ultimately the Spirit of God will reveal this to you, and you will understand clearly what I am saying, that is, if your heart is open. That means to receive this great Truth, you are going to have to want and desire it greatly, which the Holy Spirit will always honor. Otherwise, you'll read the words that I say with little understanding or meaning.

I TELL YOU OFTEN

The phrase, *"Of whom I have told you often, and now tell you even weeping,"* proclaims to us two things:

1. Due to the extreme seriousness of this matter, Paul related these great Truths to the Philippians and all others, as well, over and over again exactly as I am doing here. He did it in this manner because of all the obvious reasons.

2. What he was saying was of such moment and such consequence that if the readers failed to properly hear what he was saying, they could bring upon themselves great trouble. As well, those who tried to bypass the Cross could only lead themselves

to ultimate perdition, which means the loss of their souls.

I think one can say without fear of contradiction that this of which Paul speaks is the single most important thing. If we have an improper viewpoint of the Cross, everything else will be improper also. Always, the results will be disastrous and in a disastrous way.

THE SERIOUSNESS OF THE MATTER

The Apostle knew this. He knew the consequences, knew the seriousness of the matter, and actually knew that this was the single most important thing there is, which filled his heart with great emotion. He literally wept because he knew the end result of forsaking the Cross, or refusing to accept the Cross, would be disaster. There is only one way of Victory, and that's Jesus Christ and what He did at the Cross. If we try to divorce Christ from the Cross, which these individuals were trying to do, whomever they may have been, and which men are attempting to do today, then we have *"another Jesus," "another gospel,"* and *"another spirit"* (II Cor. 11:4). That's the reason the Apostle wept and the reason we should weep also!

ENEMIES OF THE CROSS OF CHRIST

The phrase, *"That they are the enemies of the Cross of Christ,"* refers to the results of such a course, which the next Verse proclaims, but more than all, refers to correct Doctrine.

The *"Cross"* was the instrument of death on which the Redeemer died to make Atonement for sin. As the Atonement made by Christ for sin is that which peculiarly distinguishes His Way from all others, the *"Cross"* comes to be used to denote His Way.

It is His Way because it is there that Jesus defeated all the powers of darkness and actually made a show of them openly. He satisfied the claims of Heavenly Justice because the Cross was demanded by God and definitely not by the Devil. There was only one way that man's sins could be addressed that the penalty of the broken Law might be satisfied, and that was by Christ dying on the Cross. As I've said over and over again, the Cross was not an accident or an incident; it was rather the very purpose and reason for which He came.

By the manner in which Jesus had to die in order to save man from sin, we learn and realize just how bad, how awful, how terrible, and how devastating that sin actually is. In fact, it is the cause of all the sorrow, heartache, pain, loneliness, suffering, and death on this Planet. It has filled the world with blood, with graves, with death! It is the one great cause of all heartache — sin!

WHAT IS SIN?

Sin is defined as, *"Missing the mark,"* but more particularly, missing God's Mark. It is a disobedience of His Word.

To serve as an example, we might say that all of this is summed up in the Ten Commandments. This was and is God's Standard of Righteousness, in other words, what God required of man as it regarded Righteousness.

When we read these Commandments, they seem simple enough; however, due to man's depraved, fallen nature, it was and is impossible for him within himself to keep these Commandments. It simply could not be done! And it cannot be done now within oneself. So, because of man's fallen nature, man has a tendency to substitute other gods in place of his Creator, and the church has a tendency to substitute other sacrifices in place of the Cross, which, of course, God will never accept. This is the cause of all the trouble and heartache in the world even though man refuses to recognize such.

THE PROBLEM!

Man knows that something is wrong, but he refuses to admit how wrong it actually is. In other words, he refuses to admit that he is totally wrong, completely wrong, going in the wrong direction, and in no way can find the right way by his own machinations. In fact, he doesn't even recognize the right way, i.e., Jesus Christ, when he sees it. It takes a Revelation of the Spirit by the Word on his soul for his eyes to be opened.

This means that man's problem is not merely a maladjustment, improper environment, improper education, or improper choices. It means that his problem is far, far deeper and far more widespread than all of that. As stated, man is altogether wrong, not just slightly so.

So, with man refusing to admit how wrong he actually is, he thinks he can solve his problem in various different ways. One of the greatest ways of all is humanistic psychology. This false way claims that man's problem is outward of himself instead of inward. In other words, man is actually good, and if he is not good, it is because of outside forces of some nature. Control and change these forces, whatever they might be, and then man can be good.

The Bible teaches the very opposite. It teaches that due to the Fall, man is inwardly evil, inwardly corrupt, and inwardly depraved. Consequently, there is absolutely nothing he can do to change his situation from a personal viewpoint (Rom., Chpt. 2). In other words, he is beyond rehabilitation. In fact, not only is he beyond a cure, at least from his own resources, but, as well, everything he touches, he corrupts, kills, steals, destroys, etc.

THE CROSS IS THE ONLY ANSWER

Knowing that man could not save himself, and yet, with love refusing to let him go, God would save man, but at a fearful price. As stated, the price paid, which was the Cross, tells us just how bad that sin actually is.

Man doesn't like to admit this — how bad he is or how good God is. He refuses to believe that he cannot save himself, so he keeps trying as he keeps failing.

THE CHRISTIAN AND THE CROSS

These things we have said of the world are fairly understandable as it regards the church. Unregenerate man will not admit that he is unregenerate, even though he is. However, the sadness is that the church little realizes, as well, even as Paul is addressing here, that the Cross is needed for the Believer as much as it is needed for the unbeliever. More than likely, that is the greater problem of all — the church not understanding the veracity of the Cross as it applies to our everyday living and life.

The manner in which Paul uses the statement, *"Enemies of the Cross of Christ,"* falls out to two directions. One asks, *"Does he mean enemies of the Doctrine of the Cross or of its practical influence and efficiency?"* The two are naturally connected, but here, perhaps the latter is principally intended, even as the former is intended in I Corinthians, Chapter 1. The context, especially what follows in the Apostle's description, seems to point that way.

When Christ's Cross is rightly apprehended, and when the place it claims in the mind has been cordially yielded, it becomes, as we see in the case of Paul himself, a renovating principle, the fountain of a new view and a new course.

That immense Sacrifice for our Redemption from sin decides that we are no more to live the rest of our time in the flesh to the lust of men (I Pet. 4:1).

So, Christ's Cross teaches us the slender worth, or the mere worthlessness, of much that we otherwise would idolize — in other words, it takes the luster in totality from the world.

On the other hand, it assures us of Redemption into His Likeness as a prospect to be realized in the renunciation of the *"old man,"* which refers to victory over sin and can only be achieved in this manner.

As well, it embodies an incomparable wealth of motive to persuade us to comply, for we find ourselves in fellowship with Love unspeakable, which the Cross portrays.

SELF-DENIAL

Under this influence, we take up our Cross, even as Jesus demanded (Lk. 9:23-24); which is substantially the same as renouncing or denying ourselves (Mat. 16:24). It is self-denial for Christ's Sake and after Christ's Example, accepted as a principle and carried out in the forms in which God calls us to it.

However, exactly what does the Lord mean by demanding that we deny ourselves or enter into a life of self-denial?

First, let's see what it doesn't mean:

It doesn't refer to a life of denial of all pleasure or good things, as much of the church down through the ages has thought. In the Middle Ages, many in the church took denial of the flesh or self to the place of fine art. In other words, they thought a regimen of suffering of some nature was what Christ meant by bearing the Cross. Then, certain ones began to equate such denial with holiness, etc. The more one suffered or put himself through some type of stringent physical or emotional torture of some nature, the more holy was one supposed to be, etc. None of that is what Jesus was speaking of as it regards self-denial, i.e., *"bearing the Cross"* (Lk. 9:23-24). In other words, He wasn't teaching asceticism.

Actually, the Lord was saying the very opposite. He, in effect, was saying that one cannot attain Holiness or Righteousness by this method. In other words, due to having a fallen nature, self and all of its machinations cannot bring about the desired spiritual results.

He was actually saying that we must stop all of this self-effort in this respect, and quit trying to bring about this great work within our lives, which can only be done by the Holy Spirit (Rom. 8:1).

SELF-EFFORT

The denial of self refers to taking self out of the picture, as far as self-effort is concerned, and allowing the Holy Spirit to do this which only He can do. How do we do that?

The idea is that we understand that our education, motivation, talent, ability, personal strength, etc., cannot solve the problem, which only the Holy Spirit can do. It means that we are to look to the Cross as it regards what Jesus there did on our behalf and for us, and receive its benefits. It is all done by Faith — Faith in the Cross, which means Faith in the Finished Work of Christ. That is what bearing the Cross actually means, not suffering, as many have thought!

The biggest problem for the Christian is self. By that, I mean trying to do that which only the Holy Spirit can do. There is no way that a Christian can make himself holy or righteous, irrespective of the religious works he may engage. One cannot make oneself holy and righteous by fasting, by prayer, by the study of the Word of God, by giving of money to the Work of the Lord, by witnessing to souls, by depriving oneself, etc. Now, as I've already stated, don't mistake what I've said. I'm not demeaning prayer, fasting, etc. Most of these things I've mentioned are very needful and desirable in their own right, actually, without which, the Christian cannot have a proper relationship with the Lord. However, they must never be used as *"works"* in order to bring about some desired result of Righteousness and Holiness, which God will never honor.

LOOK TO THE CROSS

The Child of God is to look to the Cross, or more particularly, to what the Cross afforded as it regards the great Sacrifice of Christ. We are to understand that every single thing we are, we need, we have, or ever will have was brought about as a result of what Jesus did at the Cross. We are to look to that, understand that, and place our Faith in that, and that's the key word — Faith. However, as I have repeatedly stated, the Object of our Faith must always be the Cross (I Cor. 1:17, 18, 23; 2:2; Gal. 6:14).

The Holy Spirit can then bring about in our lives these things which we so desperately need, but only then. That's what denying self actually means. As stated, we simply quit trying within ourselves to do this thing, which only the Holy Spirit can do. As well, He does all His Work within our hearts and lives according to what Jesus did at the Cross and our Faith in that Finished Work (Rom. 8:2). In fact, it is the Cross of Christ which has given the Holy Spirit the latitude that He now has. Under the old Economy of God, the blood of bulls and goats could not take away sins (Heb. 10:4), so that limited the Holy Spirit. Since the Cross and the fact that all sin was atoned by Christ, the Holy Spirit can now come into the heart and life of the Believer to abide forever (Jn. 14:16-17).

Actually, the Holy Spirit is so absolutely regimented to the Sacrifice of Christ that it is referred to as a *"Law."* Let's look at what Paul actually said:

THE LAW OF THE SPIRIT

"For the Law of the Spirit (the only manner in which the Spirit will work) *of Life* (this is where our life and victory come from) *in Christ Jesus* (meaning that this which the Spirit does is predicated entirely on what Jesus did at the Cross and the Resurrection. In other words, it is all in Him, meaning what He did) *has made me free from the Law of Sin and Death* (gives the Saint victory over the world, the flesh, and the Devil)*"* (Rom. 8:2). I might quickly add, the only way that the Saint is going to have victory over the *"Law of Sin and Death"* is by allowing the Holy Spirit to bring about this victory, which He always does through our Faith in the Finished Work of Christ. The *"Law of Sin and Death"* is so strong and so powerful that it is not possible to be defeated in any other manner.

WHAT DOES IT ACTUALLY MEAN?

I do not want to leave the impression that the Holy Spirit

carries out an added work regarding what Christ did at the Cross. That's not the idea at all.

The idea is, Jesus, in His Sacrificial Work on the Cross, combined with His Resurrection, carried out a completed Work. Nothing must be added as nothing needs to be added. It is all done in Christ and what He did for us at the Cross.

The Holy Spirit comes into our hearts and lives at Conversion and is there to guarantee all that Christ did. In other words, He will not allow Satan to usurp authority over the Saint of God in any regard.

However, all of this, or none of this, I should say, is an automatic process as it regards the Holy Spirit, even as we have already stated. He demands of us that we have Faith in what Jesus did at the Cross. He demands that we keep our Faith in that, understanding that all of our victory, all of our success, all of our overcoming Power, and all of our Blessings come entirely from this Source and from no other source. When our Faith is properly anchored there, the Holy Spirit then can perform His Work within our lives, which guarantees us victory over the *"Law of Sin and Death."*

As well, it is not a one-time thing but actually that which we must renew on a daily basis. This is what Jesus meant by telling us that we must *"take up our Cross daily, and follow Him"* (Lk. 9:23). Again, He is not speaking of us suffering some type of spiritual regimen, etc.

THE HOLY SPIRIT

The greatest problem of the Saint, and that which we have all faced, is that of trying to do within our lives and trying to bring about within our lives that which only the Holy Spirit can do. As a Saint of God, I want to be righteous and I want to be holy. Actually, that spirit, attitude, feeling, and desire is in the heart of every true Saint. We want to be Christlike and, in fact, more and more Christlike, but these things cannot be brought about by our own religious machinations or efforts.

However, these things fool us because, within their own right, many of them are spiritual. Because of that, when they don't bring about the desired results, but actually the very opposite, it confuses us. The actual truth is that we've turned these things, such as prayer, fasting, etc., into works, which God can never honor, and on which the Holy Spirit cannot function.

By our doing these things, whatever they might be, thinking they bring about some type of Righteousness or Holiness, whether we realize it or not, we are actually saying that Jesus did not finish the Work at the Cross, and that which He did needs something added. As we've already stated, such only seeks to frustrate the Grace of God (Gal. 2:21).

I realize that we in no way are claiming that which we are doing is adding to the Finished Work of Christ; however, whatever we think, that's the way it comes out to the Lord.

IT IS ALL BY FAITH

As the unsaved man cannot save himself by his works but can be Saved only by having Faith in what Jesus did on the Cross on his behalf (Jn. 3:16), likewise, the Christian cannot bring about a life of Holiness, or any other desired result for that matter, by his works, but only by Faith.

However, what do we mean when we say, *"By Faith"*?

We are speaking of Faith in Christ but, more particularly, what He did at the Cross and the Resurrection. Our Faith is always in Jesus, but it's not merely in Jesus but also in what He did for us. We must not forget that.

Millions of Christians have Faith in Christ, but they do not properly understand what their Faith actually is. It's sort of a nebulous Faith, sort of a shadowy Faith. In other words, they do not properly understand what the true Object of their Faith should be.

Were this question to be posed to them, what the true Object of their Faith should be, most would just simply say, *"Jesus"* or *"the Word."* While that is correct, at least as far as it goes, it leaves much to be desired.

To be sure, Paul had great Faith in Jesus immediately after his Conversion. But yet, even as the Seventh Chapter of Romans proclaims, Paul found himself failing, and failing miserably, even though he definitely had Faith in Christ. Unfortunately, millions of Christians right now are in the same situation. That's what confuses them.

They have Faith in Christ, but yet, they are failing. In other words, sin is claiming dominion over them in some manner (Rom. 6:14).

TRY HARDER?

If most Believers confide in a preacher about their particular problem, whatever it might be, and I speak of sin in one's life, they are more than likely told that they must try harder. So, they set about to do that by reading the Scriptures more, by being more faithful to church, etc. Some think that if they can just get to a certain preacher, who is supposed to have a great touch with God, and have him lay his hands on them, then their problems will be solved. If the Lord slays them in the Spirit at that time, then it's even better.

However, they find that even though these things may bless them, and even bless them greatly, they will not walk away with the victory which they desire. In other words, the same old problem will be there.

While these people definitely have Faith in Christ, even as Paul did, it is not the type of faith that's going to bring them victory.

Paul was told by the Lord that his victory, his overcoming strength, and his more Abundant Life were all found in what Jesus did at the Cross, which the Apostle gave to us in graphic detail in Romans, Chapter 6. Now, the Object of Paul's Faith is in the Cross of Christ through which the Holy Spirit can work, which brought the Apostle tremendous victory even as he records in Romans, Chapter 8.

To be sure, this was given for Paul, but it was also given for every other Believer. In other words, the Lord showed us through Paul's example how that we can walk in victory as well. Instead, too many of us attempt other things, other methods, which never bring satisfactory results, and for all the obvious reasons — obvious when one begins to understand Romans, Chapter 6.

"If you from sin are longing to be free,
"Look to the Lamb of God;
"He to redeem you, died on Calvary,
"Look to the Lamb of God."

"When Satan tempts, and doubts and fears assail,
"Look to the Lamb of God;
"You in His Strength shall over all prevail,
"Look to the Lamb of God."

"Are you weary, does the way seem long?
"Look to the Lamb of God;
"His Love will cheer and fill your heart with song,
"Look to the Lamb of God."

"Fear not when shadows on your pathway fall,
"Look to the Lamb of God;
"In joy or sorrow Christ is All in All,
"Look to the Lamb of God."

THE MESSAGE OF THE CROSS

CHAPTER

3

The Cross Of Christ Must Be The Object Of Our Faith

THE CROSS OF CHRIST MUST BE THE OBJECT OF OUR FAITH

The first thing the Believer should know and understand is that every single thing we receive from God, and I mean everything, and I speak of Salvation, the Baptism with the Holy Spirit, Divine Healing, answers to prayer, financial prosperity, communion with the Lord, etc., all and without question are made possible by the Cross. As we have been studying in the previous Chapter, the Cross of Christ is the Means by which all of these things are given to us. Now, in this Chapter we are going to look at the correct Object of Faith.

As we have previously stated, every person in the world has Faith; however, for the far greater majority, and I mean almost all, it's not Faith that God will recognize. The only Faith that He will recognize is Faith that is registered in Christ and what He did for us at the Cross. Christ and the Cross must without fail ever be the Object of our Faith.

If the Object of our Faith is mentioned, it is generally passed off with *"Faith in the Word," "Faith in God," "Faith in the Holy Spirit,"* etc. While these things are correct and right in their own way, that is not supposed to be the Object of our Faith.

The entirety of the Story of the Bible is the Story of Jesus Christ and Him Crucified (Jn. 1:1-2, 14, 29.) Every Old Testament sacrifice pictured and portrayed the Lamb of God Who would ultimately come into this world, which He did by and through the Virgin Birth. So, if we really have Faith in the Word and Faith in God, we must without fail understand that it is Christ and the Cross, which is the focal point of the entirety of the Word of God. When I speak of having Faith in Christ and the Cross, I am not speaking of the wooden beam on which Jesus died. I am speaking of what He there accomplished, which was to atone for all sin and to break the grip of sin in the heart and life of Believers. This doesn't mean sinless perfection, but it does mean that sin is not to have dominion over us as Believers (Rom. 6:14). So, let us say it again, the

Object of Faith must be the Cross of Christ, and it must remain the Cross of Christ, or else, it will be faith that God cannot recognize. In the last few years, I have read any number of books about the subject of Faith, and I do not remember one single time that one of these books, or anything said in these books, dealt with the Object of Faith. Not knowing or properly understanding what the Object of Faith is to be leaves the individual with a nebulous faith, that which is not quite understandable. Without understanding what the Object of Faith ought to be, one really cannot understand Faith; the understanding will be muddled.

PAUL

In connection with this, the great Apostle said, *"Christ sent me not to baptize, but to preach the Gospel: not with wisdom of words, lest the Cross of Christ should be made of none effect"* (I Cor. 1:17). In this Passage, we are clearly and plainly told what the Gospel of Jesus Christ actually is. It is the Cross of Christ. So, that's where the Object of our Faith must be.

The great Apostle also said, *"For the preaching of the Cross is to them who perish foolishness; but to we who are Saved it is the Power of God"* (I Cor. 1:18).

HOW IS THE PREACHING OF THE CROSS
THE POWER OF GOD?

Before we answer that, let us look at the following:

Facing the concentrated powers of Darkness, every Believer needs Power. We know that there is no power in the wooden beam on which Jesus died. In fact, there's really not even any power in the Death of Jesus per se. In fact, Paul plainly said concerning this, *"For though He was crucified through weakness, yet He lived by the Power of God."*

He then said, *"For we also are weak in Him, but we shall live with Him by the Power of God toward you"* (II Cor. 13:4).

So, that being the case, where is the Power?

The Power is in the Holy Spirit. Let me prove it from the Word of God.

Paul said, *"For the Law of the Spirit of Life in Christ Jesus has made me free from the Law of Sin and Death"* (Rom. 8:2).

The phrase, *"For the Law of the Spirit of Life in Christ Jesus,"* presents the Law which should govern the Christian and, in fact, will govern the Christian, but only with the Christian's cooperation.

LAW

Most of the time when Paul refers to *"Law,"* he is speaking of the Law of Moses (Rom. 2:12-15, 17, 20, 23, 27; 3:19-21; 4:13, 16; 5:20; 7:5-8, etc.). However, he does mention other laws, which have nothing to do with the Law of Moses.

The Holy Spirit through the Apostle uses the word, *"Law,"* in a specific sense, meaning that it is an operating and governing principle.

In fact, every law mentioned in the Bible falls into this category, even the great Law of Moses. It means that the specific *"Law"* is designed by God to operate in a particular manner, which will bring forth particular results. In other words, those results are unvarying. That's the reason it is called, *"Law."*

While the Believer doesn't want to be under the Law of Moses because Jesus has already satisfied that Law in every respect, meaning it is no longer in vogue, conversely, the Believer most definitely wants to be under *"the Law of the Spirit of Life in Christ Jesus,"* and, in fact, must be under this Law.

The *"Law of the Spirit of Life in Christ Jesus,"* which makes real to the Believer the great Victory of Jesus Christ, cannot function in the life of the Believer as intended if the Believer is frustrating that Law by obeying the *"Law of Sin"* at the same time. It is like pouring water into a tank made for gasoline and expecting the engine to continue to run. It won't!

What makes it so confusing is that the Believer's efforts to overcome sin by his own strength and abilities, i.e., *"the flesh,"* are actually bringing upon himself the *"Law of Sin and Death."* While the efforts may be of the right motivation and not necessarily sins within themselves, still, they will not work because they are of the flesh, which gives latitude to the *"Law of Sin."* Then, the *"Law of Sin"* becomes predominant in the Believer's life, which means that the sin nature is now operating at full capacity, which causes all types of problems for the Believer.

WHAT ONLY GOD CAN DO

As well, the *"Law of the Spirit of Life in Christ Jesus"* is so designed by God that it will not function or work when the Believer attempts to do for himself what only the Spirit of God can do. In other words, the Holy Spirit will not override the Believer's will, forcing him to let the Spirit take control instead of his own efforts.

• Law: this particular Law was designed by the Godhead in eternity past and will function exactly as it was designed.

• The Spirit: this is the Holy Spirit, Who is God, and Who can do anything. We are going to see how the Holy Spirit works as it regards the balance of this particular Verse.

• Of Life: all Life comes from the Lord Jesus Christ but through the Holy Spirit; hence, He is called, *"The Spirit of Life."* As well, if the Believer is trying to reach the Lord in some way other than the Cross of Christ, the Holy Spirit will actually bar access (Eph. 2:13-18).

• In Christ Jesus: whenever Paul uses this phrase, or a derivative such as *"in Christ," "in Him," "in Whom,"* etc., he is always referring to what Jesus did at the Cross. Every Believer is literally *"in Christ Jesus,"* as it regards His Death, His Burial, and His Resurrection (Rom. 6:3-5).

As well, this particular *"Law"* is the only Law in the Universe that is stronger than the *"Law of Sin and Death."* So, to have victory in our hearts and in our lives, we must function according to *"the Law of the Spirit of Life in Christ Jesus."*

This *"Law"* is merely telling us that the Work was carried out by Christ Jesus under the direction of the Holy Spirit at Calvary's Cross (Heb. 9:14). Let us say it again:

"The Law of the Spirit of Life in Christ Jesus" is the only Law to which the *"Law of Sin and Death"* will yield. This is what makes modern psychology so silly, and especially so-called preachers of the Gospel running after this shamanism.

The Laws of God, and there are several, such as *"the Law of Faith"* (Rom. 3:27; 4:3-5, 11-24), *"the Law of the Mind"* (Rom. 7:16, 21, 23), and *"the Law of Righteousness"* (Rom. 9:31), to name a few, are not so much written Laws, but rather a regulative principle which exercises control over the life of the Believer. However, this control must be given by the Believer; it will not be forcibly taken.

Upon being freely given, this regulative control is exercised by the Holy Spirit in the form of energy given to the Believer both to desire and to do God's Will, with this spiritual energy coming from the Life that God is. It is given to the Believer by reason of his position in Christ Jesus but cannot be properly realized unless he knows his position in Christ Jesus.

THE CROSS OF CHRIST IS THE FOUNDATION OF ALL BIBLICAL DOCTRINE

In fact, every Bible Doctrine, irrespective as to what it is, is built on the Foundation of the Cross. To be frank, ignoring the Cross, repudiating the Cross, or even denying the Cross is where all false doctrine begins. It is a false or erroneous interpretation of the Cross of Christ. If one wants to look at what is being preached and whoever is preaching it, one must first look at the Cross. Is the Preacher preaching the Cross? When I say, *"Preaching the Cross,"* I am not meaning that one mentions the Cross once in awhile. I mean that such a Preacher knows and understands that the Cross of Christ is the Means and the only Means by which all of these wonderful things are given to us by the Lord. If the preacher doesn't believe that, rather projecting something else, whatever it is he is preaching, he's not really preaching the Gospel, for the Cross of Christ is the Gospel.

The Bible plainly tells us that the Cross of Christ is the Foundation of all Biblical Doctrine. It says:

REDEMPTION

Peter said: *"Forasmuch as you know that you were not redeemed with corruptible things, as silver and gold, from your vain conversation* (lifestyle) *received by tradition from your fathers"* (I Pet. 1:18). Redemption presents a Work which was accomplished by Christ Jesus on Calvary and is, therefore, entirely objective, so far as we are concerned. We could have no part in it, except that we committed the sins that made it necessary, unless we had been left to die in our iniquities.

This means that Salvation is all of God and none at all of ourselves. In other words, Jesus died on the Cross whether sinful man liked it or not. However, when it comes to Regeneration or the New Birth, that is subjective. In other words, we play a part in this in that we have to evidence Faith in what Christ has already done and yield, as well, to the Holy Spirit.

It is easy to fall into the habit of preaching about the Gospel but not really preaching the Gospel itself. However, when we speak on and expound a Text like this, we are brought back to the heart of the Gospel Message of Christ. This is one way of discovering whether the message is of God or of men.

If the Message is about the Cross, which means in some way that it streams toward the Cross or proceeds from the Cross, then it is the Gospel. Otherwise, it is of men!

If we properly understand the Cross, then we understand that the entirety of the Bible is, in effect, the Story of the Cross because the Bible is the Story of the Redemption of man.

Redemption here means that we were rescued from sin and death by the Blood of Christ as the valuable consideration on account of which it was done. That is, the Blood of the Life of Christ offered as a Sacrifice effected the same purpose in regard to justice and to the maintenance of the principles of moral government, which the punishment of the sinner himself would have done.

To say it another way: it was that which God was pleased to accept in the place of the punishment of the sinner as answering to the same great ends in His Administration. The principles of His Truth and Justice could as certainly be maintained in this way as by the punishment of the guilty themselves. If so, then there is no obstacle to our Salvation, and we might, on Repentance and Faith in what Christ has done for us, be consistently pardoned.

SILVER AND GOLD

The highest form of exchange in the commerce of men is silver and gold, or that which relates to these precious metals. When Peter wrote these words, at least a third of the Roman Empire consisted of slaves. These slaves were bought with silver and gold or sold for silver and gold. So, when Peter made this statement, his words would have had even a greater meaning in his day than they do presently. It was common in those days to see slaves auctioned off to the highest bidder. Silver and gold would change hands, and the individual would then belong to a new master.

Sometime back, Frances and I were in New Orleans, Louisiana, with friends. We were standing on a street corner, waiting for a restaurant to open. I looked up to my right and spotted one of the historical markers that are quite common in certain parts of our nation. This marker, however, somewhat startled me because it spoke of the fact that on that particular corner the slave market of New Orleans once stood.

It was here that Abraham Lincoln, the Illinois rail-splitter, stood and watched the proceedings, proceedings, incidentally, of extreme cruelty, and vowed in his heart, *"God, if You will give me the ability, I will smite this curse that plagues this land."*

God took this man at his word and made him the President of the United States. A bloody Civil War was fought with over 600,000 men killed, but Lincoln stood true to his word. During his time in office, Congress produced the Emancipation Proclamation, which, in effect, outlawed the terrible scourge of slavery in this nation.

SLAVERY

The sad fact is, there is a far worse slavery that is incumbent upon all men than even the slavery which I have just mentioned. It is the slavery of sin, which gives Satan the right to hold men in bondage.

In the United States alone, it is said that there are 20 million alcoholics. As well, it is said that there are approximately 20 million men and women addicted to gambling. There are about 25 million drug addicts in this nation. But yet, every human being who doesn't know Christ is a slave to their passions in some way, whether it's these mentioned or not.

Of course, unredeemed man bristles at the idea that he is a slave. In fact, he claims in the loudest voice possible that he is his own man, free to do what he likes. In reality, he is free to do what Satan likes and no more!

As a result of the Fall, man is born in original sin, which, in effect, means that he is born a slave — a slave to passions and pride. We do have a problem!

Even though lost and therefore in slavery, the soul of each one of these individuals, whomever and wherever they might be, is of such value as to defy all description. In fact, it is so valuable that Jesus said: *"For what is a man profited, if he shall gain the whole world, and lose his own soul? or what shall a man give in exchange for his soul?"* (Mat. 16:26).

Because of this great worth, there is nothing on the Earth that can redeem a lost soul. So, if man, God's Highest Creation, is to be redeemed, God will have to perform the task from the worth of Himself. It will have to be a worth of far greater value than silver and gold. What could that be?

JESUS CHRIST

God became Man, i.e., *"the Lord Jesus Christ."* He did so for many reasons, but the main reason of all was that He might pay this price for dying humanity, which He Alone could pay, the payment of which would be His Own Life. God is a Spirit, and He cannot die; therefore, in order to die, He would have to become Man.

The price that was demanded was high, higher than we could ever begin to comprehend; however, inasmuch as God paid the price Himself, man is left with no quarrel or argument. So, to meet this need, Jesus Christ died as a Sacrifice for sin. Let the reader understand that this was the reason He came, the reason He lived, and the reason He died. It was for sin — our sin and not His.

This is the only satisfactory account which can be given of that most wonderful of all events — the Death, the violent Death, the shameful, painful, accursed Death of the innocent, the Perfect, Incarnate, only-begotten of God. This event would have been utterly inexplicable had we not been informed in a plain, well-accredited, Divine Revelation that this Immaculately Holy, this Absolutely Perfect, this Infinitely Dignified Person, who was occupied by Divine appointment to gain the most important and otherwise unattainable objects in the moral government of the Universe, the place of guilty men. In occupying our place, He met with our desert, did what we were bound to do, suffered what we deserved to suffer, and did and suffered all that was necessary in the estimation of infinite Wisdom and Righteousness, to lay a foundation for our pardon and Salvation.

"We all, like sheep, have gone astray; we have turned every one to his own way; and the LORD has laid on Him," as the destined victim, *"the iniquities of us all."* The consequence was, *"Exaction was made, and He became answerable. It pleased*

the Lord to bruise Him," instead of destroying us; and *"He was wounded for our transgressions, He was bruised for our iniquities: the chastisement of our peace was upon Him; and by His Stripes we are healed. He did bear our sins in His Own Body on the Tree; was made sin in our stead,"* died as *"the Just One, in the stead of the unjust"*; *"redeemed us from the Curse of the broken Law by being made a Curse in our stead."*

The direct and primary end of this Sacrifice, so far as man is concerned, was to effect a change in his relation to God — to lay a foundation for an alteration in our state — to secure pardon and Restoration to the enjoyment of the Divine favor. However, the ultimate and most important end of this Sacrifice in reference to man was, through this change of relation, to effect a change of disposition, through this alteration of state, to secure a transformation of character.

TRADITION

The phrase, *"From your vain conversation* (lifestyle) *received by tradition from your fathers,"* proclaims the vast difference by comparison to what we have received from our Heavenly Father.

Even though Peter was speaking directly of the Mosaic Law, still, the word, *"Fathers,"* refers also to the whole of humanity in that all babies are born in the likeness of Adam, which speaks of total depravity as a result of the Fall (Gen., Chpt. 5).

When the Blood of Christ was shed as a victim for sin, it was to deliver men from this *"vain lifestyle,"* which is the best that our earthly fathers could do. Even the great Law of God that was given to Moses, which, of course, was perfect in every respect, was taken by man and twisted and perverted until it was hardly recognizable. It had succumbed to the place of mere *"tradition."*

DELIVERANCE FROM DEPRAVITY

Deliverance from depravity is an essential part, the most

important part in some points of view, of the Christian Salvation. Deliverance from guilt and that Sacrifice, which was necessary, and is sufficient to secure deliverance from guilt, is the grand means of securing this deliverance from depravity.

As well, the connection of the Atonement with Sanctification, which we've been dealing with again and again in this Volume, is frequently stated in Scripture, and is one of the most peculiar and important principles of the Christian Faith. *"Christ gave Himself for us, that He might redeem us from all iniquity, and purify unto Himself a peculiar people, zealous of good works"* (Titus 2:13-14). *"Christ gave Himself for us, that He might redeem us from this present evil world"* (Gal. 1:4). Christ *"sanctified Himself,"* one might say, devoted Himself to suffer as a Sacrificial Victim so that His People might be *"sanctified through the Truth"* (Jn. 17:19). *"When He died for all, all died in Him; and He died for us, that we might not live unto ourselves, but to Him Who died and rose again"* (II Cor. 5:15).

"Christ has redeemed us from the curse of the Law, having become a curse in our place," not only *"that the Blessing of Abraham"* — a full and free Justification — *"should come upon us Gentiles,"* but that *"we also might obtain the Promised Holy Spirit,"* the Source of all true Holiness, *"by believing"* (Gal. 3:13-14).

THE PRECIOUS BLOOD OF CHRIST

Peter said: *"But with the Precious Blood of Christ, as of a Lamb without blemish and without spot"* (I Pet. 1:19).

The phrase, *"But with the Precious Blood of Christ,"* presents the payment, which proclaims the poured-out Life of Christ, all on behalf of sinners.

The manner in which the shedding of the Blood of Jesus Christ as the great Sacrificial Victim secures the holiness of all who believe in Him may be stated in a few words, though fully and satisfactorily to illustrate it would require more space than we can here devote to it.

By making the Atonement consistent with the Divine Justice to confer Spiritual Blessings on sinners, it removes out of the way of their Sanctification obstacles otherwise insurmountable. By procuring for the Saviour, as one part of the reward of His Generous Labors and the cause of God's Glory, the Power of dispensing Divine influence, it secures what is at once absolutely necessary and completely sufficient for making men holy. Finally, the statement of the truth about Christ, the Son of God, suffering and dying in the place of sinners, which is contained in the Scriptures, when understood and believed, is under Divine influence the grand means of destroying in the sinner's mind that enmity against God. This enmity against God is the elementary principle of all depravity and of kindling up in his heart the Love of God, which is the elementary principle of all Holiness — of delivering man from the demoralizing influence of *"the present evil world," "things seen as temporal,"* in bringing him under the sanctifying influence of *"things unseen and eternal."*

This then is the Apostle's statement: *"The Blood of Christ has been shed to redeem you from your vain lifestyle received by tradition from your fathers. The Son of God has died as a Sacrifice for sin in order to secure your Holiness."*

THE CHRISTIAN AND REDEMPTION

Surely it does not require many words to show what Christ has done for us, especially considering the price that He has paid, to provide an all-powerful motive, and to place our Faith totally in His Great Finished Work. Has deliverance from depravity been secured at such a cost, and shall I pour contempt on the Divine generosity by looking elsewhere as it regards Sanctification? Shall I counteract the great design of the Death of Christ?

Though He shed His Blood that I might be redeemed from my former vain lifestyle, shall I still fashion myself according to my former lusts in my ignorance? Shall I still hug the chains to break asunder which the Lord of Glory toiled, bled, and died that I might be free? Considering this, how can I, in whose room Christ died for sin, live any longer in sin? Reckoning myself as — if I believe the Truth, I well may — to have died to sin in Christ Jesus and to be alive in Christ Jesus to God (Rom. 6:11). Surely it is the most unnatural and incongruous of all things in me to allow sin (the sin) to *"reign in my mortal body, so that I should obey it by its desires."* Surely I should not *"yield my members to sin as instruments of unrighteousness; but I should yield myself to God, as one alive from the dead, and my members to Him as instruments of Righteousness"* (Rom. 6:12-14).

THE ANSWER

This is the answer, in fact, the only answer, for all the enticements of sin and of the world. Except you can offer my soul something beyond the price that was given for it on the Cross, I cannot hearken to you. Far be it from me that I should prefer a base lust, or anything in this world, for I owe it all to Him Who gave Himself to death for me and paid my ransom with His Blood. His Matchless Love has freed me from the miserable captivity of sin and has forever fastened me to the sweet yoke of obedience. Let Him Alone to dwell and rule in me and let Him never go forth from my heart, Who, for my sake, refused to come down from the Cross (Brown).[1]

BLOOD IN THE EYES OF GOD

In Genesis, Chapter 9, God says that man is not to eat flesh with blood in it because life is in the blood. Blood is precious to God; it is given on the Altar as an Atonement for our souls. In the Mosaic Legislation, the people were prohibited from eating things strangled because the blood was still in the flesh. The blood was used upon the Altar, poured out at the base of the Altar for an Atonement for sin. The life of the flesh, as stated, is in the blood, and *"I have given it to you upon the Altar to make an Atonement for your souls: for it is the blood that makes an atonement for the soul"* (Lev. 17:11).

When the Lord looked upon the crimson of life poured out, even though it was that of a bullock or a lamb, in God's Sight, it was precious because it was a symbol of the Blood which would be shed by His Only Son.

The blood of a man is even more precious in His Sight than that of an animal, as would be obvious. In Genesis, Chapter 9, God says that if a man's life is taken in cold blood, the person who took his life must pay for it with his own blood (Gen. 9:6). In the Book of Numbers, God says the shedding of blood by violence, by murder, defiles the land (Num. 35:33). It cries to God as the blood of Abel cried to the Lord of Heaven (Gen. 4:10).

PRECIOUS BLOOD

If the blood of animals and the blood of men is precious to God, what shall we say about the Blood of God's Son, our Redeeming Saviour? In Acts 20:28, the Apostle Paul says that our Church was purchased by the Blood of Christ. This is an amazing and astonishing expression. In fact, everything about the Atonement is beyond comprehension. If there is anything that defies description, it is the Atoning Death of Christ. How does the Blood wash away our sins? What are the Sufferings of Christ into which we can hardly enter?

To be frank, we can but little enter into the mysteries of the Atoning Grace of God in Jesus Christ.

The first thing we must know is that the Blood of Christ brings to us God's Atoning Grace. The Law says, *"This do and you shall live."* We are to obey this Commandment, and we will have Eternal Life, but how does a man keep the Law of God? How can he learn to be perfect in all his ways when his every effort is characterized by mistake and sin?

THE SACRIFICE

So, under the old Economy of God, man brought for his sin

a sacrifice. He came before God with a bullock or a lamb but had to come again and again. So, his life was one of perpetual memory of his sin and shortcomings.

Likewise, the High Priest went into the Holy of Holies with the blood of expatiation, and he returned again. In fact, it had to be done every year. There was no end. What does the Blood of Christ do for us?

Paul writes in Romans 10:4: *"For Christ is the end of the Law for Righteousness to everyone who believes."* In Romans 5:9, he tells us that we are now *"justified by His Blood,"* and *"we shall be Saved from wrath through Him."*

Christ is the end of the Law, which means that He has satisfied the demands of the broken Law. If we look in Faith to Him, His Blood will redeem us from the Wrath and Judgment of God upon our sins. Outside of Christ, we are slaves to the tyrant of the Law. The Law threatens us, curses us, and judges us. There is no righteous man before the Law. All have sinned and come short of the Expectation of God. What does a man do, therefore, who finds himself always a sinner?

The Blood of Christ brings to him the Grace of God. Under the shelter of God's Love, Mercy, and Grace, the Judgments have been placated. Calvary did this for me!

THE BLOOD OF CHRIST AND
THE WASHING OF SINS

It is through the Blood of Christ, and the Blood of Christ only, that our sins are washed away. We are not saved by His Miraculous Birth, even though that was absolutely necessary, by His Beautiful Life, even though that was necessary, or by His Miracles that could even change the course of nature, even though that was necessary. Neither were we saved by His Great Words of Wisdom, though never a man spoke like this Man, but we are Saved rather by the Blood of the Cross.

As well, the Death of Christ is not exemplary. In other words, He did not die to teach us as an example. He did not die for our inspiration, but He died for our sins according to the Scriptures. What God seeks in us is a response of humility, Repentance, and acceptance so that through the Blood of the Son of God, we might be cleansed, and we might be acceptable in His Sight, which is the only way we can be acceptable. As well, this is not accident in history, nor is it something that just sort of happened as it regards the Plan of God. The Apostle says that the spilling of the Precious Blood of Christ was fore-ordained before the foundation of the world, before God flung the stars and the planets into space, and before He created this Earth. Christ died for our sins according to the Foreknowledge and Sovereign Elective Grace of God. It is in the Blood of Christ that we are justified. It is in the Blood of Christ that the Church is born. It is in the Blood of Christ that we have hope of forgiveness for sins. By the Blood of Christ, He has quenched all the altar fires on the Earth.

THE ALTAR?

It is difficult for us in this modern day to realize that in the day of the Egyptian, the Babylonian, the Assyrian, the Greek, and the Roman that the entire Earth was covered with altars and the smoke of fires ascending up to Heaven. As far as I know, there is not one altar burning in the Earth today. Why?

The Atoning Grace of God in Christ Jesus quenched all the altar fires on the Earth. There are no more priestly orders, for He is our High Priest, making Intercession for us in the Sanctuary of God.

Our Lord was obedient to the Law for us in His Life. In Death, He paid the penalty of sin for us. In His Death, He was the scapegoat that carried away the sins of His People. In His Resurrection, He not only was declared to be the Son of God, but He also brought Justification to declare us righteous in His Presence when He comes again. In His Return, He will bring to us a complete Salvation. It will be the completed Redemption of the purchased possession, a resurrected, immortalized body as well as a redeemed and blood-bought soul.

THE BLOOD OF CHRIST AND REGENERATION

What has the Blood of Jesus Christ done for us? It has brought to us not only God's Grace and Forgiveness for our sins, but the Blood of Christ also brings to us the promise and the power of a glorious, redeemed, and regenerated life.

It is a marvelous thing that in the poured-out Blood of our Lord, we have the poured-out Blessings of God and of Heaven upon us. The Life of our Lord literally was poured out into this world, and that Love and Grace comes even to us.

When the soldiers smote the Son of God, they struck the Rock from which flows the Living Waters. When they pierced His Hands and His Feet, they opened the resources of Grace, Power, and Glory from Heaven, and when they pierced His Side, they opened the Fountain of God's Love, Grace, and Mercy. Not only that, but in that Gift of God's Love in the Life of His Son, there came with it that cleansing, regenerating Power that makes us new men and women, new Creations in God's Sight.

THE BLOOD OF CHRIST FOR ME

Have you ever noticed how we categorize sins? Do you see that man over there? He is a violent sinner. Do you see that one over there? He's the dregs of the Earth. Do you see this one here? He is as dirt and filth.

We have a tendency to gather our righteous skirts around us and talk about how sinful other people are. Then we remember the Word of the Lord in which God says all have sinned — all. There is not one of us who is righteous by his own means — no, not one. One man may have sinned in one category and another in a different category, but I also have sinned in my categories. My life is full of blemish and wrong, and I need to be Saved just as the next person does.

I also need to cast myself upon the Mercies of God. I, too, need to say, *"Lord, be merciful to me, a sinner."* Praise God, the same loving Grace that was extended to others is extended to me. Under the Blood, we all are Saved. *"When I see the Blood, I will pass over you."*

There is no more condemnation to those who are in Christ Jesus (Rom. 8:1). We are free. We are washed. We are redeemed. We are justified by the Blood of the Crucified One. I come openly and unashamedly, confessing my Faith in the Son of Glory.

(The writer owes a debt of gratitude to Dr. W. A. Criswell for the above material regarding the Blood of Christ).

WITHOUT SPOT OR BLEMISH

The phrase, *"As of a lamb without blemish and without spot,"* harks back to the lambs which were offered in the old Jewish economy.

At the beginning of the Ministry of Christ, John the Baptist used the term when introducing Christ: *"Behold the Lamb of God, which takes away the sin of the world"* (Jn. 1:29). John, of course, said this at the behest of the Holy Spirit. The meaning was clear.

Of all the untold millions of lambs which had been offered up from the very beginning, starting, it seems, with Abel (Gen., Chpt. 4), and then increasing greatly with the advent of the Sacrificial system in the Levitical Law, all and without exception typified the coming Son of God. While the blood of bulls and goats could not take away sins, it did serve as a stopgap measure until Christ would come.

We find the practice began, as stated, with Abel, continued with Noah some 1,600 years later (Gen. 8:20), with the practice taken up by Abraham, in fact, to such a degree that Abraham was referred to as the, *"Altar builder"* (Gen. 12:8; 13:4; 22:13-14), continued by Isaac (Gen. 26:25), and then Jacob (Gen. 35:7). Of course, when the Levitical system came into force under Moses, the offering of lambs as sacrifices was constant. Two were offered each day, 9 a.m. and 3 p.m., with that doubled on the Sabbath. As well, at the time of the great Feasts, and especially at Passover, many thousands were offered up. Josephus said that as many as 250,000 were offered during the last Passover week attended by Christ. While not that many, many hundreds, if not thousands, were offered up on the other Feast Days, as well, during the course of the year. Then again, Israelites were constantly coming and offering up sacrifices. In fact, the Altar fires were to never go out on the great Brazen Altar.

All of this, as stated, typified Christ Who was to come (Isa., Chpt. 53).

EGYPT

Quite possibly the greatest example of the offering up of sacrifices is found in the Deliverance of the Children of Israel from Egyptian bondage. It is recorded in Exodus, Chapter 12.

A lamb was to be killed for each house, roasted with fire, and eaten with bitter herbs. The blood of the lamb was to be placed on the doorposts and the lintels of each house, which would ensure safety and protection for the Israelites inside. The death Angel was to come through and in each house which did not have the blood applied, the firstborn would die. However, the Scripture plainly said: *"And the blood shall be to you for a token upon the houses where you are: and when I see the blood, I will pass over you"* (Ex. 12:13).

While the Miracles, as performed by Moses, did not deliver the Children of Israel from Egyptian bondage, *"the slain lamb"* did!

THE METHOD

It is said that when each lamb was offered up in the daily sacrifices by the Priests, after the little animal was killed and its hide stripped from its body, the Priest would take a razor sharp knife and lay the flesh open all the way down the backbone. It would be pulled open where the Priest would minutely inspect it for discoloration. If the flesh was found to be discolored or to have any blemish at all, that carcass would be rejected, and another lamb would take its place. The Scripture plainly said, *"Your lamb shall be without blemish, a male of the first year: you shall take it out from the sheep, or from the goats"* (Ex. 12:5).

All of this typified Christ and, in fact, was meant to typify Christ, hence, John the Baptist saying to our Lord: *"Behold the Lamb of God, which takes away the sin of the world"* (Jn. 1:29).

Jesus was Perfect in every respect — Perfect in His physical Body, Perfect in His Character, Perfect in His Spirit, Perfect in His Life, Perfect in His Keeping of the Law, and, above all, Perfect in the Sacrifice of Himself.

FOREORDAINED

Peter said, *"Who verily was foreordained before the foundation of the world, but was manifest in these last times for you"* (I Pet. 1:20).

The phrase, *"Who verily was foreordained,"* refers to the fact that God in His Omniscience planned the Redemption of humanity, as Peter mentions here, even before man was created and, in fact, before the Universe was created. Of course, only one with perfect knowledge, past, present, and future, could do such a thing. That's the reason that we say that the Sacrifice of Christ was objective. Inasmuch as all of this was designed by the Lord, it means that it is unchangeable. I should think it would be understood that man could have absolutely nothing to do with the origination of anything designed before man was ever even created.

Again, as we've already stated, the acceptance of this great Redemption Plan, as it regards being Born-Again, is, however, very subjective. It depends upon our obedience and Faith.

When it came to what Jesus did on the Cross to redeem humanity, man had no part in that, therefore, can claim no part. All is of God!

THE FOUNDATION OF THE WORLD

The phrase, *"Before the foundation of the world,"* refers to the time before the Universe was created. To be frank, this is beyond our comprehension and thinking. This tells us that the Incarnation was no mere episode, consequent upon the fall of man, but it is also the Doctrine that, *"Before the foundation of the world,"* God had foreknown and decided to allow the Fall itself.

In effect, the Apostle is telling those to whom he is writing, and us, as well, that they must not treat their share in the Gospel liberation as if it were, at best, a piece of good luck and so learn to despise it. They must, as well, think of it as if Paul and Silas were preaching to them a novel invention at discord with the spirit of the Old Covenant under which they had previously been. God knew from all eternity Who was to be His Messiah and His Lamb, but for reasons known to Himself, the particular and personal declaration of Christ was reserved until now.

In effect, the Apostle is telling the Early Church that for you has been kept the Revelation of a secret which underlay the whole Old Testament system. The foreknowledge includes not only the knowledge and decision that Jesus should be the Christ, but that His History should be what it was. This is what made His Rejection so awful and beyond words.

It is one thing to reject that which is devised by men, as right as it might be, but to reject that which was instituted by God, and done so even before the foundation of the world, is beyond comprehension.

CHRIST WAS MANIFESTED

The phrase, *"But was manifest in these last times for you,"* refers to the invisible God, Who, in the Person of the Son, was made visible to human eyesight by assuming a human body and human limitations. All of this was for the purpose of carrying out the great Plan of God as it referred to Redemption, which necessitated such an act in order that Christ could die on the Cross. God, as stated, cannot die; therefore, He would have to become Man in order that this act of Sacrifice might be carried out.

In Christ, many things were manifested; however, all of these things led up to the main event, which was the Sacrificial Offering of Himself on the Cross as payment for sin. Consequently, the Cross must ever be the central focus of our Faith, and it must remain the central focus of our Faith. Everything Christ did was of immeasurable significance, as should be obvious. However, even though these things contributed toward the Redemption of humanity, and I speak of His Healings and Miracles, plus His Words of Life, still, it was the Cross and the Cross Alone which effected Redemption!

WRONG DIRECTION

A short time ago, in looking at a Commentary regarding these particular Scriptures, the Brother stated, *"If the Christian is to live a victorious life, he is going to have to have a resolute determination,"* or words to that effect. Regrettably, that is where most of the church presently is in their doctrine concerning victorious, overcoming, Christian living.

While it is definitely true that the Christian must have a resolute determination, the other side of that truth is that this alone is woefully insufficient. But yet, that's about the only advice that most preachers can give Christians as it regards walking in victory. The Seventh Chapter of Romans describes Paul's personal experience immediately after being Saved and baptized with the Holy Spirit. The timeframe may have lasted several years. This Chapter lets us know that a resolute determination is not strong enough to bring about the desired result.

The Scriptural Truth is that the only manner of victory which God has prescribed is our Faith in what Christ has done at the Cross on our behalf. This gives the Holy Spirit the latitude to work within our lives (Rom. 8:1-2). Consequently, the three main ingredients regarding the Christian's life and walk are *"the Cross," "our Faith,"* and *"the Holy Spirit."* The Cross is the Means by which all things come to us from God. As a result, our Faith is to rest in that Finished Work. This done, the Holy Spirit, Who functions entirely within the parameters of the Sacrifice of Christ, will grandly help us (Rom. 8:11).

ROMANS, CHAPTER SIX

The entire Sixth Chapter of Romans proclaims to us the manner in which we are placed into the Crucifixion of Christ and what it means to us. The Eighth Chapter of Romans proclaims what the Holy Spirit does for us and with us after the Believer understands Romans, Chapter 6. As someone has said, *"Romans, Chapter 6, presents the mechanics of the Holy Spirit"* while *"Romans, Chapter 8, presents the dynamics of the Holy Spirit."*

The Sacrifice has been offered, and it has not been offered in vain. Had not the Death of Christ served its purpose, it could not have been followed by His Resurrection. If He had not risen, then would we have had reason to conclude, *"We are yet in our sins,"* with our guilt unexpiated and the fetters of depravity unbroken. However, we have abundant ground for concluding that *"Messiah, cut off, but not for Himself,"* has *"finished transgression, made an end of sin."* If He died *"for our offenses,"* He has been *"raised again for our Justification."*

"It is finished," said the dying Saviour on the Cross; and from the Throne of His Glory, when He broke the bands of death, the Father responded, *"It is finished."*

BEAR WITH ME

Paul said, *"Would to God you would bear with me a little in my folly: and indeed bear with me"* (II Cor. 11:1).

This section is unique in all of Paul's writing. It has been well called the most magnificent and, yet, destructive thing that Paul has done in the way of irony. Like an actor on the ancient stage, he puts on a mask in order to act a part. The part which he acts is that of a fool, of a fellow who has no sense, but it is only he himself who feels that he is acting a fool.

He asked his readers for once to allow him to do this. He feels that he is inflicting something on them, something sense-less, but yet, something that is needed. He asked them to toler-ate it for a little while.

What makes Paul feel that he is acting the role of a fool is the fact that he boasts about his own person. This is what he dislikes. However, the Corinthians themselves have crowded him into assuming so unpleasant a role.

He takes this role because of his great concern for them because of the attacks made upon his person in order to injure not merely him but, most of all, the Corinthians themselves, their Faith, and their entire Spiritual Lives.

Paul's whole motive and aim are not self-aggrandizement but complete frustration at the attempts of the false apostles who have already done much to hurt the Corinthians.

PAUL'S FEELINGS

He feels like a fool also because he seems to descend to the level of these false apostles whose great asset was self-recom-mendation and boasting about themselves. Is Paul now not advertising himself in the same way after he has exposed these men's folly as being senseless?

Ah, but these men are not playing a role as is Paul; their whole lives and activities are this very folly. Paul only ap-parently stoops to their level by now boasting about himself. Their boasts are entirely hollow. Behind the great show which they make is nothing, mere empty air. Behind that show and pretense of great excellence and power is in stark reality only secret viciousness, which they would not dare to let the Corinthians see.

When Paul now takes the boaster's role, it is only a role, just a role. All that he will say and boast of himself is true, not a sham, not a pretense, not false, and not lying. It is the straight fact and the simple reality from beginning to end, something which the false apostles cannot say.

In fact, the Corinthians cannot verify a single boast of the false apostle. They have nothing but the simple word of these boasters, whose greatness lies in comparing themselves with themselves.

Every word of Paul's boasting, the Corinthians can verify. Yes, most of what he will say, they have long ago verified. Truth does not like to boast; lies must boast. Truth can truly boast; lies can boast only by lying.

THE HOLY SPIRIT ALLOWED THIS FOLLY

The phrase, *"Would to God you would bear with me a little in my folly,"* expresses earnest desire; however, the appeal is not to God but to the Corinthians.

The idea seems to be, *"I know that boasting is generally foolish, and that it is not to be indulged in; but though it is to be generally regarded as folly, yet circumstances compel me to it, and I ask your indulgence."*

As we've already stated, this situation was far more than a Preacher merely defending himself. Actually, in most circumstances, we should not defend ourselves, leaving that to the Lord. He is our defense. And yet, the Holy Spirit not only allowed this by Paul, but sanctioned it as well!

Whatever it may look like to the reader, the facts are that this was an attack by Satan against the Prescribed Order of God, in essence, the Government of God. It was an attack against the one the Lord had chosen, namely Paul in this instance. The truth is, the church is very seldom satisfied with the ones chosen by God, whomever they might be. The simple reason is that most religious denominations have long since abrogated the Headship of Christ, consequently, serving as the head themselves. So, if they do not choose the person, they automatically oppose the person. To be sure, those in that particular, unscriptural position of so-called leadership will never choose that which God has chosen, and for all the obvious reasons. Basically, the abrogation of the Headship of Christ is Satan's means of destroying denominations, even those which began correctly.

To be led by the Lord demands a consecrated prayer life, a constant study of the Word of God, and above all, proper Faith in Christ and the Cross, which maintains a broken and contrite spirit. Many do not desire to do that, so they either attempt to take over the Headship of Christ themselves, or else, they look to other men for leadership, which makes up most of the modern church.

A SUBVERSION OF THE GOSPEL

Along with the abrogation of the Headship of Christ, and we speak of Christ as the Head of the Church, almost always, if not always, a subversion of the Gospel takes place as well.

These false apostles were Judaizers who were attempting to attach Law to Grace, which, of course, is basely unscriptural. So, I personally think it is impossible for the Government of God to be replaced without, at the same time, the Gospel being subverted. So, there was far more here than just a Preacher merely defending himself.

NECESSITY

The phrase, *"And indeed bear with me,"* presents the Apostle repeating himself for the simple reason that he doesn't enjoy the tact he is forced to take.

The things about which he was writing were the subject of scrutiny at Corinth. Certain workers (false apostles) had come to Corinth after Paul left and had set about to institute their own false gospel. To do this, they felt they had to discredit Paul and his work, which is generally the tact taken by such who do Satan's work. Paul's appeal for the approval of the Corinthians was the sincerity of his service. As we have repeatedly stated, it is an insult of the highest order for this Man of God to have to prove himself to the very people he has brought to Christ.

JUSTIFICATION

There is a sense in which our Justification is twofold. In God's Sight, Faith justifies. In man's sight, work justifies. In fact, the Scriptures say, *"Faith without works is dead."* This is the point at which Law and Grace are reconciled. The New Testament way of life is not the Old Testament way. We are Saved by Grace, but when Grace saves, it produces in its place the fulfillment of the Law.

This does not mean that the old Mosaic Commandments are revived and that we are to be regimented, as Israel of old, by a system of legalistic obedience. It does mean, however, that the inner Law of Grace supersedes the outer Law of Commandments. At the same time, the evidence of Faith is in works, but it is works inspired by Faith. Works are the effect of Faith and not the cause of it.

FAITH

Thus, the only way to show our Faith to men is by our works. God sees the quality of our Faith in His Own Divine Knowledge, while man sees the reality of our Faith by his human observation.

The saving element of Faith is in our believing, while the evidential element of Faith is in our doing. When Abraham believed God, he was justified in God's Sight. However, Abraham did not prove his Faith until he offered Isaac in sacrifice, or at least proceeded to do so but was stopped by the Lord. Faith is not only a feeling, it is also an act.

We must be careful to preserve the distinction between Faith and works. We are justified when we believe, but not until we live out that inner Justification will men count us as just men. The cause of Justification is Faith, while the effect of Justification is works.

So far as God was concerned, He accepted Paul's service because of his Faith, but so far as man was concerned, He accepted Paul's service because of his works.

One of the most convincing evidences was the Apostle's sincerity. His motives were not personal. He was actually jealous for the spiritual progress of his Converts. He had espoused them to Christ and could not be content unless he saw them continuing in Blessing and growth.

As well, he knew that if they bought into this doctrine of Law being added to Grace, it would ultimately destroy them spiritually.

THE CORRECT OBJECT OF FAITH

Faith is probably the major topic of the Church; however, it must be understood that unless our Faith is anchored in the correct Object, which is Christ and the Cross, it is simply faith that God will not recognize. The Cross of Christ must, and without fail, be the Object of our Faith. When that is done, we are truly having Faith in the Word, Faith in the Lord, etc.

JEALOUS

Paul also said, *"For I am jealous over you with godly jealousy: for I have espoused you to one husband, that I may present you as a chaste virgin to Christ"* (II Cor. 11:2).

In this Verse, Paul gives us the reason for his actions. It is, as stated, the Corinthians themselves. They must not be lost to false doctrine.

The phrase, *"For I am jealous over you with godly jealousy,"* refers to the *"Jealousy of God"* (Ex. 20:5; 34:14; Nah. 1:2).

In both the Old and New Testaments, jealously can refer to an exclusive, single-mindedness of emotion, which may be morally blameworthy or praiseworthy, depending on whether the object of the jealousy is self or some cause beyond self.

In the former case, the result is envy or hatred of others (Gen. 30:1; Prov. 3:31; Ezek. 31:9), which, for the New Testament, is the antithesis of love and, hence, the enemy of true Christian fellowship (I Cor. 13:4; II Cor. 12:20; James 3:14).

The Bible, however, also represents the other possibility of a *"Divine jealousy,"* which is actually the subject of this Scripture. It is a consuming, single-minded pursuit of a good end, which Paul exhibited toward the Corinthians (Ex. 20:5; I Ki. 19:10; I Cor. 12:31).

This positive usage is frequently associated with the marriage relationship, which, in a sense, Paul uses here, where a jealousy for the exclusiveness of the relationship is the necessary condition of its permanence (Num. 5:11; Ezek. 16:38; II Cor. 11:2).

GOD IS A JEALOUS GOD

Jealousy, as stated, is referred to God as well as men (Ex. 20:5; 34:14; Nah. 1:2). Difficulty is sometimes felt with this due to principally the way in which the negative connotations of the term have come to predominance in common English usage.

Scripture, however, also witnesses to a positive application of jealousy and finds in this idea a highly relevant term to denote God's Holy Zeal for the honor of His Name and the good of His People who are bound to Him in the marriage of the covenant — whether the Old, which represented Israel, or the New, which represents the Church (Deut. 32:16, 21; II Ki. 19:31; Ezek. 36:5; Zech. 1:14; Jn. 2:17).

In this sense, the Jealousy of God is of the essence of His Moral Character, a major cause for worship and confidence on the part of His People and a ground for fear on the part of His Enemies.

BECAUSE HE LOVED THEM

It was because Paul loved these Corinthians, and because
he feared that they were in danger of being seduced from the
simplicity of the Gospel, that he writes these words and takes
this tact. Actually, the phrase, *"I am jealous,"* means properly,
I ardently love you; I am full of tender attachment to you. In
fact, the word was usual and common among the Greeks to
denote an ardent affection of any kind.

In making these statements, Paul reverts in his mind to the
tenderness of the marriage relation, unto the possibility that in
that relation, the affections might be estranged. Consequently,
he makes use of this figure.

HIS MOTIVE

As we see here, in back of the proposed foolishness, which
Paul mentioned in the first Verse, lies the deepest seriousness.
Paul reveals his motive and his aim at once and thus excludes
all wrong ideas about *"a little something of foolishness"* that is
now to be employed.

When the purpose is so serious, any folly or foolishness
which serves that purpose will certainly not be frivolous, su-
perficial, or objectionable in any way.

Three parties are most deeply concerned: Paul, the Corinthians, and Christ. What unites them is Paul's great and holy
office. As well, we have that office shown here in a new and most
lovely light. Here there are the three who are concerned in that
office, all in their actual relation. Here the motives and the purposes, all intertwined, so supreme for all concerned, are shown
for the welfare of the Corinthians, and you and me as well.

THE ONE HUSBAND, CHRIST

The phrase, *"For I have espoused you to one husband,"*

proclaims the fact that the Apostle was not jealous of the affection of the Corinthians for himself but of their affection for Christ.

The picture is that of a father who has betrothed his daughter to the noblest of bridegrooms. Soon the nuptials will be celebrated. Soon the father is to lead his daughter to the altar (we use our modern language).

This father can lead her there only as a pure virgin. The point and pivot of the whole imagery lies in this term: *"a virgin pure."* Hence, we have the preamble: *"I am jealous over you with God's Jealously."* I watch over you with jealous eyes and see that you ever remain pure for that great day of presentation to Christ.

As far as we are able to say, this imagery is borrowed from the oriental style betrothal in which the bride was pledged to the groom by the parents, which made the two man and wife, yet so that a longer or a shorter interval intervened before the groom came to claim his bride, to carry her to his own home in grand state, there to consummate his marriage.

The word, *"Espoused,"* as Paul uses it here, means properly to adapt, to fit, to join together, hence, to join in wedlock, to marry. Paul is here forming a connection between the Corinthians and the Saviour similar to the marriage connection, which actually all Believers fit. Jesus is the *"Husband,"* and the Church is the *"Bride,"* at least as Paul uses the analogy here.

A CHASTE VIRGIN

The phrase, *"That I may present you as a chaste virgin to Christ,"* tells us several things:

• They were not to befoul themselves with spiritual adultery, which is what would happen if they accepted the teaching of the false apostles.

• *"Present you,"* actually refers to a *"presentation,"* which will take place at the Rapture of the Church and, more particularly, at the *"Marriage Supper of the Lamb"* (Rev. 19:7-9).

Even though Paul was Jewish but, more particularly, an Apostle to the Gentiles, still, his thinking was in Jewish terms, hence, the manner in which he presents this subject.

I FEAR

Paul said, *"But I fear, lest by any means, as the serpent beguiled Eve through his subtilty, so your minds should be corrupted from the simplicity that is in Christ"* (II Cor. 11:3).

Paul has just compared the Church to a Virgin soon to be presented as a Bride to the Redeemer. The mention of this seems to have suggested to him the fact that the first woman, Eve, was deceived and led astray by the Tempter, and that the same thing might occur in regard to the Church, which he was so desirous should be preserved pure.

The phrase, *"But I fear,"* as it correlates with the following statements, presents the grounds of his fear. They were:

• That Satan had seduced the first woman, thus demonstrating that the most holy were in danger of being led astray by temptation.

• That special efforts were being made to seduce them from the Faith. He had reason to suppose that the persuasive arts of the false teachers, the power of philosophy, and the attractive and corrupting influences of the world might be employed to seduce them from simple attachment to Christ.

• All other deceptions are the repetitions of the original in the Garden of Eden and are very effective. Its practitioners will use the basest means, any and all such means, to gain one's evil ends — *"craftiness."*

SEDUCTION

The phrase, *"As the serpent beguiled Eve,"* goes back, as we have stated, to the original seduction (Gen. 3:1-11).

The word, *"Serpent,"* here refers to Satan, who was the agent by whom Eve was beguiled (Jn. 8:44; I Jn. 3:8; Rev. 12:9; 20:2).

Paul did not mean that the Corinthians were in danger of being corrupted in the same way but that similar efforts would be made to seduce them. Satan adapts his temptations to the character and circumstances of the tempted. He varies them from age to age and applies them in such a way as best to secure his object. Hence, all should be on their guard.

No one knows the mode in which he will approach him, but all may know for certain that he will approach them in some way.

SUBTILTY

The phrase, *"Through his subtilty,"* refers to the strategy of Satan.

"Subtilty" in the Greek is, *"Panourgia,"* and means, *"Shrewdness, cunning, and craft."* A tempter always employs cunning to accomplish his object. This can fall out to many directions. If one is lying, they can go in any direction after any manner. Truth has only one direction while lies can chart their own course. This is the method Satan used against Eve (Gen. 3:1).

We will find in this Chapter that Satan is to be dreaded as a lion (I Pet. 5:8); more to be dreaded as a serpent, even as this Verse proclaims; and most to be dreaded as an Angel of light (Vs. 14).

Jesus referred to this in John 8:44. It is so effective because it is the first deception that entered our world and because its results were so terrible. All other deceptions are the repetitions of this original, most fatal one, which is the outcome of radical deception.

Paul says, *"Eve,"* and not, *"Adam,"* in this connection because he wants to designate the *"serpent"* as the deceiver as he dealt with Eve. He says, *"The serpent,"* and not, *"Satan,"* because he desires to bring out the full baseness of the act in its similarity to what the false prophets were doing in Corinth. They crawled into Corinth as Satan did into Eden; they were like serpents.

They used the same *"craftiness."* They too intended to slay the innocent; consequently, these deceivers in Corinth were doing the Devil's serpent work. Paul desires to arouse all the horror of the serpent in the Corinthians. Like a flash, this word, *"Serpent,"* reveals all the deadly danger from which the Corinthians should flee.

MODERN SEDUCTION

During Paul's time, the Church under his teaching had been brought in correctly. Jesus Christ is the New Covenant, and the meaning of that New Covenant was given to Paul, the meaning of which is the Cross of Christ. False apostles were coming and trying to swing the Believers toward Law, which, of course, Law and Grace cannot mix. Paul knew if they accepted the subtle approach of these deceivers, they would wreck themselves.

Today it is different. The church as a whole knows almost nothing about the Cross of Christ as it regards our everyday living for God. They have knowledge as it regards Salvation, with the words, *"Jesus died for me,"* the most often used, and rightly so. However, when it comes to living for God, the modern church has almost no understanding whatsoever regarding the part the Cross plays in this most important subject.

THE SONLIFE BROADCASTING NETWORK

The Lord is beginning to bring this Message of the Cross back to the Church. Of course, as there was opposition in the times of Paul, there is opposition now. Nevertheless, there are some Preachers who are hearing what is being said and are accepting it, which changes their Ministries altogether.

We must understand that ninety-five percent of Paul's teaching, as it regards the Cross of Christ, had to do with our everyday living for God. It is the very opposite now, with most teaching done regarding Salvation. Regrettably, even that is falling by the wayside. When you remove the Cross out of the church, you are left with nothing but a vapid philosophy. In other words, Christianity then becomes a religion instead of a relationship. However, I think one can say that preachers who try to pull the people away from the Cross presently are being used of Satan exactly as these false apostles were in the times of Paul.

ERROR

Late Jewish fiction and speculation regarded the fall of Eve as a sexual sin, in other words, that Satan as a fallen Angel had sexual intercourse with the first woman.

Some of the commentators collect all of the Jewish statements on this subject on the supposition that they cast light on Paul's reference to Eve, that Paul might at least have had such in mind since he pictures the Corinthians as a pure virgin who may not be found pure at her presentation to her bridegroom. We decline to follow them.

There is nothing of sex in Paul's words, and neither do his statements even slightly hint at such a thing. Eve's seduction had nothing to do with sexual immorality, but rather an immorality of the spirit, which fell out to disobedience regarding the Word of God.

CUNNING!

The *"subtilty"* mentioned here by Paul assumed an attractive form to be sure. It was a fascinating manner, a manner fitted to charm, in order to seduce these Corinthians. To be frank, it almost succeeded! In fact, considering that these people had been Saved under Paul, and that he was, without a doubt, one of the greatest men of God in the world of that day, the fact that they could be turned against Paul, which they almost were, tells us how powerful this *"subtilty"* was and is.

THE SIMPLICITY THAT IS IN CHRIST

The phrase, *"So your minds should be corrupted from the*

simplicity that is in Christ," proclaims the fact that Paul feared for his own Converts that they may be turned away from Christ, as Eve was beguiled by Satan to turn away from God. Let me say it plainly and clearly: any preacher who tries to turn people from the Cross of Christ is in the same category as these false apostles in the time of Paul.

The idea is that all the individual members of the Church should be holy. They, as individuals, are soon to be presented in Heaven as the Fruit of the Labors of the Son of God and as entitled to His Eternal Love. How pure should be the lips that are soon to speak His Praise in Heaven! How pure the eyes that are soon to behold His Glory! How holy the feet that are soon to tread His Courts in the Heavenly World!

YOUR MINDS

As Paul uses the word, *"Minds,"* it speaks of the thoughts being perverted. The mind is corrupted when the affections are alienated from the proper object, and when the soul is filled with unholy plans, purposes, and desires.

This speaks of devotion to Christ, and Christ Alone. Satan will try to use the world or false doctrine to turn people away from their love for Christ. However, anyway it is sliced, a departure from the ways of Christ impacts, of necessity, our love for Christ.

Jesus said in connection with *"false prophets,"* which would arise and *"deceive many,"* that *"the love of many shall wax cold"* (Mat. 24:11-12).

To be sure, the time of which Jesus spoke in this Twenty-fourth Chapter of Matthew pertains to the very times in which we presently live.

The word, *"Minds,"* as well, refers to *"single-mindedness,"* as it refers to Christ.

The mind and all its thoughts are set solely and singly upon Him in love, loyalty, and devotion, and there is no duplicity which secretly turns to another.

As well, the word, *"Purity,"* can be added to this meaning as it refers back to the figure of *"a virgin pure."* The thoughts are to be without a stain or a smudge of disloyalty of any kind.

In his craftiness, the serpent aims to introduce duplicity into our thoughts, which are directed to Christ, and, thereby, to defile our thoughts regarding Him. In other words, we are no longer to be Christ's Alone in our thoughts; secretly, in our hidden thoughts, we are to hanker after another or something else.

Figuratively, we should thus no longer be a bride loyal and pure in heart for our blessed marriage presentation to Christ.

Consequently, an admonition underlies Paul's words, which urges the Corinthians to flee any contact with false apostles. What a shame to pretend to be loyal to Christ while disloyalty has crept into the heart through the serpent's agency, which used the false apostles.

CORRUPTED

"Corrupted," in the Greek is, *"Phthio,"* and means, *"To spoil by any process, or shrivel or wither, to ruin, to destroy."*

The fact is there is a great danger concerning all Believers of being corrupted from the simplicity that is in Christ. Satan desires to destroy us and his great object is readily accomplished if he can seduce Christians from the simple devotion to the Redeemer; if he can secure corruption in doctrine or in the manner of worship, and can produce conformity in dress and in style of living to this world.

Formally, he excited persecution, but in that, he was foiled. The more the Church was persecuted, the more it grew. Then he changed his ground. What he could not do by persecution, he sought to do by corrupting the Church, and in this, he has been by far more successful.

This can be done slowly but certainly, even effectually, but without exciting suspicion. It matters not to Satan whether the Church is crippled by persecution or its zeal destroyed by false doctrine and by conformity to the world. His aim is secured and the power of the Church destroyed. In fact, the form in which he now assails the Church is by attempting to seduce it by simple and hearty attachment to the Saviour. To be frank, he is by and large successful!

SIMPLICITY

One of the greatest tricks of Satan presently and, in fact, that which he has always used, even as Paul outlines here, is the pretense of leading Believers into higher enlightenment.

One propagator of the greed message made the statement the other day, *"Our ministry is not to get people saved, but to enlighten them after they get saved."* However, his so-called enlightenment is, pure and simple, *"another Jesus, another spirit, and another Gospel"* (II Cor. 11:4).

The following will provide some of the means by which Satan attempts to destroy the simplicity that is in Christ:

• From the pure Doctrines of the Word of God: by the admixture of philosophy and by the opinions of the world, there was danger that their minds should be turned away from that hold on the simple Truths which Christ had taught, in other words, to get the Church to abandon the Cross.

• Christ had a single aim; He was free from all guile; was purely honest; never made use of any improper arts; never resorted to false appearances, and never deceived. His Followers should in like manner be in the same capacity.

There should be no cunning, no tricks, and no craft in advancing our purposes. There should be nothing but honesty and truth in all that we say.

Paul was afraid that the Corinthians would lose this beautiful simplicity and artlessness of character and manner. As well, he was afraid that they would insensibly be led to adopt the maxims of mere cunning, policy, expediency, and seductive arts, which prevail so much in the world — a danger which was immanent among the shrewd and cunning people of Greece, but which is confined to no time and place.

Christians should be more guileless than even children are; as pure and free from tricks as was the Redeemer Himself.

The modern church is rife with these *"tricks"* as it embraces the Hebraic movement, the greed message, and humanistic psychology.

• From the simplicity and worship, which the Lord Jesus commended and required:

The worship which the Redeemer desired to establish was simple, unostentatious, and pure — strongly in contrast with the gorgeousness and corruption of the pagan worship, and even with the imposing splendor of the Jewish Temple service.

WORSHIP

The Lord through the Holy Spirit intended that worship should be adapted to all lands, and such as should be offered by all classes of men — a pure worship, claiming first the homage of the heart, and then such simple external expressions as should best exhibit that homage.

How easily might this be corrupted and, in fact, has been corrupted!

What temptations there were to attempt to corrupt it by those who had been accustomed to the magnificence of the Temple service, and who would suppose that this of the Messiah could not be less gorgeous than that which was designed to shadow forth His Coming. As well, those who had been accustomed to the splendid rites of the pagan worship might well suppose also that the worship of Christ must be at least as splendid as these false religions had been!

Sadly, according to the history of the Church, for a considerable part of its existence, its beautiful, simple worship of the Lord, instituted by the Redeemer, has been corrupted until all that is left is ceremony and ritual. Or else, we have thought that great noise and activity constituted such when it really doesn't.

So, I think one could easily say that this which Satan attempts to corrupt regarding simplicity is our love for Christ, the pure Doctrine of Christ, and the worship of Christ. He seeks to alienate the love, infiltrate the Doctrine, and adulterate the worship.

HE WHO COMES

Paul said, *"For if he who comes preaching another Jesus, whom we have not preached, or if you receive another spirit, which you have not received, or another Gospel, which you have not accepted, you might well bear with him"* (II Cor. 11:4).

Why does Paul then not attack these false apostles on what would thus be the chief issue, their false gospel? Why does Paul fight about the issue of his own person, as he does in these Chapters, as if this were the chief issue? He tells us throughout.

These false apostles made Paul's person the supreme issue. They used *"craftiness"* in this. They intended to establish themselves as the genuine Apostles of Christ. Paul would later say that this is no marvel, for Satan tries to appear, as well, as an Angel of light.

There is some evidence that they may have held their real teaching, which was, no doubt, Judaism, in abeyance until they should have destroyed Paul's standing in Corinth and have fully established themselves. This accomplished, it seems that they planned to come out into the open with their false gospel. For this reason, Paul compares them to the serpent and to Satan.

It seems that the Corinthians were still in the dark as to what these liars really taught in regard to the Gospel. Paul rightly joins the issue which they drew on his own person. This alone stood in the open; the other was concealed and could thus be evaded if it were attacked by Paul.

A PARTICULAR INDIVIDUAL

The phrase, *"For if he who comes,"* is not meant to portray a hypothetical situation, but rather a particular individual, or else, the ringleader of several, who had come into the Church at Corinth with devious purposes in mind.

Perhaps several such had come to Corinth, and many others who may yet come are included in Paul's indictment. As well, that which he says is meant not only for that particular time but, in fact, is an admonition for the Church for all time. As false prophets were rife during the old Economy of God (the Old Testament), false apostles fit that category now under the New.

ANOTHER JESUS

The phrase, *"Preaches another Jesus, whom we have not preached,"* presents the core effect of Satan's deception. If *"another Jesus"* is preached, *"another spirit"* will be received and *"another gospel"* believed, all bogus.

What does Paul mean by *"another Jesus"*?

Paul preached *"Jesus Christ and Him Crucified"* as the answer for hurting, dying humanity. In fact, he said, *"But God forbid that I should glory, save in the Cross of our Lord Jesus Christ, by Whom the world is crucified unto me, and I unto the world"* (Gal. 6:14).

So, to preach Jesus in any other capacity than the Crucified, Resurrected One is to preach another Jesus. This means that a historical Jesus is bogus. It means that if we make Jesus the provider of money as our primary message, we are plainly and simply preaching another Jesus. In other words, if we preach Jesus in any capacity except Him Crucified, which means that the Offering of Himself satisfied the claims of Heavenly Justice, making it possible for sinners to be Saved, we are preaching a bogus gospel. It is not just Jesus, but rather, *"Jesus and Him Crucified"* (I Cor. 2:2).

JESUS THE SAVIOUR

Jesus is not an economist; He is a Saviour. Jesus is not a

psychologist; He is a Saviour. Jesus is not a doctor; He is a Saviour. Jesus is not a sociologist; He is a Saviour. Jesus is not a politician; He is a Saviour. In fact, He is the Saviour, which means there is no other.

While all the things mentioned are definitely affected by Christ in a positive way, that is not His Primary Objective, it being the Salvation of the soul.

The Jesus that Paul preached, *"Christ and Him Crucified,"* sets captives free. It saves souls while at the same time destroying the powers of darkness. Man's real problem is sin, and that's the problem Jesus addressed as Saviour, and did so by the Cross.

All of this means that if the preacher is preaching anything other than the Cross, or if the Believer has set his affections on anything except the Cross of Christ, the end result will always be *"another Jesus."* That is what the modern church is by and large preaching — *"another Jesus."*

The Jesus of the Bible came to this world specifically to go to the Cross. This means that the Cross was not an incident, not an assassination, not an accident, and not an execution, but rather a Sacrifice. If man wants to be Saved, this is the way it had to be. However, the modern church no longer even preaches against sin. So, if you do not recognize sin as man's problem, then you don't need the solution, which is *"Jesus Christ and Him Crucified."* So, let me say it again, *"What is being preached in modern churches is 'another Jesus.'"*

FALSE APOSTLES

The false apostle whom Paul describes preached *"another Jesus."* He speaks of the same person and uses the same name but makes him altogether *"other"* than Paul does. Thus, *"another"* is in place. Such a Jesus would send a *"different spirit,"* who would also employ a *"different gospel."* This is the major problem in the modern church.

Much of the Charismatic world, whether through ignorance

or otherwise, repudiates the Cross. While some of them admit its necessity for Salvation, and even that is beginning to fall by the wayside, they repudiate its effectiveness thereafter. In other words, they go beyond the Cross, which means it is *"another Jesus."*

As well, when most Pentecostals, and I am Pentecostal, opt for humanistic psychology in place of the Cross, which is the answer for all of the ills of man, they are, pure and simple, preaching *"another Jesus."* Regrettably, almost the entirety of the church world has fallen for this humanistic lie. That particular Jesus, this *"another Jesus,"* saves no one and delivers no one; consequently, we have churches full of unconverted people.

THE GOSPEL AS PREACHED BY PAUL

By Paul using the phrase, *"Whom we have not preached,"* he proclaims the fact and the truth that the Holy Spirit gave him his Message and, thereby, sanctioned his Message of the Cross, that the Cross of Christ must ever be the Object of our Faith. In other words, if we do not preach the Gospel as Paul preached the Gospel, which is *"Jesus Christ and Him Crucified,"* the fact is, we are not preaching the Gospel. We should think this over very carefully and as Paul also said, *"Examine yourselves, whether you be in the Faith"* (II Cor. 13:5).

ANOTHER SPIRIT

The phrase, *"Or if you receive another spirit, which you have not received,"* proclaims the ultimate result of *"another Jesus."* If *"another Jesus"* is presented, and this can be explained as a Jesus not of the Cross, it is guaranteed that *"another spirit"* will be the result. In other words, even though it may look like it's the Holy Spirit, in fact, it will not be the Holy Spirit, but rather a spirit of darkness.

By Paul using the phrase, *"Which you have not received,"* he is referring to the fact that what set them free from the terrible bondages of sin was the Holy Spirit of God and not some bogus spirit. However, the insinuation is, if they kept listening to these false apostles preaching *"another Jesus,"* they would find themselves back in the bondage from whence they had previously been delivered. It is a frightening prospect!

THE PRESENT TIME

Many things are happening presently in the church, which purports to be *"Revival,"* a *"Moving of the Holy Spirit,"* etc. While the Believer definitely does not want to reject something which is actually of Christ, neither does he want to accept something which is not of Christ.

As we've already stated, Satan coming as a roaring lion is overly obvious and does not pertain to deception (I Pet. 5:8). However, him coming as a *"serpent"* definitely does pertain to deception (II Cor. 11:3), and he is most dangerous as *"an Angel of light"* (II Cor. 11:14).

We are hearing reports at this time of people who are supposed to be in the Spirit who are barking like dogs, roaring like lions, crowing like roosters, etc. Women are supposedly going through some type of spiritual labor, actually imitating a physical birth, claiming that they are giving birth to revival, a Moving of the Holy Spirit, etc.

Let the reader understand that the Holy Spirit does not bark like a dog, roar like a lion, or crow like a rooster. Neither does He go through indecent contortions claiming that it is a *"spiritual birthing."* All of this is bogus. In fact, it is *"another spirit."*

THE WORD OF GOD

One will look in vain in the Word of God, which must always be the criteria, for such antics. However, if that is not bad enough, to claim that such is of the Spirit of God makes the sin even worse, and sin it is, even gross sin.

In fact, even with something that may possibly be Scriptural in its own right, if it is taken out of context or undue preeminence is given, the Holy Spirit simply will not function in that capacity. Paul said, *"If therefore the whole Church be come together into one place, and all speak with Tongues,"* or one might quickly add, *"all convulse in laughter,"* or any number of things, *"and there come in those who are unlearned, or unbelievers, will they not say that you are mad?"* (I Cor. 14:23).

While the Lord at times definitely can come upon a person until he can no longer stand, or come upon one with laughter, etc., if, in fact, a Believer goes to church solely for such to happen, he will soon get into *"another spirit."*

ANOTHER GOSPEL

The phrase, *"Or another gospel, which you have not accepted,"* means the Gospel that first set you free, and if you revert to this *"other gospel,"* which repudiates the Cross, you will go back into bondage.

The false apostle comes and preaches another Jesus — you thus get a different spirit, one that you did not get from us — and a different gospel, which you did not receive from us.

The True Gospel of Jesus Christ, which is the Message of the Cross, gets people Saved, lives changed, bondages broken, sick bodies healed, and Believers baptized with the Holy Spirit, which radically changes everything for the better. There is no higher enlightenment than that, which these liars profess to have. That goes for now as well as then. Any ministry that does not fit in somewhere with the things we have stated, which is a mirror of the Book of Acts and the Epistles, is not a true ministry. To say it another way: the Church today must have some of the earmarks of the Book of Acts. If it doesn't, in the Eyes of God, it's not really church but something else altogether.

Paul also said, *"For I determined not to know anything among you, save Jesus Christ, and Him Crucified"* (I Cor. 2:2).

The Cross of Christ, as here plainly stated, was Paul's

Message. It was given to him by the Holy Spirit, and he gave it to us in his Epistles. If the preacher is not preaching the Cross, he is not preaching the gospel. If one doesn't have his faith entirely in Christ and the Cross, and maintained entirely in Christ and the Cross, one will find oneself then living in a state of spiritual adultery. Ladies and gentlemen, it is *"The Cross"*! *"The Cross"*! *"The Cross"*!

"The whole world was lost in the darkness of sin,
"The Light of the world is Jesus;
"Like sunshine at noonday His Glory shone in,
"The Light of the world is Jesus."

"No darkness have we who in Jesus abide,
"The Light of the world is Jesus;
"We walk in the Light when we follow our Guide,
"The Light of the world is Jesus."

"You dwellers in darkness with sin blinded eyes,
"The Light of the world is Jesus;
"Go, wash at His Bidding, and Light will arise,
"The Light of the world is Jesus."

"No need of the sunlight in Heaven we're told,
"The Light of the world is Jesus;
"The Lamb is the Light in the City of Gold,
"The Light of the world is Jesus."

THE MESSAGE OF THE CROSS

4

The Holy Spirit Superintends The Entire Process

THE HOLY SPIRIT SUPERINTENDS THE ENTIRE PROCESS

The Holy Spirit Alone can bring that which is required of the Believer, a life of Righteousness and Holiness (Rom. 8:1-11). To make it easier to understand, it is impossible for the Believer to sanctify himself, at least according to the New Covenant. What we have to do and what we have to be can only be brought about by the Holy Spirit. He Alone is able to carry out the process, to make us what we ought to be, and to effect the change within our lives that must be brought about.

As the Holy Spirit comes into our hearts and lives at Conversion, He is there for many purposes, but the chief purpose of all is to rid us of all sin. In fact, as James put it, *"The Spirit Who dwells in us lusts to envy?"* (James 4:5).

This refers to the Holy Spirit, which means that the word, *"Spirit,"* should have been capitalized in the King James Text. The word, *"Lusts,"* here means, *"To earnestly or passionately desire."* Of what is the Holy Spirit envious, and what does He passionately desire? The Holy Spirit is envious of any control the fallen nature might have over the Believer, and is passionately desirous that He control all our thoughts, words, and deeds. He is desirous of having the Believer depend upon Him for His Ministry to him so that He might discharge His Responsibility to the one Who sent Him, namely God the Father.

As we go forward, we will see that the Holy Spirit works exclusively within the parameters, so to speak, of the Finished Work of Christ. In fact, it is the Cross of Christ which has given and does give the legal means to the Holy Spirit to do all that He does. So, the Holy Spirit works exclusively within the confines of the Finished Work of Christ, in other words and as stated, it is the Cross which has given the Holy Spirit the legal means to do all that He does. Considering this, it is imperative that the Object of our Faith ever be Christ and the Cross. That's why Paul said that he determined not to know anything save Christ and Him Crucified. That was his subject matter in some way of any and every sermon he preached. It is *"The Cross!" "The Cross!" "The Cross!"*

HOW THE HOLY SPIRIT WORKS

If you were to ask most Christians, even preachers, as to how the Holy Spirit works in the heart and life of the Believer, most would probably give you a blank stare. The truth is, they don't know. He is somewhat taken for granted in religious circles. Even Pentecostals who claim to know more about the Holy Spirit, for the most part, simply do not know how He works.

If they tried to give you an answer, they would talk about some of the things that He does, such as giving one the utterance of speaking in Tongues, and they might even talk about His Power. However, that really speaks of what He does and not how He does it. So, how does He work?

Let me give to you that which the Lord gave to me as it regards this great Truth. As someone has well said, and rightly so, all Revelation is preceded by desperation. I don't know if that is true in all cases, but it most definitely was true in my case.

I WILL SHOW YOU THINGS ABOUT
THE HOLY SPIRIT YOU DO NOT NOW KNOW

That's what the Lord said to me.

The day in question, which was in March, 1988, if I remember the month correctly, presented a heartbreaking time.

Our house sits on some 20 acres of property, with Donnie's house right next to ours. I had gone to the back of the property so I would have some privacy where I could pray.

That particular morning, it seemed like the powers of darkness would almost pull me apart. I even remonstrated to the Lord that I felt He was allowing Satan too much latitude. I went on to say to Him, *"No human being can stand this."*

It seemed like there was a thousand pounds on my shoulders crushing me to the ground as I attempted to force my way through this onslaught of the Evil One. Then, all of a sudden, it changed.

One moment I was being crushed, and the next moment it was like I was walking on clouds. The Spirit of God covered my heart and began to flow into my very being. Then the Lord spoke to me. He said:

"I will show you things about the Holy Spirit you do not now know."

My thoughts instantly went to the fact that the Holy Spirit is God, and there are all types of things that we don't know about Him; however, I also felt in my spirit that what the Lord was addressing was the matter at hand.

I had no doubt that the Lord had spoken to me and had given me a promise. However, there was nothing that took place in the coming days, weeks, months, and even as it rolled into one, two, and three years, that I could label as the Lord having given me information regarding the Holy Spirit that I did not then know.

I was baptized with the Holy Spirit with the evidence of speaking with other Tongues when I was eight years of age. The Lord had anointed me to preach the Gospel in that hundreds of thousands, and I exaggerate not, had been brought to a Saving Knowledge of Jesus Christ. I depended on Him, looked to Him, and sought the Lord for Guidance and Leading by the Holy Spirit, which He was always so generous to give. So, what did the Lord mean by the statement, *"I will show you things about the Holy Spirit you do not now know"*?

THE WORD OF THE LORD CAME TO PASS

Some nine years had passed. It was now 1997. I was in my office that morning even before daylight, getting ready for the program over our SonLife radio stations. I was studying the Book of Romans, actually, the Sixth Chapter.

Then the Lord began to open up to me the meaning of the sin nature, which is cataloged by the Apostle Paul in the Sixth

Chapter of Romans. To be frank, I had not known before then what the sin nature actually was, but it was like the Lord just placarded this upon my spirit to help me to understand the basic reason for failure among Christians. It is because they do not understand the sin nature.

I won't go into any detail regarding this now, in order to save time and space. As well, we have dealt with it at length in our Commentaries and also in one of the Study Guides.

At any rate, I walked the floor back and forth in my office, with tears streaming down my face, all because I finally understood the reason. When one fails the Lord and is doing everything within his power not to fail, but fails anyway, and doesn't know why, it leaves one in a terrible state of mind. The questions fly thick and fast, but there are no answers. Now I knew why the failure.

Now, don't misunderstand, the failure is the fault of the individual, but it's not a fault as most people think of such. If a person is truly Saved, that person doesn't want to sin. In fact, sin is abhorrent to him. While the flesh may want something that's wrong, the inner man doesn't! However, if the Believer doesn't understand *"the Law of the Spirit of Life in Christ Jesus,"* then such a Believer will ultimately be overcome and controlled by *"the Law of Sin and Death"* working through the sin nature.

On that particular morning, even though the Lord had opened up to me information that I had not previously known, He did not give me any solution for the problem, that to come later.

It was several days later, if I remember correctly. It was the time of our morning prayer meeting at 10 a.m. Probably 10 or 15 people had gathered, and I was always with them as it regards prayer. This took place every morning, Monday through Friday, at 10 a.m.

THE CROSS OF CHRIST

While in prayer that morning, I was thanking the Lord

for what He had shown me some days earlier, and then asking Him for the solution to the problem. As stated, He had explained to me what the sin nature was, how it worked, and how it could control the Believer, if the Believer didn't understand certain things. However, He did not explain to me how to have victory over this thing. It was to come that morning.

The Lord said to me three simple things which revolutionized my life and Ministry. He said:

1. The answer for which you seek is found in the Cross.
2. The solution for which you seek is found in the Cross.
3. The answer for which you seek is found only in the Cross.

In other words, the answer to the sin nature and the answer to sin in any capacity is the Cross of Christ and only the Cross of Christ. I knew the Lord had given me something special. It was to change my heart, my life, my Ministry, and, in fact, everything. In a sense, it was the beginning of the Message of the Cross.

However, the Lord did not say anything about the Holy Spirit. I knew that the Holy Spirit had a part to play in all of this, but the Lord never told me what it was.

THE HOLY SPIRIT

I even asked the Lord that morning, *"How does the Holy Spirit work in all of this?"* but no answer then was forthcoming. To be frank, I was so overjoyed, so thrilled, and so excited by what the Lord had told me about the Cross that I did not press the issue.

But yet, in the days that followed, I sought the Lord earnestly about this matter because I knew the Holy Spirit had to be very prominent in this effort.

In fact, every single thing done on this Earth, with the exception of Jesus going to Calvary, has been carried out by the Person, Ministry, and Office of the Holy Spirit. He is the One of the Godhead Who carries out the Work of God on Earth, as stated, with the exception of what Jesus did at Calvary. And yet, even then, He superintended every part and parcel of the Conception, the Birth, the Life and Living, the Ministry, and the Death and Resurrection of Christ. In fact, on the Cross, our Lord did not die until the Holy Spirit told Him that He could then die. It would be at 3 p.m., the time of the evening sacrifice (Heb. 9:14).

The days went into several weeks. I had begun attempting to teach the great Message of the Cross to our radio audience as well as our television audience.

It was radio that morning. Loren Larson was on the program with me.

It was about 15 minutes until the time would end for the program, and then something happened of which I have no explanation.

HOW THE HOLY SPIRIT WORKS

There was a pause in the teaching for a moment, and then something came out of my mouth that was a total surprise. I made the statement:

"The Holy Spirit works entirely within the framework of the Finished Work of Christ and will not work outside of that framework."

Where did that come from? I had not thought on that subject, had never heard the statement before in my life, and had not read it in a book anywhere. The Lord instantly gave it to me, and without any explanation.

That has never happened to me before or since like that. When I made the statement, I sat there in silence for a moment or two. Loren spoke up and said, *"Can you give me Scripture for that?"*

How could I give him Scripture when it was not something I had known, studied, or read in a book somewhere? It had come out of the blue, actually, from the Lord.

Then I looked down at my Bible, and it was opened to Romans 8:2.

Those words leaped out at me:

"The Law of the Spirit of Life in Christ Jesus has made me free from the Law of Sin and Death."

I quoted that Scripture, knowing that it was the Scriptural answer for that which I had stated.

The program ended a few minutes after that. I arose from the table and turned to my right to walk out of the door when the Spirit of God came over me.

A PROMISE KEPT

As I stood there for a few moments as the Spirit of the Lord washed over me, the Lord spoke to my heart saying, *"Do you remember that morning in 1988 when I told you that I would show you things about the Holy Spirit you did not then know?"*

Of course, I remembered!

He then said, *"Well, I have just kept My Word to you. What I have given you regarding how the Holy Spirit works is a great Truth."*

THE LAW OF THE SPIRIT OF LIFE IN CHRIST JESUS

What is this Law?

It is a Law of God devised by the Godhead in eternity past. Because it is a Law, which pertains to a principle of operation within our hearts and lives, to be sure, it will work exactly as designed. This we must understand. These spiritual Laws given to us in the Seventh and Eighth Chapters of Romans function in the spiritual realm just as much as the laws of physics or mathematics, all designed originally by God.

THE SPIRIT

This is the Holy Spirit, which, in brief, tells us how He works. As is obvious, the Holy Spirit is God. As such, He is Omnipotent (all-powerful), Omniscient (all-knowing), and Omnipresent (everywhere).

LIFE

All Life comes from Christ, but it comes through the Holy Spirit. In other words and as previously stated, everything the Godhead does on this Earth goes through the Office and the Person of the Holy Spirit. God the Father is in Heaven, and God the Son is there as well. The Holy Spirit is on this Earth carrying out the Work of the Godhead. And yet, all three are everywhere because they are God.

IN CHRIST JESUS

Even though I have not personally counted them, it is said that the Apostle Paul uses the phrase, *"In Christ Jesus,"* or one of its derivatives, such as, *"In Him," "In Christ," "In the Lord,"* etc., some 170 times. Irrespective as to how the phrase is used, without exception, it refers to Jesus Christ and what He did at the Cross of Calvary. In a sense, this tells us how that the Holy Spirit works. As previously stated, He works entirely within the framework of the Cross of Christ.

Before the Cross, the Holy Spirit was very limited as to what He could do. The reason was, the blood of bulls and goats could not take away sins (Heb. 10:4), meaning that the sin debt remained with even the godliest individuals of Old Testament times. Due to that fact, this limited the Holy Spirit, Who could not associate with sin in any fashion.

As a result, whenever Believers in Old Testament times died, their souls and spirits were not taken to Heaven, but rather they went down into Paradise, actually as a captive of Satan. To be sure, he could not hurt them because the Bible says they were comforted, but, still, they were his captives. They were there waiting for the Cross, which would free them from this place, which it did.

Now, when a Believer dies, his soul and spirit instantly go to be with the Lord Jesus Christ because the sin debt was forever lifted at Calvary's Cross.

So, when Jesus paid that terrible sin debt, that made it possible for the Holy Spirit to instantly come into the heart and life of the believing sinner at the moment of Conversion, which He does, there to abide forever (Jn. 14:16-17).

The Eighth Chapter of Romans presents the great Holy Spirit Chapter of the Bible as it regards how the Holy Spirit works within the heart and life of the Believer.

NO CONDEMNATION

Paul said, *"There is therefore now no condemnation to them which are in Christ Jesus, who walk not after the flesh, but after the Spirit"* (Rom. 8:1).

The phrase, *"There is therefore now no condemnation* (guilt) *to them which are in Christ Jesus,"* opens this great Chapter, which some have called the *"Dynamics of the Holy Spirit."*

As the subject of Romans, Chapter 3, is God declaring the sinner righteous, so the theme of this Eighth Chapter of Romans is God making the Believer holy. The former Chapter deals with Christ's Work for the sinner, i.e., Justification; this Eighth Chapter deals with Christ's Work in the Believer, i.e., Sanctification.

This Chapter opens with *"no condemnation,"* and closes with *"no separation."*

The subject of Romans 5:12-21 is *"condemnation"* for all who are in Adam; the theme of this Eighth Chapter of Romans is *"no condemnation"* for all who are in Christ.

The special Greek word used for *"condemnation"* occurs only in Romans 5:16, 18, and Romans 8:1. It, therefore, links these two Passages.

The divided state of the Believer is glaringly obvious in Romans, Chapter 7, which speaks of a terrible struggle due to the Believer not knowing or understanding what Christ has actually done for him at Calvary and his standing in that Finished Work. However, this divided state ends in the glorious triumph of the Spirit over the flesh — that is, if the Believer tenaciously clings to Christ and the Cross.

"Condemnation" in the Greek is, *"Katakrima,"* and means, *"An adverse sentence, the verdict."*

WHAT ADVERSE SENTENCE OR
VERDICT IS PAUL TALKING ABOUT?

He is dealing with the struggle between the flesh and the Holy Spirit in the life of the Believer. Unless the admonition of Romans, Chapter 8, is followed regarding the Work of the Holy Spirit, the flesh will triumph, which always brings condemnation. In other words, the Believer fails despite the fact that he does not want to do so and is trying with all his strength not to do so. That is the flavor of the struggle in Chapter 7 of Romans, which tells us in no uncertain terms that the Believer's efforts to overcome sin within his own strength are pointless and futile. Even though a new Creature in Christ Jesus, he is simply no match, at least within himself, against this monster of sin.

However, the Believer who knows the Truth acts upon that Truth. This allows the Holy Spirit to perform His Office Work, so to speak, which He can only do relative to Truth. The Believer is then guaranteed victory irrespective as to how bad the sin or bondage may be. As the Believer within himself is no match for sin, sin, Satan, and death are no match for the Holy Spirit. So, there is *"no condemnation"* because in following the Holy Spirit, there is no failure. As well, the word, *"Now,"* tells us that this condemnation-free state is available this moment.

WHY DID PAUL USE THE WORD, *"NOW"*?

Due to repeated failure, many have come to believe that total victory is not possible in this life, such awaiting the coming Resurrection when we shall be changed. However, the Holy Spirit through the Apostle is loudly debunking that erroneous thought by declaring that victory is possible now! To follow the Prescribed Methods of the Holy Spirit is to guarantee victory.

To ignore those methods is to invite disaster.

The word, *"Now,"* emphasizes the struggle-free Christian experience offered by Christ when He said, *"Come unto Me, all you who labor and are heavy laden, and I will give you rest"* (Mat. 11:28).

IN CHRIST JESUS THE SIN DEBT IS PAID

If one is to notice, Paul uses the word, *"In,"* relative to the Believer and his relationship with Christ Jesus. He didn't say, *"With,"* but rather, *"In,"* and for purpose and reason.

He is referring to the fact that one must understand and believe that when Jesus died on Calvary, the sinner, upon his Faith, is literally *"baptized into Christ Jesus,"* actually *"baptized into His Death"* (Rom. 6:3). In other words, Jesus did this for the sinner, and the sinner is actually in Christ as Christ dies on Calvary.

The reader must understand that even though Paul used the word, *"Baptized,"* he is not speaking here of water, but rather the Crucifixion of Christ. In fact, the word, *"Baptized,"* or, *"Baptism,"* can be used figuratively or literally. Paul is here using it figuratively. Let's look at a Passage with the use of the word both figuratively and literally. John the Baptist said:

"I indeed baptize you with water unto Repentance (here he uses the word literally)*: but He* (Christ) *Who comes after me is mightier than I, Whose Shoes I am not worthy to bear: He shall baptize you with the Holy Spirit, and with Fire* (here he uses it figuratively)*"* (Mat. 3:11). Unfortunately, almost all of the modern church thinks that Paul is speaking of Water Baptism. They, therefore, miss the entirety of the meaning of at least one of the greatest Chapters in the entirety of the Word of God, Romans, Chapter 6.

In the Death of Christ, which refers to the poured-out, Perfect Life of Jesus represented in His Precious Shed Blood, the terrible sin debt of humanity was satisfied (paid). This means that the believing sinner no longer has a debt of sin against him. Consequently, Satan has no more hold or claim; therefore, the terrible wages of sin, which is death (spiritual death — separation from God), is no longer applicable to the believing sinner. He is now united with God, which means the enmity has been removed, and is called the *"Born-Again experience"* (Jn. 3:3). However, as great and wonderful as that is, it is only the first part.

DOMINION OF SIN IS BROKEN

The second part relates to Jesus breaking the dominion of sin, which also occurred in this great Sacrifice. This is primarily what is meant by Paul referring to the Believer being *"in Christ."*

Regarding Salvation, Jesus died for the sinner. Regarding dominion over sin, the Believer died in Christ. The Believer must know and understand that, which, regrettably, most don't, I think! As Jesus dying for the sinner guaranteed Salvation, the sinner dying in Jesus guarantees sin's dominion is broken, thereby, victory over sin. So, as we have repeatedly stated, the Work of Christ at Calvary was, in effect, a *"Double Work,"* or a *"Double Cure."*

The first part of Jesus dying for the sinner on Calvary is known by all true Believers. However, the second Finished Work, which actually took place at the same time as the first Finished Work, is not so readily known or understood by most Believers. Consequently, the terrible struggle of Romans, Chapter 7 ensues.

The phrase, *"Who walk not after the flesh, but after the Spirit,"* plainly tells us that those who know and understand this second great Finished Work, meaning they were *"in Christ"* when He died, and depend on this great Truth, will always have the Help of the Holy Spirit and, therefore, no failure.

AFTER THE FLESH

Let's see what the flesh actually is, as Paul uses the word.

The flesh pertains to that which is indicative to a human being, in other words, what a human being can do. It speaks of our education, motivation, personal ability, personal strength, talent, etc. These things within themselves aren't sinful or wrong, but the fact is, if we try to live for God by the means of these things, i.e., *"the flesh,"* we are doomed to failure. It cannot be done.

So, the question is, *"Why cannot it be done in that fashion?"* Paul gave us the answer to that as well:

"And if Christ *be* in you *(He is in you through the Power and Person of the Spirit [Gal. 2:20])*, the body *is* dead because of sin *(means that the physical body has been rendered helpless because of the Fall; consequently, the Believer trying to overcome by willpower presents a fruitless task)*; but the Spirit *is* Life because of Righteousness *(only the Holy Spirit can make us what we ought to be, which means we cannot do it ourselves; once again, He performs all that He does within the confines of the Finished Work of Christ)*" (Rom. 8:10).

So, if we are to live for God and do so successfully, we must do this thing God's Way, and that Way is the Cross.

Therefore, to *"walk after the flesh"* is to depend on one's personal strength and ability, or else, great religious efforts, in order to overcome sin. This guarantees failure no matter how sincere, motivated, or consecrated the person may be. One would surely have to say that the Apostle Paul was all of these things and more. And yet, until this great Truth of *"in Christ,"* which was brought about by the Cross, was revealed to him, that part of his Christian experience was a total failure, even as Romans, Chapter 7, portrays. Paul went into detail concerning his own personal experience that you and I may not have to follow and walk the same path. Regrettably, however, most of us seem to have to learn this lesson the hard way, even as did Paul.

The word, *"Walk,"* in the Greek is, *"Peripateo,"* and means,

"To live, to deport oneself, to follow." It speaks of our everyday walk, life, and living before God, in other words, how we order our behavior, which pertains to the totality of our Christian experience. As we have stated, this Eighth Chapter concerns the Sanctification of the Believer.

THE GLAD TIDINGS OF THE GOSPEL

Christ took the position of bearing the sin penalty at Calvary even though He had never sinned but, in effect, paying the sin debt of all humanity. To do this, He had to die. However, being God, He rose from among the dead and ascended above the highest heavens, having by His Death destroyed death (Heb. 2:14), broke the back of sin (Heb. 9:26), and exhausted the curse of the Law (Gal. 3:13).

The Glad Tidings of the Gospel consist in the declaration that for all who by Faith in Christ died and rose with Him, there is no person and no thing that can condemn them. For Christ, there is now no condemnation. He suffered its full intensity at Calvary, but He suffered that condemnation there on behalf of, and for the benefit of, all who believe upon Him. Hence, there is no condemnation for them.

They are in a new position entirely beyond and above the reach of everything to which condemnation attaches. Where Christ and His Members now stand, there can be no question of sin, wrath, condemnation, or imputation. All such questions were settled before He ascended thither. He is now at the Throne of God, with His Person and Work accepted, because these questions were settled at Calvary.

The glorious Truth that liberates the Believer's heart is that he is there in that Glory with Christ where nothing that condemns can reach him (Eph. 2:6).

A LIFE OF POWER, HOLINESS, AND VICTORY

This is not only a new position in the Last Adam as contrasted with the old position in the first Adam, it is also a New Life — a Life of Power, Holiness, and Victory. The Christian Faith is not a scheme of Salvation intellectually accepted, but a Life of Power and Holiness experimentally enjoyed.

Emmanuel's Destruction of sin at Calvary may become to Faith a moral reality now as it will become in the New Heavens and the New Earth a physical fact, for in them, Righteousness alone will dwell.

WHAT THE LAW COULD NOT DO

Paul said: *"For what the Law could not do, in that it was weak through the flesh, God sending His Own Son in the likeness of sinful flesh, and for sin, condemned sin in the flesh"* (Rom. 8:3).

The phrase, *"For what the Law could not do,"* speaks of the Law of Moses. In other words, the Law of Moses could not condemn sin (destroy sin) but could only condemn the sinner, and this it did grandly. The phrase, *"What the Law could not do,"* could be rendered literally from the Greek, *"The impossible of the Law."* This was an impossible thing on the part of the Law, that it could condemn sin by giving power to sinners in order to overcome this monster. This it could not do! In other words, the Law of Moses demanded obedience, even as does all law, but furnished man no power to obey its injunctions.

And yet, this is exactly what Israel tried to force it to do. Except for a small Remnant, the entirety of generation after generation was lost in this capacity, until finally it grew so bad that they murdered their Messiah, with the resultant loss of the entirety of nationhood. As a result, they wandered as vagabonds for about 1,900 years until finally becoming a Nation again in 1948.

Regrettably, as Israel tried to force the Law of Moses into a posture it was never intended, many of their modern disciples attempt to force Faith into the same mold. God's Word must never be used against Himself, in other words, attempting to force it into that which it was never intended.

What exactly do we mean by that?

Some in the modern church teach that Believers can confess anything they want into existence. No, you cannot! You can confess anything He wants into existence, but not anything that we want. As stated, God will not allow His Word to be used against Himself against His Will. The foolishness that anything we Believers do is the Will of God is foolish indeed!

WEAK THROUGH THE FLESH

The phrase, *"In that it was weak through the flesh,"* means that the only power the person had in order to keep the Law as given by God was his own willpower, which was woefully insufficient. The *"flesh"* refers to the human frailties of each and all people. Man is so weak, in fact, that he is not able, at least within his own power, to even keep the simple Laws of God laid down by the Creator, much less save himself.

"Weak" in the Greek is, *"Astheneo,"* and means, *"Impotent, without strength."*

The Law of Moses was like a mirror that showed man what he was but gave man no power to change what he was; consequently, there was no victory over sin in the Law (Rom. 7:7-12).

The phrase, *"God sending His Own Son,"* refers to man's helpless condition, unable to save himself, unable to keep even a simple Law, and, therefore, in dire need of a Saviour.

God sending His Only Son tells us two things:

1. The tremendous Love of God for lost humanity.

2. The terrible power of the bondage of sin, which could not be broken any other way than by and through Jesus Christ and what He did for us at the Cross. God had to deliver man, that is, if man was to be delivered, which He did through the Cross, and through the Cross Alone. There is no deliverance in any other direction (Rom. 6:3-5).

The phrase, *"In the likeness of sinful flesh,"* says literally, *"Of the flesh of sin."* The choice of words is especially noteworthy:

Paul does not say simply, *"He* (Jesus) *came in the flesh"* (I Tim. 3:16; I Jn. 4:2), for this would have expressed a bond between Christ's Manhood and sin.

Neither did he say, *"In the flesh of sin,"* which would have represented Him as partaking of sin, which He did not.

Nor did he say, *"In the likeness of flesh,"* since He was really and intensely human; but, *"In the likeness of the flesh of sin."*

FULLY HUMAN BUT YET GOD

This means that Jesus was really human, conformed in appearance to the flesh, the characteristic of which is sin, yet sinless.

Dickson said, *"Christ appeared in a Body which was like that of other men insofar as it consisted of flesh, and was unlike insofar as the flesh was not 'flesh of sin'."*[1]

The phrase, *"And for sin,"* means, *"To Atone for sin, to destroy its power, and to save and sanctify its victims."* In other words, that was His Purpose for coming, and to be sure, He carried out His Purpose in totality.

CONDEMNED SIN IN THE FLESH

The phrase, *"Condemned sin in the flesh,"* means that as a Man, in fact, the Last Adam, He faced all the power of sin, Satan, death, and everything that man faces and more, and much more, we might quickly add, and never failed one time. As well, He not only did not fail, but He also destroyed the power of sin, dethroned death, and defeated Satan. In other words, He condemned sin and all its power, breaking its hold over the human race.

Also, He did this not as a Deity, for such would not have sufficed, but as a Man, The Man Christ Jesus. The only help He had was the Holy Spirit, Who is available to all Believers as well.

In fact, at least as far as man was concerned, the only way that God could defeat sin and its results, which is death, is by God becoming Man. Inasmuch as dominion was vested in the first Adam (Gen. 1:28; Ps. 8), and then lost through forfeiture, which, in effect, gave Satan dominion, it had to be purchased back by another Adam, in effect, *"The Last Adam."* All was lost in this manner and only could it be purchased back in this manner.

THE RIGHTEOUSNESS OF THE LAW

Paul said, *"That the Righteousness of the Law might be fulfilled in us, who walk not after the flesh, but after the Spirit"* (Rom. 8:4).

The phrase, *"That the Righteousness of the Law might be fulfilled in us,"* tells us that the Law of Moses contained Righteousness, as should be obvious, considering that it was given by God. However, for its Righteousness to be obtained by man, perfect obedience had to be rendered, which was impossible because of the *"weakness of the flesh."*

The phrase, *"Might be fulfilled in us,"* could be translated, *"Find its full accomplishment in us,"* not merely, *"Be performed by us."* The Apostle had a much deeper meaning, namely that the Aim of God in giving the Law might be accomplished in us, in our Sanctification, which is the ultimate end of our Redemption (Eph. 2:10; Col. 1:22).

THE SIGNIFICANCE OF THE LAW

I think we surely should understand from this Verse just how significant the Law of Moses actually was. Even though it was given exclusively to the Jews for a particular purpose and reason, still, it was meant for the entirety of the world. These were God's Laws, and they applied to all. I speak primarily of the moral Law, i.e., *"Ten Commandments."* As well, this moral Law could not pass out of existence because it is moral truth, and moral truth never changes. For instance, it was wrong to steal 4,000 years ago, and it is wrong to steal presently. In fact, it will always be wrong to steal, etc. So, God's Law was righteous, and, as well, it had a Righteousness, which could be obtained by obedience, but not by man in his fallen condition. However, Jesus, as the Second Man and the Last Adam, totally kept the moral Law in every respect, even throughout thirty-three and one-half years of public life and being contested by Satan at every turn, as well, He took the penalty of the broken Law on the Cross of Calvary. He did this as the Representative Man, and Faith in Him (Jn. 3:16) grants the Believer a satisfied Judgment and the position of perfect Law-keeper. Upon Faith in Him, His Victory becomes our Victory, which is intended.

RIGHTEOUSNESS

Upon simple Faith in Him, the vilest of human beings can become, and, in fact, do become instantly righteous. Of course, the world can little accept this, thinking they can somehow earn this place and position; however, their efforts are doomed to failure, for such is impossible!

Sometime ago, Frances and I took a few days off. During this time of rest, I was studying this very Passage that we are now addressing, and when I read the words, *"That the Righteousness of the Law might be fulfilled in us,"* the Presence of God came all over me. I sat there for a few moments weeping as I sensed the Lord impressing upon me the significance of this statement. It is something that only Christ can do and something which He gloriously did do. As a result, that for which He paid such a price can now be ours by the simple act of Faith.

WALK

The phrase, *"Who walk not after the flesh, but after the Spirit,"* emphatically portrays to us that the *"Righteousness of the Law"* cannot be had by anyone who attempts to attain such by his own efforts.

The word, *"Walk,"* as we have previously stated, refers to *"the ordering of one's behavior or conduct."*

"Flesh" can mean the frailty of human endeavors, but in this case, it refers to the *"indwelling evil nature."* Of course, the *"Spirit"* refers to the *"Holy Spirit."*

"After" in the Greek is, *"Kata,"* and has as its root meaning, *"Down,"* which suggests domination.

Wuest says, *"In other words, a Christian is one who orders his behavior in such a way that it is not dominated by the evil nature (Sin Nature), but by the Holy Spirit."*[2]

THE BELIEVER AND THE TWO NATURES

As a great portion of this Chapter constantly warns the Believer as to the possibility and danger of walking after the flesh, etc., such presents the great moral fact of the existence of these two natures in the Believer, and is actually the theme of this Chapter.

In a sense, the Believer is dead, for he was crucified with Christ. As a partner with Christ, he, therefore, enjoys all of the advantages of the partnership acquired by Christ before he was brought into it. This is not necessarily an experience; it is rather a Divine operation apprehended and enjoyed by Faith.

However, the Believer is always very conscious that his carnal nature is not dead, but that between it and the new Spiritual Nature he received at Conversion (Eph. 1:13), there is a deadly warfare that really never stops.

If the carnal nature were actually dead, it would not be necessary to urge Christian people not to make provision to gratify its appetites (Rom. 13:14).

THE TEACHING OF THE NEW NATURE

This New Nature is received by every believing sinner at Conversion. It is energized by the Holy Spirit, hence, our walking after Him, which teaches that the Christian may enjoy such victory. It is actually a moral experience so liberating that the fact of indwelling sin may become to him only a matter of knowledge — because the Word of God asserts its existence — but not a painful fact of consciousness.

In other words, while it is true that this contest between the flesh and the Spirit is unending, if we follow after Christ exactly as we should, we are made to enjoy a *"rest"* that is actually beyond comprehension. While we do fight, it is only the *"good fight of Faith."*

Regrettably, most Christians have the opposite and, therefore, sad experience. We are painfully conscious of this principle of evil lodged in our nature, while the existence of the New Nature within us is a matter of belief because it is declared in the Scriptures but not fully enjoyed at all!

Thus, Verse 2 of this Chapter forms its key note. It asserts the existence of these two natures in the Believer but declares that the new Spiritual Nature liberates from the old carnal nature.

So, the object of the Chapter is not the forgiveness of sins or justification from them, but rather liberation from the power of sin in order to live a life of Sanctification.

THE SPIRIT OF LIFE

To the Believer, *"the Spirit of Life"* is imparted, which is the new Spiritual Nature. That Nature operates with a regularity of a law just as the principle of sin operates as a law in its sphere. The Holy Spirit issues Life, the other, death.

The Law of Moses could not make a man holy, not because of its impotency, but because of the impotency of man on whom it acted. As an example, if an old-fashioned railway engine were built of paper, steam would be powerless to move it, not because of any weakness in the power of steam, but because of the weakness of the material of which the engine was built.

However, God does what the Law could not do, i.e., pardon the transgressor and give him a New Nature. In the sinless flesh of His Beloved Son, He first destroyed sin, condemning it to death, and then, the impartation of the Divine Nature to the Believer causes him by faultless conduct to satisfy all the righteous requirements of the Law.

These righteous requirements cannot be satisfied by anyone who walks *"after the flesh,"* who is controlled by the principle of sin in the flesh, but only by him who is controlled by
the Holy Spirit.

THE HOLY SPIRIT

One cannot help but notice the emphasis that Paul places
on the Holy Spirit in this Eighth Chapter. As we have stated, it
is called by some, *"The Dynamics of the Holy Spirit,"* and yet, I
am concerned that many do not know or understand properly
what Paul is saying and what he meant respecting the involvement of the Holy Spirit.

For instance, many in the modern church do not subscribe
to the Baptism with the Holy Spirit with the evidence of speaking with other Tongues (Acts 2:4). They claim that one re-
ceives the Holy Spirit at Conversion and there is no more to
receive. They are wrong!

While the Holy Spirit is definitely involved in the Salvation
process, even as He is involved in every single thing done by
God on Earth, other than conviction, His participation in the
New Birth is in the realm of Regeneration. However, if the Be-
liever then does not go on and be baptized with the Holy Spirit,
which will always be accompanied by the speaking with other
Tongues, the Holy Spirit is left pretty much dormant in the
Believer's life, unable really to do much more (Acts 1:8; 2:4).

I think this is emphasized by the insistence in the Book of
Acts of Believers being baptized with the Holy Spirit. In fact,
this is of such necessity that Jesus, in effect, told His Followers
not to go do anything for Him concerning His Work until they
first received *"the Promise of the Father."* He was speaking of
the Holy Spirit, actually saying, *"For John truly baptized with
water; but you shall be baptized with the Holy Spirit not many
days hence"* (Acts 1:4-5). Of course, Acts, Chapter 2, portrays
that momentous occasion when they were filled.

THE URGENCY OF BEING BAPTIZED
WITH THE HOLY SPIRIT

Chapter Eight of the Book of Acts portrays this necessity to such an extent that Peter and John were sent to Samaria immediately to pray for those who had recently been Saved under the Ministry of Philip that they might be baptized with the Holy Spirit, which they were.

In Acts, Chapter 9, the Lord sent Ananias to the newly-converted Paul that, among other things, he might *"be filled with the Holy Spirit"* (Acts 9:17).

In Acts, Chapter 10, Cornelius and his household were all filled immediately after they were Born-Again.

Acts, Chapter 19, portrays Paul sensing the absence of the Holy Spirit activity in some Ephesians, immediately asking them, *"Have you received the Holy Spirit since you believed?"* (Acts 19:2).

Paul prayed for them and all 12 were instantly filled.

Even though the Baptism with the Holy Spirit is definitely intended for Power (Acts 1:8), and done so to continue the Works of Christ, much more is involved here as well. Without the Baptism with the Holy Spirit, I feel that the Scripture is replete with the fact that all He can do and desires to do in the hearts and lives of Believers can little be done at all unless the Believer is baptized with the Holy Spirit with the evidence of speaking with other Tongues. Paul says as much with the statement, *"In Whom* (Jesus) *you also are built together for an habitation of God through the Spirit"* (Eph. 2:22).

So, I little think that all of this work mentioned by Paul, which only the Holy Spirit can carry out, can actually be done without the Holy Spirit Baptism. The insistence by Jesus and the Spirit Himself in the Book of Acts, I think, is replete.

SPIRIT-FILLED BELIEVERS

Now we come to those who are Spirit-filled. Just because a

person has been baptized with the Holy Spirit, does that mean he automatically has the benefit of the great Truths spoken of by Paul? The answer to that should be obvious, *"No, he doesn't"*!

Paul was Saved and baptized with the Holy Spirit himself and did not at the beginning have this great victory within his life which he portrays to us in these particular Chapters. The Seventh Chapter of Romans bears this out. So, what was or what is the trouble in this area?

Being baptized with the Holy Spirit actually guarantees little, but really rather portrays the potential of what can be, that is, if the Believer will cooperate with the Spirit of God.

Were you to ask Spirit-filled Believers if they understood what Paul was saying in the Eighth Chapter of Romans, most would probably nod in the affirmative. They have been baptized with the Holy Spirit, so they automatically think that such within itself is all that is needed. They could not be more wrong.

The truth is, due to the paucity of teaching on this subject, most Spirit-filled Believers little know or understand that of which Paul speaks as it regards all Victory being in the Cross of Christ (I Cor. 1:17, 18, 23; 2:2). In fact, there are many, even the far greater majority of those who are actually baptized with the Holy Spirit, even with Gifts of the Spirit working through them, who don't understand this Truth. In other words, they are being used by the Lord but, at the same time, living lives of spiritual failure. They are frustrated! They do not know why! Nevertheless, the failure is ever present, and the situation does not seem to get better, but rather worse.

In fact, that is true! It is getting worse. These people know they are Saved, they know they are Spirit-filled, and they love the Lord, and so, they cannot understand the failure, especially considering that they are trying so hard not to fail. Let me say it another way:

There are millions presently baptized with the Holy Spirit who speak in other Tongues almost daily but still are living lives of spiritual failure. This is so simply because they do not understand the Message of the Cross as it regards our everyday living for God. They have understanding respecting the Cross of Christ concerning Salvation. However, as it regards our Sanctification, how we live for God on a daily basis, and how we have victory over the world, the flesh, and the Devil, of that, they do not understand or know. Consequently, despite being filled with the Spirit, as stated, they are living lives of spiritual failure.

HOLY SPIRIT INVOLVEMENT

The manner in which the Holy Spirit works in this situation is to energize the great Truths of Calvary in the heart and life of the Believer, bringing him to his full potential that he may realize this great Victory purchased by Christ, and purchased, I might quickly add, at the Cross. However, if the Believer does not know this *"Truth,"* there is very little the Holy Spirit can do (Jn. 8:32).

To make the matter worse, which further ties His Hands, so to speak, the Believer at times is working furiously within his own strength, attempting to bring about victory, and yet, constantly failing. Please remember, we are speaking of people who truly love the Lord, are truly trying to serve Him to the best of their ability, and, in many ways, are even used by the Lord, sometimes greatly. However, with such a Believer not knowing or understanding the great Truth of the Cross as it regards our Sanctification, it keeps the Holy Spirit from doing what He Alone can do. Almost every time such a Believer is striving with all of his strength to live as he ought to live but is still failing, which, as we have stated, greatly frustrates such a person.

TRYING HARDER BUT STILL FAILING

It is somewhat like a swimmer who is drowning. He is flailing his arms and head with all his strength, attempting to keep his head above water. Whenever others come to rescue him, sometimes they find it very difficult because of him fighting so severely. In other words, the drowning swimmer actually hinders his rescue by the person who has come to save him.

If he would just relax and quit fighting, the rescue would be much easier; otherwise, it is almost impossible. In fact, some drowning swimmers have actually had to be knocked out physically before they could be rescued.

The Christian who is struggling in the flesh, even though very sincere, is not really helping the situation but, as the drowning swimmer, is actually severely hurting his cause.

Once the Believer knows the Truth of what Christ has done at the Cross and has Faith in that Great and Wondrous Work, the Holy Spirit can then take over and do all that needs to be done, making this Christian life a tremendously pleasurable experience. Otherwise, it can be Hell on Earth, and that is not an exaggeration!

Why do you think it was for Paul before he learned this great Truth, when he said, *"O wretched man that I am! Who shall deliver me from the body of this death?"* (Rom. 7:24).

THE FLESH

The great Apostle now says, *"For they who are after the flesh do mind the things of the flesh; but they who are after the Spirit the things of the Spirit"* (Rom. 8:5).

The phrase, *"For they who are after the flesh do mind the things of the flesh,"* certainly does refer to the unsaved, but it refers also to Christians. Actually, the thrust of the entirety of Paul's dissertation is to the Believer, which portrays the struggle between the flesh and the Spirit, and how that the Believer is either in one or the other or somewhere in-between.

The Greek has it, *"For those who are habitually dominated by the flesh put their mind on the things of the flesh."* The *"flesh,"* as it is here used, pertains to the sin nature. In other words, the Christian is dominated by the sin nature.

AGAIN, WHAT IS THE FLESH?

Even though we have already explained this elsewhere, due

to its vast significance, please bear with our repetition.

The flesh is that which is indicative to a human being. It pertains to our education, motivation, personal talent and ability, personal strength, willpower, etc. These things are not wrong within themselves, and Paul also said:

"For though we walk in the flesh (because we are human beings)*, we do not war after the flesh: (for the weapons of our warfare are not carnal, but mighty through God to the pulling down of strong holds)"* (II Cor. 10:3-4).

To repeat myself, he is saying that we cannot live for God by the same means that we do everything else as a human being. In fact, we can only live for the Lord, at least successfully, in one way. That one way is that our Faith be placed exclusively in Christ and what Christ did for us at the Cross (Lk. 9:23).

However, it is very hard for Believers to admit that due to the fact that they are Born-Again, even Spirit-filled, they, within themselves, cannot live this life. But, you cannot. The powers of darkness are too strong. To be frank, we greatly insult Christ when we try to do something that He has already told us we cannot do. Furthermore, at great price, and I mean great price, He made a way. He made a way for us to live this life as it ought to be lived, which pertains to what He did at the Cross. At the Cross!

• He atoned for all sin, past, present, and future, at least for all who will believe (Jn. 3:16).

• He broke the grip of sin that it not dominate us. While the Bible does not teach sinless perfection, it most definitely does teach that sin is not to have dominion over us (Rom. 6:14). However, if our Faith is in anything other than Christ and the Cross, the Sin Nature will most definitely control us despite the fact that we are Spirit-filled, etc. The way the Lord has prepared for us is *"The Cross! The Cross! The Cross!"*

DOMINATED BY THE SIN NATURE

"Dominated" in the Greek is, *"Kata,"* and means, *"Down."*

The manner in which it is used refers to the state being con-
tinuous. This speaks of a person who is habitually dominated
by the indwelling sinful nature.

This does not at all mean that the Christian desires this,
but that it is happening (the domination) because of trusting in
the flesh, i.e., self-efforts for victory, which cannot be gained in
that fashion. It must ever be remembered that the flesh cannot
deliver from the flesh.

Paul also said, *"Do mind the things of the flesh."* *"Mind"* in
the Greek is, *"Phroneo,"* and means, *"To exercise the mind, or
have a sentiment or opinion."* Consequently, it means that the
Believer who is dominated by the sin nature has an improper
understanding of the Word of God concerning this tremendous problem and is, therefore, attempting to gain victory in
the wrong way. He is not necessarily doing it purposely or
intentionally; nevertheless, the end result is the same, domination by the sin nature.

The phrase, *"But they who are after the Spirit the things of
the Spirit,"* presents the very opposite of the previous phrase.

AFTER THE SPIRIT

That which is *"after the Spirit"* is that which is according
to the Word of God. He cannot nor will He function except
according to the blueprint, which is the Word. While He will
definitely help the seeking Believer find the Truth, He will not
force such upon the disinterested.

What are the *"things of the Spirit?"*

"Things" in the Greek is, *"Logos,"* and means, *"Something
said, including the thought, by implication a topic (subject of
discourse), also reasoning (the mental faculty) or motive, and
above all the Divine expression, i.e., Christ."*

So, Who Jesus is, what Jesus said, and what Jesus did is
the Eternal Logos, i.e., the Things of the Spirit. Even though
it pertains to all things relative to Christ, more particularly, it
refers to the great Truth of Him breaking the dominion of sin,

at least in this case.

If the Believer sets his *"mind"* upon this of what Jesus has done and believes it with all his heart, he will receive the *"Things of the Spirit,"* which are total victory, and in this case, over sin.

While the word, *"Things,"* has the same connotation or meaning concerning the *"flesh,"* it is there inverted. It presents the Believer who should be speaking the Words of Christ or the Spirit, but rather is speaking words of the *"flesh,"* which pertains to error, and most likely, religious error. It is difficult to explain, but in its most simplistic form, it means that the Believer speaks the Words of Christ versus the Believer who does not. However, the manner in which Paul made the statement needs more explanation.

MENTAL AFFIRMATION

It is possible for a Believer to know this Truth as laid out in Romans, Chapters 6, 7, and 8, but actually know it only in his intellect. Consequently, he gives a mental assent or affirmation to this Truth, but really does not know it experimentally. In other words, it is not in his heart and, consequently, will bring forth few results.

To be frank, there are many who mistake mental affirmation for Faith and are confused when it does not bring forth positive results. True knowledge of the things of God pertains not only to knowledge of the intellect but, as well, that which gets down into one's spirit. That is how true Faith springs forth.

So, the favorite statement of many people, *"I've tried that and it doesn't work,"* is the tip-off that true Faith is lacking, with the individual only giving mental assent to the subject at hand, in this case, the Cross of Christ. Many people attempt to learn the Things of God, and above all, the Word of God, even as they would learn arithmetic, etc. It is not to be learned or understood in that fashion.

Jesus as the Eternal Logos must become a part of one's

very spirit and being. In fact, when one truly has true Faith in God, it is quite possible they can exhibit Faith but little explain what they are exhibiting. On the other hand, oftentimes, those who have a mere mental assent can, in fact, properly explain what they believe but obtain few results.

A WAY OF LIFE

"After the Spirit" is a way of life. That's the reason Paul used the term, *"After the Spirit."* The word, *"After,"* should have been translated, *"Dominated,"* for that is the actual Greek word used here.

Consequently, it could be translated, *"For they who are dominated by the flesh do mind the things of the flesh; but they who are dominated by the Spirit the things of the Spirit."* However, there is a difference in the way the word, *"Dominated,"* is used.

The dominion of the flesh sooner or later goes into compulsion. In other words, the individual is compelled by this domination to do those things which are wrong, which Paul outlines in Romans 7:15.

However, the word, *"Dominated,"* as it is used concerning the Holy Spirit, is the exact opposite. While the Holy Spirit will definitely dominate the Believer, it is only when the Believer freely gives control to the Spirit. In essence, the Spirit will never force a Believer to give Him control.

As well, the Holy Spirit dominates the Believer only in the sense of that which is good for the Believer, which is the very opposite of the flesh. He has our good at heart and constantly pushes forth toward the realization of such good.

How wonderful it is to be led by the Spirit, guided by the Spirit, empowered by the Spirit, taught by the Spirit, and, in fact, to be *"after the Spirit."*

THE WILL OF THE BELIEVER

If the Believer's Faith is in the wrong object, in other words, something other than the Cross of Christ, the will of the Believer can be forced by Satan to do something wrong against that persons will. In fact, it is happening millions of times a day all over the world, and we continue to speak of Believers.

While the will is very important, as the Scripture uses the term, *"Whosoever will,"* still, it within itself is not capable of overthrowing the powers of darkness. Unfortunately, most Christians are trying to live for God by the means of willpower, which is not God's Way. As stated, while the will is important, it within itself is not strong enough to overcome the powers of darkness.

That's what Paul was talking about when he said, *"For sin shall not have dominion over you: for you are not under the Law, but under Grace"* (Rom. 6:14). The very fact that the Apostle says that it is not supposed to have dominion tells us that it most definitely can have dominion. As already stated, the word, *"Dominion,"* is strong, meaning that a person's will is being dominated by an outside force, in this case, Satan.

Where the will is very, very important, and, in fact, the only place that it has preeminence, is when it makes the decision to place one's Faith in the Cross of Christ or to put that faith somewhere else. If the choice is wrong, Satan can dominate a person's will, forcing him into a course of action that he doesn't want to do.

Now, stop and think a moment, when you sinned, whenever that was and whatever it was, did you want to do it? While the flesh may want some things that are wrong, the inner man of the Believer doesn't want to sin. In fact, sin is abhorrent to any Believer. If it isn't, the person needs to get Saved.

Now, the Believer must understand that even though Satan forces a person's will, forcing him to do things that he doesn't want to do, still, that person is most definitely responsible. However, he is responsible in a different way than most would think.

As we've already stated, the responsibility goes back to the time he makes the decision to follow the Word of God as it regards the Cross, thereby, placing his Faith in that Finished

Work, or placing his faith somewhere else.

A SUPER WILLPOWER

Many Christians have the idea that when they got Saved, the Lord gave them a super willpower. As one man told me once, *"Brother Swaggart, before I was saved I could not say 'no' to the Devil, but now that I know Christ, I can say 'no' to his temptations, etc."* No, one cannot make it in that capacity.

A person's will is no stronger after he is Saved than before he is Saved. So, if you think that the Lord gives Believers some super willpower, that's not true at all. As stated, we are not meant to try to live for God by the means of willpower. We are meant to live for the Lord by the means of Faith, but it must be Faith in Christ and what He did for us at the Cross.

I remember when the Lord first began to open this great Truth up to me. I preached it at Family Worship Center. One of our Preachers on staff grew very angry at me regarding the Message. He was denying that one's will could be overrun by Satan, with that Believer being forced into a course of action he did not want to go. And yet, I knew the man would lock himself into a room in fits of depression, sometimes staying there in the darkness for days. Did he want to do that? No! He didn't want to do that. It was Satan overriding his will, forcing him into that situation. Let me say it again:

The Lord's Way is the Cross of Christ, which demands our Faith in that Finished Work, and that Finished Work Alone. When we place our Faith in Christ and the Cross exclusively, the Holy Spirit will help us grandly, as only He can do. When our faith is placed elsewhere, this is a state of spiritual adultery, which the Holy Spirit cannot abide. Thank God, He doesn't leave us in situations of this nature, but He is greatly hindered in what He can do for us. That confuses many Christians. They are Spirit-filled, and they don't understand why the Holy Spirit doesn't help them. In truth, He is helping them all that He can, but He is greatly limited, as stated, because their Faith is in the wrong object.

CARNALLY MINDED

Paul said, *"For to be carnally minded is death: but to be Spiritually Minded is life and peace"* (Rom. 8:6).

The phrase, *"For to be carnally minded is death,"* springs back to the *"flesh"* of Verse 5.

"Carnally minded" in the Greek is, *"Tophronema tes sarkos,"* and means literally, *"The mind of the flesh."* Again, *"flesh"* refers to the evil or sin nature. It means that the mind is possessed by, thus, controlled or dominated by the evil nature, the description of an unsaved person or a Believer who is not dominated by the Spirit of God.

The word, *"Death,"* speaks of spiritual death, i.e., separated from God. So, the question must be asked, *"Can the Believer continue indefinitely following after the flesh?"*

Of course, the answer to that is, *"No!"* But yet, there is no line drawn in the sand, so to speak, respecting that far and no further. Anytime anyone asks the Lord to forgive him, irrespective as to how bad the sin may be or how many times he has been forgiven for that same sin, if he is truly sincere, God will always forgive (I Jn. 1:9). He puts no limitations on forgiveness, Mercy, Grace, or His Love. Nevertheless, sinning and repenting, even though God's Provision is definitely not His Will, which should be overly obvious.

THE FLESH AND DEATH

Irrespective of the things just said, the Believer must always understand that the *"flesh"* always leads to *"death."* That's why it is called, *"The Law of Sin and Death"* (Vs. 2). That means that while the Believer is under the domination of the sin nature, he is plagued by misery, heartache, disappointment, frustration, pain, suffering, hurt, hopelessness, plus shame and humiliation. So, even though God will always forgive as long as the penitent is sincere, still, the price is incredibly high. Consequently, irrespective of the struggle, the Believer who is caught in this snare must never give up and must never respond to hopelessness. It is my belief, and I think borne out by the experience of the Apostle Paul, that the seeking soul will always find the answer to that for which he seeks. The Lord, I believe, has promised that (Lk. 11:9-13).

PATIENCE

I write these words primarily to those of you who would attempt to help Believers who are caught in this snare. They do not want that thing which dominates them and are trying with all their strength to overcome but so oftentimes in the wrong way. I am cautioning you, the reader, to be patient with them, loving, kind, compassionate, and considerate. Point out the great Truths given in these three Chapters, but never condemn. Who knows, you may be speaking to another Apostle Paul!

If you are reading these words and find yourself dominated by the terrible sin nature, prayerfully, the Lord has helped us to properly explain these great Truths to such an extent that the victory which you have long sought will now be yours. That is why Jesus came down here to die on Calvary. He paid such a price, and He did it for you and me. He wants you to be free. He is not dangling a carrot in front of you and then pulling it away at the last moment. Actually, He has brought you to this very place as you hold this book in your hands. He has had me to write these very words to you and for you.

SPIRITUALLY MINDED

The victory you have so long sought is now yours. You know and understand what Jesus has done for you, and that by Faith, you were actually in Him when He was crucified, even baptized into His Death. As such, sin shall not have dominion over you anymore. Once you know this Truth, and it is something you now know, Satan dare not usurp authority over the Holy Spirit. He will now operate in Power in your heart and life because you now know the Truth, the Truth of the Cross. Actually, the phrase, *"But to be spiritually minded is Life and Peace,"* is now yours. It is that for which you have sought and longed. It is without money and without price, but yet, purchased at such price; it is yours!

The phrase, *"But to be spiritually minded is Life and Peace,"* presents the most glorious, wonderful, fulfilling life that one could ever know. This is what living is really all about. This is that which only God can give, and He reserves it for those who love Him and believe in His Great and Glorious Name. While it is for anyone, still, the requirements of Faith must be met.

The words, *"Spiritually minded,"* in the Greek are, *"To phronema tou pneumatos,"* and means literally, *"The mind possessed by the Spirit,"* thus, a mind controlled or dominated by the Holy Spirit.

Such a person possesses the Life that God is, Life and Peace.

LIFE AND PEACE

Wuest said, *"The word 'Peace' as it is here used, means 'to bind together that which has been separated,'"*[3] thus, the believing sinner bound together with God and His Life after having been separated by sin.

The *"Life and Peace"* here spoken cannot be purchased by money, attained by education, discovered by scientific theory, or earned by religious works. It is a free Gift from God. As stated, it comes beautifully and simply by the vehicle of Faith, but it must have the correct Object of Faith, which is the Cross of Christ.

However, even though we have said it several times, please allow us to say it again:

One cannot have faith in something of which one has no knowledge. While God doesn't require much, He does require some things. He requires that you know and understand that

Jesus Christ not only paid the sin debt, but He also broke the dominion of sin, and He did it for you and me. This is given to us in Romans 6:3-7. Actually, the entirety of the Sixth Chapter portrays this great Truth, plus Chapters 7 and 8.

TWO WILLS

There are two wills contrasted in Verses 5-8.
1. The will of the carnal nature.
2. The Will of God.
The carnal will, being independent of God's Will, is consequently hostile to it and cannot be otherwise.

Therefore, all who are governed by the carnal will cannot, so long as they are thus governed, please God, be they ever so religious, moral, cultivated, or noble. It is not that God takes no pleasure in noble actions performed by unconverted men, but that He cannot take pleasure in and accept religious worship and meritorious actions designed to purchase His Favor, which are prompted by the carnal mind. Hence, the Lord rejected Cain's worship and offerings.

All who are controlled by the carnal will set their affections upon gratifying it. The opposite is true in the case of those controlled by the Divine Will. The one control ends in death; the other in life.

ENMITY AGAINST GOD

Paul said, *"Because the carnal mind is enmity against God: for it is not subject to the Law of God, neither indeed can be"* (Rom. 8:7).

The phrase, *"Because the carnal mind is enmity against God,"* means that anything that is not of God and used in the manner in which God has intended, in effect, creates hostility toward God. As we have stated, the *"carnal mind"* is *"the mind of the flesh."* Again, it refers to the sin nature. In putting this in its proper focus, hopefully, as the Spirit of God intended through Paul, please allow me to say it in this manner.

In effect, Paul is here explaining two things:

1. WORLDLINESS

He is warning all Believers of the danger of all things which are not totally of the Lord. To be sure, this covers a wide area. It speaks of the Believers' consecration and dedication. It speaks of their sincerity before God. It speaks of one's relationship with Christ, in other words, every facet of one's being in the Lord.

As well, it speaks of worldliness. By that I mean the things of this world, which, if engaged, will put one in the frame of a carnal mind and will ultimately lead to spiritual death. Unfortunately, churches are full of people of this nature. They know far more about sporting events, Hollywood, Wall Street, or a hundred other things, which may not actually be sin within itself, than they know about God. Such shows a *"carnal mind,"* at least a mind that is leaning in that direction. The interest of such a person, even though claiming Christ, is not really on the Lord but on worldly things. Such is in the carnal direction and will ultimately lead to a carnal mind, if not already!

2. THE WORD OF GOD

Paul is also speaking of the Believer who does not know the Truth of Romans, Chapters 6, 7, and 8, and is, thereby, overtaken by the sin nature, therefore, dominated by sin. Such a situation is miserable, to say the least, irrespective of how hard he may be trying to overcome this thing. However, the harder the person tries, the worse the situation becomes.

The weapons being used are his willpower, or even spiritual things, which are good within themselves, but will not perform the intended task of freedom.

Even though the Believer does not think as such, attempting to use his willpower to overcome sin constitutes a *"carnal mind."* It would actually be the same were he using quite legitimate principles such as *"confession,"* the *"laying on of hands,"* etc. One could name several other great Biblical principles also.

We are certainly not saying that these things are wrong when, in reality, they are right, and even very much right. However, to use such attributes in the capacity of that of which we speak, even as valuable as they are, is the same as a carpenter attempting to use a handsaw instead of a hammer to drive nails. It simply won't work because it was not made for that purpose.

DECEPTION

Satan tricks us by these things simply because they are very good and actually bless us greatly. I speak of fasting, prayer, witnessing to souls, giving money to the Work of God, etc. All these things are greatly beneficial to the Believer, but the truth is, they will not give one victory over sin. In other words, one cannot fast one's way to victory over the sin nature; it simply cannot be done. The Cross Alone is the answer for sin.

But yet, the reader may ask, *"How could these things which are so right within themselves, even though used wrongly, be declared as 'enmity against God?'"*

Enmity in the Greek is *"echthra,"* and means, *"Hostility,"* and, in this case, *"Against God."*

The reader who is caught in this trap might quickly exclaim that he has no hostility against God, but rather the very opposite. That is correct but, at the same time, incorrect. The answer is found in the next phrase.

"For it is not subject to the Law of God, neither indeed can be," in its simplest form means that what is being done, whatever it may be, is not in God's Prescribed Order and, therefore, presents the person not going God's Way, which generates hostility whether intended or not. In other words, every single thing that is not exactly as God intends for it to be is, in effect, at war with Him, whether the Believer understands that or not.

THE DIVINE ORDER

"Subject" in the Greek is, *"Hupotasso,"* and is actually a military term meaning, *"To arrange in order under."* In other

words, God has a Divine Order, and all Believers are to come under that *"Order."* Such speaks of humility and, therefore, deals with the *"mind."* For instance, *"Let this mind be in you, which was also in Christ Jesus:*

"Who . . . made Himself of no reputation, and took upon Him the form of a servant, and was made in the likeness of men . . . He humbled Himself, and became obedient unto death, even the death of the Cross" (Phil. 2:5-8).

So, the *"carnal mind"* is not a *"spiritual mind,"* and the reason is that it is not a *"humble mind."*

We find here that one of the reasons for the *"carnal mind"* is a lack of humility and brokenness before God. I greatly suspect that this problem is so acute that the best among us, whomever that may be, has far more spiritual pride, which is the worst type of all, than any of us realize (Isa. 66:2).

WHAT IS THE LAW OF GOD

It is the Word of God! It must be carefully and faithfully followed. That's the reason that it is so absolutely imperative that Believers know the Bible. As well, one must always understand that it is virtually impossible to exhaust its treasures and resources. Considering that it is the Living Word of God, its meanings continue to enlarge and grow.

So, if the Believer takes the position that he already knows the Word and, therefore, further study is little needed, he is greatly shortchanging himself, so much so, in fact, that it beggars description. Ever how much one may know, there is much more to know.

FAITH IN THAT WHICH IS OF GOD

Paul continues, *"So then they who are in the flesh cannot please God"* (Rom. 8:8).

Hebrews 11:6 says, *"But without Faith it is impossible to please Him."* So, we are told that *"Faith"* pleases God while the *"flesh"* displeases God.

Everything that God has, does, and uses, in regards to the human family, originates totally, absolutely, completely, and altogether with Him. In other words, Salvation is all of God and not of man. That would include all of the nuances of Salvation, as well, which pertain to Divine Healing, Sanctification, Righteousness, Leading and Guidance by the Holy Spirit, etc.

That also means that every single Word in the Bible, although penned by men and, therefore, used as instruments, is, in fact and in totality, authored by the Holy Spirit (Mat. 4:4; II Pet. 1:21).

Inasmuch as everything originates with God and is of a worth far beyond our capacity to grasp or understand, there is no way that sinful man can earn anything which is of God. Consequently, the only way anything can be obtained from the Lord is through the vehicle of Faith. In other words, man believes what God has said, taking it at face value. As well, true Faith in God also consecrates itself to do the Will of God in every respect that is humanly possible. That sounds very complicated, but actually, about all that man can do respecting the absolute Will of God is to furnish a willing mind and obedient heart (II Cor. 8:12).

God does not look for ability, talent, resources, or self-will in man as a requirement, but rather the very opposite, which is a brokenness before Him. This, in effect, says that man knows that within himself he deserves nothing good from God (Isa. 66:2; Lk. 18:14). Actually, Bible Faith does not really function very well outside the sphere of Biblical humility. As well, if it is true Faith, it must be Faith that's in the correct Object, which is *"Jesus Christ and Him Crucified."* Then the Holy Spirit can work in one's life, bringing about that which must be brought about, and which He Alone can do.

THE FLESH AND DISPLEASING GOD

As we have previously stated, the *"flesh"* basically speaks of man's frailty, inability, and weakness, even impossibility, regarding spiritual things. This is a result of the Fall in the Garden of Eden (Rom. 8:10). Inasmuch as humanity is fallen, that means that within the *"flesh,"* man has nothing good, can do nothing good, and cannot come up with anything which pleases God, as should be obvious. And yet, we seem to keep trying.

The whole idea is that if man tries anything within himself, whether Believer or otherwise, God simply cannot accept such. This is at least one of the reasons that God hates self-righteousness to such an extent, because it originates with the flesh, i.e., *"man's self-efforts, self-will."* Consequently, the effort is coming from a poisoned source, which can never be accepted by God.

As well, if self-righteousness becomes the attitude of a Believer, the *"flesh"* from such a source is just as hateful to God as it is in an unbeliever, actually far, far worse!

In fact, every direction other than the Cross always and without exception leads to self-righteousness. It is the Cross alone which answers this terrible question and this great problem.

THE FLESH IS THE GREATEST
HINDRANCE TO THE BELIEVER

The Believer should know that everything he has which is any good has come from God and God Alone, which means it originated totally with God. This means that God does not need any help and, in fact, if man, even converted man, attempts to help God in these areas, which all of us have tried to do at one time or the other, it only tends to frustrate the Grace of God and, therefore, sully that which the Holy Spirit is attempting to do within our hearts and lives.

As the *"flesh"* keeps much of the human family from coming to God, likewise, the *"flesh"* is the greatest hindrance to the Believer. The temptation is always very heavy to add something to what Jesus has already done at Calvary's Cross, to take away from what He has already done, or to substitute something else altogether in its place, which is the great sin of the Church, and in fact, all of us for that matter. However, no matter how consecrated such an effort may be, it does not please God and, in fact, cannot please God for the obvious reasons.

THE PERSONAL EXPERIENCE OF PAUL

When Paul wrote these words, and we especially speak of Chapters 6, 7, and 8 of Romans, he was writing something of which he knew firsthand. For a particular time in his Christian life, he attempted to overcome sin with the efforts of the *"flesh,"* his own willpower, ability, etc. It did not work, even as it cannot work. So, he knew firsthand of the terrible dangers and the futility of such an effort and, as well, how it displeases God for His Children to attempt such. I look back at my own life, and I tend to grieve when I realize how I have personally fallen into this trap so many times, and how it caused me so much heartache, troubles, and difficulty.

Paul learned that every effort by the flesh, no matter how well motivated, how well intentioned, and how loaded down with Scriptures and religious effort, only tends to make the situation worse, with sin even more pronounced. In other words, instead of climbing out of the hole, he only tended to sink deeper (Rom. 7:15).

WHAT JESUS DID AT CALVARY

There are many reasons for this: as we have stated, when one tends to make this effort, one is attempting to solve the problems of the flesh with the flesh, which is impossible. He is attempting to assuage a poisoned situation with water, so to speak, from a poisoned spring. Irrespective of that, even if it was not poisoned and polluted, man simply does not have the strength to overcome sin within himself. It just cannot be done. The problem is of far greater magnitude than any human being could ever begin to realize. It is so bad, in fact, that God had to become Man, literally becoming a human Sacrifice, i.e., a Sin-Offering, in order for the terrible sin debt to be paid and its dominion broken.

As well, what Jesus did at Calvary completed the task of Victory and Deliverance over sin in totality. Nothing can be added to that, even as nothing needs to be added. In fact, when we try to add something, we are insulting God.

AN EXAMPLE

To use a crude analogy, let's say that a man owed one billion dollars at the bank and had absolutely no way to pay this terrible debt, actually being flat broke. A wealthy benefactor then steps in and pays the entirety of the debt. As well, he deposits one billion dollars in cash in the same bank and tells the bank administrators that this man, who had formerly owed this terrible debt, is now free to write checks to his heart's content on this new account.

Of course, the man is now very elated that this terrible debt has been paid, with him no longer owing anything. He is, as well, told of the tremendous amount of money that's in the bank, on which account he is free to write checks for whatever he needs.

The man then has to purchase a piece of land which costs one million dollars. To purchase this land, he goes to the bank and opens a new account, depositing $10, which is separate from the huge account that's already available to him in the bank. He then writes the one million dollar check on his new account to pay for the land when, in reality, he only has $10 in the bank, at least in his separate account, which he has just recently opened.

THE BANKER

The banker says to him, *"Why are you doing this? Your $10 in the bank will not cover a one million dollar check, and you* *don't need to do this anyway considering that we have one billion dollars in this bank on which you can write as many checks as you like. I have also been told by your benefactor that if you exhaust this one billion dollars, he will instantly replenish it with as much as is needed."*

Considering what the benefactor has done for this man, hypothetically speaking, of course, I should think that it would be obvious that the benefactor would not be too very much pleased at the foolish personal actions of this individual regarding finances. It is the same with the Lord.

Even though our illustration is crude, this is exactly what we Believers have done many times. We have tried to take our two cents and purchase what only one billion dollars could obtain, and which has already been provided, at least if we are allowed to use such an illustration.

Everything we need has already been done by Christ, by the Sacrificial Offering of Himself on the Cross, which paid all debt and, in turn, made Eternal Life possible. So, why do we insult Him by attempting to do it all over again ourselves, which is impossible anyway?

IN THE SPIRIT

Paul continues, *"But you are not in the flesh, but in the Spirit, if so be that the Spirit of God dwell in you. Now if any man have not the Spirit of Christ, he is none of His"* (Rom. 8:9).

The phrase, *"But you are not in the flesh,"* in one sense of the word, is asking the question, *"Since you are now a Believer and no longer depending on the flesh, why are you resorting to the flesh?"*

The phrase, *"But in the Spirit,"* in effect, is saying, *"You now have the Holy Spirit to help you."*

It is the Holy Spirit Who makes these great Truths real to the heart of the Believer, but as we have repeatedly stated, He cannot make any Truth real which the Believer does not know, nor can He work on our behalf when we are attempting to do the thing ourselves, which we cannot do. This is what Paul is talking about.

The phrase, *"If so be that the Spirit of God dwell in you,"* in essence, says, *"Provided that,"* or *"Assuming that."* That is, assuming that the Spirit of God dwells in you, that is an indication that you are not in the sphere of the evil nature.

"Dwell" in the Greek is, *"Oikeo,"* and means, *"To live or dwell in a certain place as your home."* The Spirit is not only resident in the Believer in the sense of position in him, but He is actively at home in him, living in him as His Home.

A MINISTRY TO PERFORM

It further means that the Holy Spirit is not abiding in the Believer just to be there, but rather has a Ministry to perform in the Believer, namely to give the Believer victory over sin and then to produce the Fruit of the Spirit. He gives the Believer victory over sin by making real to him and energizing within him the great Truth and Fact of what Christ did for him at Calvary and the Resurrection.

This together with the presence of the imparted Divine Nature in the Believer, and the fact that God has broken the power of the evil nature, puts the Believer out of the sphere of the evil nature and within the sphere of the Holy Spirit. Consequently, the Believer is, therefore, not in the grip of the evil nature, but under the control of the Holy Spirit as he yields himself to Him.

However, these things of which we have said are the ideal, meaning what is supposed to be. Too often the Believer does not know the full Truth of what Christ has done for him at Calvary, giving the Holy Spirit little to work on and work with. As well, most Believers do not yield to the Holy Spirit too very well either, taking control out of His Hands. So, the truth is that the Holy Spirit in most Believers can only do and be to a limited degree in comparison to what really can be done. In other words, most of us live so far beneath what we can

truly be in Christ. We tie the Hands of the Holy Spirit, griev-
ing Him, wounding Him, and actually allowing Him very little
latitude within our lives. That's the reason that we have said
that His Work is potential — only what we will allow Him to
do, which too often is not very much.

In fact, even as we have stated, if the Believer doesn't understand the Cross of Christ as it regards our everyday living,
irrespective of what other direction we might take or how religious it might be, we then greatly limit the Holy Spirit.

THE SPIRIT OF CHRIST

The phrase, *"Now if any man have not the Spirit of Christ,
he is none of His,"* actually refers to the Holy Spirit. In other
words, it is not possible for a person to be truly Saved without
the Holy Spirit dwelling in him.

Some have thought that the *"Spirit of Christ"* referred to
Christ's Personal Spirit; however, that is incorrect.

Paul is merely saying that the Holy Spirit coming in to
dwell within the heart and life of the Believer is made possible only by what Christ did at Calvary and the Resurrection.
There Jesus satisfied the terrible sin debt, which means that
Satan no longer holds a claim on anyone who evidences Faith
in Christ. Consequently, since the Day of Pentecost, the Spirit
of God does not merely come to be with Believers, but rather
in Believers (Jn. 14:17).

So, Paul is saying to failing Believers that if they claim the
Holy Spirit is not within their lives helping them, that means
they are not even Saved, because if they are Saved, the Holy
Spirit is there and is ready to do what He is there to do.

THE BAPTISM WITH THE HOLY SPIRIT

As we have said several times and which I believe the Book
of Acts and the Epistles bear out, the Believer must go on after
Conversion and be baptized with the Holy Spirit, which will
always be accompanied by speaking with other Tongues as the

Spirit of God gives the utterance. Without this Baptism, the Holy Spirit is held somewhat dormant in the heart and life of the Believer, even though present. I realize that virtually all in the non-Pentecostal sector of the Church would strongly deny this, but I feel the Scripture bears it out graphically so.

THE EXAMPLE OF THE WORD OF GOD

One must understand that the Word of God must stand as the criteria for all Faith and belief. Agreeing upon that, our next task is to rightly divide the Word of Truth.

I believe the example of the Book of Acts and the Epistles, as well, are replete with the fact that Believers in the Early Church had as the foundation of their Faith Salvation by Faith, the Baptism with the Holy Spirit with the evidence of speaking with other Tongues, the mighty Power of God evidenced in the healing of the sick and the working of Miracles, and the great Truth that Jesus Christ is coming again to set up a Kingdom on this Earth. If, in fact, that is the flavor of the Early Church, and it is, then our Churches should at least be similar at present. If not, then it's not truly church, at least as God calls such. In other words, the Church ought to have the earmarks of the Church of the Book of Acts and the Epistles.

It is the Holy Spirit Who makes real to the Believer all that Christ has done for the Believer. Therefore, if we ignore Him, disbelieve Him, or fail to give Him the latitude which He wants and seeks, He simply cannot do what needs to be done in our hearts and lives. It is absolutely imperative that the Holy Spirit have His Way. Regrettably and sadly, most Pentecostals and Charismatics, who, in fact, are baptized with the Holy Spirit, give Him very little latitude. As a result, they have but little of what He can really do.

THE HOLY SPIRIT AND THE CROSS

And yet, if the Believer, although Spirit-filled, does not understand the Cross of Christ relative to our Sanctification, such a Believer cannot live a victorious life irrespective of being filled. In other words, a Believer can be baptized with the Holy Spirit with the evidence of speaking with other Tongues and exercise that privilege of speaking in Tongues everyday, and even be used by the Holy Spirit, but still live a life of spiritual failure. In other words, the Baptism with the Holy Spirit does not guarantee victory. That comes solely by our Faith in Christ and what He did for us at the Cross (Rom. 6:1-14; 8:1-11; I Cor. 1:17, 18, 23; 2:2; Gal. 2:20-21; 6:14; Col. 2:10-15).

That's at least one of the reasons that we have Spirit-filled Preachers recommending humanistic psychology. They had been led to believe that the Baptism with the Holy Spirit was the solution to all victorious living. Not experiencing victorious living because of not understanding the Cross of Christ relative to Sanctification, they have turned to humanistic psychology, which affords no help at all.

The answer, and the only answer, for the sins, perversions, bondages, and problems of humanity is the Cross of Christ. It alone is the answer.

THE BODY IS DEAD BECAUSE OF SIN

Paul said, *"And if Christ be in you, the body is dead because of sin; but the Spirit is Life because of Righteousness"* (Rom. 8:10).

The phrase, *"And if Christ be in you,"* refers to a person having accepted Jesus as one's own personal Saviour; consequently, the Divine Nature, which is the Nature of God, is instantly deposited in such a Believer. As well, and as we have just studied, the Holy Spirit has also taken up residence within the Child of God.

The phrase, *"The body is dead because of sin,"* speaks of the human body. Paul says it this way in order that the Believer know and understand that he must not try to gain victory over sin by the means of his own physical body, i.e., self-will, willpower, personal efforts, one's own personal strength, etc.

The Believer's human body is dead in the sense that it has death in it because of sin, which speaks of Adam's sin, which brought both spiritual and physical death to each member of the race. In view of that, and as Paul has already adequately explained, one's willpower alone, which has to do with the human body and the human mind, simply cannot bring about the needed results because of the Fall in the Garden of Eden. Actually, it can only hinder what the Spirit of God Alone can do. As we've tried to explain, that which activates the Spirit, so to speak, is our Faith in Christ and what Christ has done for us at the Cross.

So, Paul is saying that one is foolish to resort to these pitiful measures when he already has tremendous firepower within his heart and life in the form of Christ and the Holy Spirit to bring about what is needed.

The phrase, *"But the Spirit is Life because of Righteousness,"* tells us several things:

THE SPIRIT

Paul is speaking of the Holy Spirit, which is obvious. He is God and, as a result, can do anything. In other words, He is Almighty. So, one is not to think that his situation is so bad that the Holy Spirit is insufficient.

I remind the Believer that this is the same Spirit of God Who *"moved upon the face of the waters"* in Genesis 1:2. The Earth at that time *"was without form, and void,"* and in six days' time, He brought it back to a habitable state as well as creating all animals, fouls, fish, and human beings.

Understanding that, I think that the Holy Spirit has the Power to do whatever is necessary.

THE SPIRIT OF LIFE

The Holy Spirit has *"Life"* and, in fact, *"is Life."*
Man has no spiritual life within himself due to his spiritual

death. Even the life which the Believer has is that which is imparted by the Holy Spirit, all made possible by the Lord Jesus Christ and what He did for us at the Cross. So, to attempt to bring life out of death (the physical body of the human being) is a futile effort. All Life is in the Spirit, and all Life emanates from the Spirit, and, as stated, it is all made possible by Christ and what He did at the Cross. This *"Life"* is obtained by evidencing Faith in Christ and what He did for humanity at Calvary.

RIGHTEOUSNESS

The *"Righteousness"* addressed here is the Righteousness of God, which is given instantly to any sinner upon Faith in Christ.

Within himself, man has no righteousness, despite the fact that he attempts constantly to manufacture such, which the Bible calls *"self-righteousness"* (Lk. 18:9-14). Let's say it again another way:

Every effort that we make to live for God, other than Faith in Christ and the Cross, always and without fail leads to self-righteousness. That's the reason that, sadly and regrettably, the modern church is the most self-righteous that it has been at any time since the Reformation.

What is Righteousness?

Righteousness is simply that which is right, but it's right according to God's definition and not the definition given by man. As well, it is the Standard set by God and not by man. It is the only Righteousness that God recognizes, and as such, He is instantly angry at man's efforts at self-righteousness, which God calls *"wicked"* (Ps. 7:11; Rom. 1:18).

THE HOLY SPIRIT

Now Paul says, *"But if the Spirit of Him Who raised up Jesus from the dead dwell in you, He Who raised up Christ from the dead shall also quicken your mortal bodies by His Spirit Who dwells in you"* (Rom. 8:11).

The phrase, *"But if the Spirit of Him Who raised up Jesus from the dead dwell in you,"* tells us two things:

1. The same Power of the Holy Spirit which raised Jesus from the dead dwells in Believers and is available for our use. This is what Paul is saying.

The idea is that there is no temptation of sin so black, binding, or destructive but that the Spirit of God can handle it, that is, if we know the truth respecting the Finished Work of Calvary. That same Resurrecting Power is available to all Believers.

2. That's the same Power that is dwelling in the Believer, and we are assured that He will use whatever part of it is necessary in order that we might have the victory for which we seek.

What a Promise!

However, again I emphasize that all of this is predicated on the Cross of Christ and the Cross ever being the Object of our Faith. The Holy Spirit works exclusively within the parameters, so to speak, of the Finished Work of Christ, and will not work any other way. In other words, it is the Cross which has given and does give the Holy Spirit the legal means to do all that He does for us. That's the reason it is called, *"The Law of the Spirit of Life in Christ Jesus"* (Rom. 8:2).

SHALL MAKE ALIVE YOUR MORTAL BODIES

The phrase, *"He Who raised up Christ from the dead shall also quicken your mortal bodies by His Spirit Who dwells in you,"* continues to express these two points:

1. Many claim that Paul is speaking here exclusively of the coming Resurrection. While he is definitely speaking of that coming great event, still, by the use of the word, *"Mortal,"* he is also speaking of our present experience in Christ. In other words, the Holy Spirit will impart whatever Power is needed to our present physical bodies (mortal) in order that we may

have victory in any and every capacity of our life and living.

"*Quicken*" in the Greek is, "*Zooporeo,*" and means, "*To cause to live, make alive, give life.*" So, He will infuse Spiritual Life into these physical bodies, which always takes precedence over the "*death*" that is already there due to Adam's fall.

Paul is dealing here not only with the fact of sin, which we face everyday in our physical bodies, but also in the fact of original sin, which is the cause of the problem in the first place.

He imparts enough Life into these physical bodies, which overcomes the death and gives us strength to say, "*Yes,*" to Christ in whatever capacity that He requires.

2. Even though this of which we have stated is the thrust of Paul's statement, nevertheless, in a secondary sense, he also is speaking of the coming Resurrection of Life when the Holy Spirit will also at that time give every Believer a new body (I Cor. 15:38, 51-57).

RESURRECTION LIFE

Resurrection Life, which can be had by every Believer, was paid for at Calvary's Cross. In order to have it, it only requires Faith. Paul also said concerning this:

"*For if we have been planted together in the likeness of His Death, we shall also be in the likeness of His Resurrection*" (Rom. 6:5). In other words, Paul is here saying that Resurrection Life, how we live this life, how we conduct ourselves, and how we order our behavior is all predicated on our understanding that all of this is made possible by what Jesus did at the Cross. It is the Cross! The Cross! The Cross! And only the Cross!

In brief, what the entirety of this book is all about is in the following:

1. Jesus Christ is the Source of all things we receive from God (Jn. 1:1, 14, 29; 14:6, 20; Col. 2:10).

2. The Cross of Christ is the Means, and the only Means, by which all of these wonderful things are given to us (Rom.

6:1-14; Col. 2:10-15).

3. With Christ as our Source and the Cross as our Means, the Object of Faith must always be, and without exception, the Cross of Christ (I Cor. 1:17, 18, 21, 23; 2:2).

4. With Christ as our Source and the Cross as our Means, and the Cross of Christ the Object of our Faith, the Holy Spirit, Who works exclusively within the parameters, so to speak, of the Finished Work of Christ, will then work mightily on our behalf. In fact, He Alone can make of us what we are to be. But again, I emphasize that He works exclusively within the framework of the Cross of Christ and will not work outside of those parameters, which requires that our Faith be exclusively in Christ and what He did for us at the Cross (Rom. 8:1-14; Eph. 2:13-18).

BIBLIOGRAPHY

CHAPTER 1
George Williams, *William's Complete Bible Commentary*, Grand Rapids, Kregel Publications, 1994, pg. 777.
H.D.M. Spence, *The Pulpit Commentary: Vol. 1*, Grand Rapids, Eerdmans Publishing Company, 1978.
George Williams, *William's Complete Bible Commentary*, Grand Rapids, Kregel Publications, 1994, pg. 777.
H.D.M. Spence, *The Pulpit Commentary: Vol. 1, Grand Rapids*, Eerdmans Publishing Company, 1978.
Ibid.
Kenneth S. Wuest, *Wuest's Word Studies in the Greek New Testament: Philippians 2:6*, Grand Rapids, Eerdmans Publishing Company, 1942.
Ibid.
Ibid.
H.D.M. Spence, *The Pulpit Commentary: Philippians 2:7*, Grand Rapids, Eerdmans Publishing Company, 1978.
George Williams, *William's Complete Bible Commentary*, Grand Rapids, Kregel Publications, 1994, pg. 931.
Kenneth S. Wuest, *Wuest's Word Studies in the Greek New Testament: Philippians 2:7*, Grand Rapids, Eerdmans Publishing Company, 1942.
Ibid.
H.J. Paton, *The Modern Predicament*, London, Blackfriars Press Limited, 1955, pg. 233.

CHAPTER 2
Alexander MacLaren, *The Epistles of St. Paul to the Colossians and Philemon*, New York, A. C. Armstrong and Son, 1905, Pg. 220.
Ibid., Pg. 225.
Kenneth S. Wuest, *Wuest's Word Studies in the Greek New Testament: Philippians 3:15*, Grand Rapids, Eerdmans Publishing Company, 1942.

CHAPTER 3
John Brown, *Expository Discourses on the First Epistle of Peter: Vol. I*, William Oliphant and Sons, Edinburgh, Pg. 144.

CHAPTER 4
Kenneth Wuest, *Wuest's Word Studies in the Greek New Testament*, Grand Rapids, Eerdmans Publishing Company, 1955.
Ibid.
Kenneth S. Wuest, *Wuest's Word Studies in the Greek New Testament: Romans 8:6*, Grand Rapids, Eerdmans Publishing Company, 1942.

NOTES

NOTES

NOTES

NOTES